Maurice Thompson

The King of Honey Island

Maurice Thompson

The King of Honey Island

ISBN/EAN: 9783743313637

Manufactured in Europe, USA, Canada, Australia, Japa

Cover: Foto ©ninafisch / pixelio.de

Manufactured and distributed by brebook publishing software (www.brebook.com)

Maurice Thompson

The King of Honey Island

THE KING OF HONEY ISLAND.

CHAPTER I.

SOME INTRODUCTORY ADVENTURES.

JULES VERNON with his wife, who was much younger than himself, and his only child Pauline went to the Vernon plantation house, or Vernon Place, as it was called at Bay Saint Louis, to spend some months. There were few residents on that wild, lonely and lovely shore in those days; for our story begins at the time when war with England, commonly called the War of 1812, was at its high-tide. Why Mr. Vernon had sought this isolation will be disclosed, perhaps, in due time; at present we must be content to know him with only such a glimpse of his character and motives as circumstances permit.

He is a man of giant stature; and his face, almost

covered with grizzly beard, wears that look of rugged strength which perfect health often gives to the countenance of an aged man whose life has been spent at sea. His shoulders are square-set and powerful, his head large, shaggy, leonine, his arms heavy and muscular. When he laughs, there is a suggestion of sea-roar in his voice—a mellow hoarseness not unlike the beating of long swells on a reef.

His wife is a bright, clear-faced, volatile creole, just beginning to show the lines of age in her pretty face, albeit her hair is almost snow-white.

As for Pauline, she is lovely, a girl to catch the eye and heart of almost any man, with her regular features, her expression of modest simplicity, lighted up with a charming vivacity, her plump, supple figure and her luxuriance of shining hair.

Here they are, these three, living for the time a life of utter loneliness in a large, rudely built house, in the most out-of-the-way nook to be found on the wild gulf coast.

It was not as strange as it seems romantic, that they were thus isolated; for in those days men ventured without fear and risked everything without hesitation.

Mr. Vernon was a very rich man, who, since he abandoned sea-faring life, had been one of the chief leaders of affairs in New Orleans. His business relations had been many and far-reaching. Perhaps he now wished to get rid of some of them, and had come to this lonely plantation with the hope of breaking away from entanglements which had become irksome to him.

But it is impossible in this life to know just how we may slip away from disagreeable entanglements, or just where and when we are to encounter the persons who shall cast the strongest influences into our affairs.

A tall, slender, emaciated, but yet seemingly vigorous old man, one stormy March night, sought the hospitality of the Vernon household. Of course, as was the old Southern custom, they took him in, although his actions were mysterious to the point of suggesting a doubt as to his sanity. He had crossed the bay in a little open boat, which capsized with him near the shore; and when he entered the house it was evident that he had suffered much. Next morning he was ill, and for many days he seemed at the point of death.

In this extremity, he confided his life-secret to Mr. Vernon. Simply told it was this: His orphan grand-daughter, a sweet and beautiful girl, while yet scarcely more than a mere child, had been influenced by a daring young scapegrace to elope with him and become his wife. This was in Scotland. The old man, who gave his name as Max Burns, did not disclose the name of his granddaughter's abductor. Perhaps he had good reasons for keeping it a secret; but he went on to tell a touching and almost incredible story of how he had spent many years and a large fortune in trying to find and in some way take back his wandering grandchild Margaret. The young man, immediately after marrying the girl, took her to Italy, where he became a robber. The grandfather followed him, only to find that he had fled to Spain. There, too, he was an outlaw; and after some years of picturesque and terrible adventure, he was so closely pushed by the authorities that he left the country and was next heard of in San Domingo. From there, at length, he came to New Orleans.

All this time Max Burns, who was a Presbyterian preacher, had followed him as best he could, making every effort that money and tireless energy could sustain to capture the man and regain Margaret.

And now, almost penniless, his fortune dissipated in his vain endeavors, his health badly broken and with old age gripping his vitals, he was once more close upon the object of his long and apparently hopeless quest.

"And so," he went on in a feeble, panting tone, "just as I can almost reach him it seems that I must die. Oh, Margaret, Margaret!" and he lay gazing at the ceiling as if in prayer.

The story was so strange that, told under the peculiar and pathetic circumstances, it filled the hearts of the Vernon household with inexpressible sadness.

No one hearing the old man speak could doubt the truth of what he said; there was the unmistakable stamp of sincerity and deep, absolutely poignant feeling on every word as it came from his feeble lips.

But contrary to every probability, Burns got well and departed as mysteriously as he came, going off on foot in the direction of the Pearl River and Honey Island, a region which at that time was the home of a robber-band the most desperate and powerful ever known in our country.

The old saying is it never rains but pours. Scarcely had old Max Burns gone away leaving behind him the almost weird impression of his strange story and of his mysterious personality, when another wanderer thrust himself into the life of the Vernons; and this time it was a young man of distinguished bearing, handsome, winning and withal not devoid of most that goes to add romance to character.

Pauline had been out to the cabin of one Lapin, the overseer of her father's slaves, to see Lizette, the overseer's daughter, who had been ill. Returning thence on horseback and followed by a negro groom, she was making her pony gallop briskly when at a turn in the path he suddenly scared, whirled about and flung her off.

The object which had frightened the fiery little animal proved to be an easel roughly improvised by an artist who had been sketching a cluster of moss-hung trees. The artist himself was near by, and ran to Pauline's assistance.

The fall, though hard, had rather dazed than hurt the astonished girl, and before she fairly realized what had happened, she found herself upborne in the arms of a strange, handsome young man, who held her as if she had been a little child.

"Are you hurt?" he inquired, his face close to hers, his eyes tenderly regarding her.

At first she could make no answer, and she was too weak from fright to struggle. The groom hastened to the spot ; but seeing his young mistress in the possession of a stalwart, heavily armed white man, was afraid to say a word or move a hand. The pony freed of its burden, had run home at full speed, and the thoroughly frightened negro after glaring a moment whipped his own cob and rushed away in the same direction, leaving Pauline a helpless captive in the clasp of her rescuer.

Mr. Vernon chanced to be at the house when the groom, wild-eyed and gasping, arrived with his but half-coherent story of the adventure.

"Pierre Rameau!" he hoarsely cried in a half-whisper. "Pierre Rameau done got Miss Pauline! Oh, de good Lor', de good Lor', Marse Vernon run dar quick!"

Mr. Vernon did not need to be twice told. He snatched a brace of heavy pistols, mounted the groom's horse and galloped toward the scene of the tragedy.

Pierre Rameau was a terrible name in the Gulf-coast region in those days, more terrible even than that of John A. Murrell became a few years later. Indeed, Rameau was reputed to be the leader of all the robbers, pirates and creole *forbans* in the whole Southwest. His deeds had hung a fascinating mist of romance about him which appealed to the imagination of the people.

Little wonder, then, that Mr. Vernon felt, as he urged the clumsy horse along the vague bridle path under the trees, a terrible whirl of mingling and, so to say, crashing emotions. His daughter was his idol; he worshiped her as only an aged man can worship an only child, the offspring of a belated marriage.

Pauline in the hands of Pierre Rameau! The thought was absolutely unbearable, and yet it had to be borne, at least for a few minutes; and the strain upon the old man's feelings showed in the swelling veins of his neck and forehead as he leaned forward over his horse's shoulders and seemed trying to pierce the dark, thick woods with his gaze.

When he turned a sharp curve of the way and looked down a straight stretch between heavy live-oaks and under gray festoons of Spanish moss, he saw something which, as a picture, hung ever after in his memory.

It was Pauline walking side by side with a tall young man, who, armed like a brigand, with rifle and pistols, and bearing an artist's portfolio, sauntered with the careless ease and grace of one at home in any place. The two seemed quite on good terms with each other, and were coming toward Mr. Vernon, who checked his horse in time and glowered darkly at them.

Pauline ran forward to meet her father, her face beaming.

"Papa, this gentleman is Mr. Fairfax, of Virginia; when my pony threw me a moment ago, he came to my aid." She spoke rapidly and in French. "He is an artist, and is staying at Monsieur Vasseur's. I hope you will thank him for his kindness to me."

The young man came up just then, and Mr. Vernon bent upon him a steady, searching look.

"Are you Mr. Burton Fairfax, sir?" he demanded, putting away the pistol that he had been holding for deadly use.

"Yes, sir." Evidently the young man was surprised. His face showed it.

"The negro told me that a robber had caught my daughter, so I was scarcely prepared to see the son of my old friend, Colonel Stirling Fairfax."

Mr. Vernon had regained perfect composure, and was now smiling kindly.

"You knew my father?" inquired Fairfax.

"Many, many years ago, in England. We were the best of friends, and I am proud now to see his son and to thank him for his gallant kindness to my daughter."

"You give me the deepest pleasure," Fairfax said, the strangeness of the situation preventing a clear understanding of it.

"Your mother was a Burton," Mr. Vernon went on. He dismounted and took the young man's hand. "Fine old families, the Burtons and the Fairfaxes—fine old families. Glad to take your hand, sir."

Pauline stood by, looking on. It was a picturesque group, and evidently the young girl felt deeply the romance of the occasion. Her feelings heightened her beauty.

Mr. Vernon pressed the young man to go to Vernon Place, and the three walked thither along the woodland road, the horse following after them.

When they reached the house, the two gentlemen were quite like old acquaintances. Mrs. Vernon was glad to see the son of her husband's old friend, and thus Fairfax found himself the center of charming attentions.

It was like a leaf from some old romance, like being cast into a nook where the poetry of life still survived and where scarcely a ripple of the new order of things was ever heard.

Rich, fatherless, motherless, without a tie to bind him to any spot, the young man, after much travel and many adventures, had come to New Orleans, whence, in search of whatever was new or sketchable, he pressed on into the wilderness, and finally found his way to the lonely shore of Bay Saint Louis, where he was glad to make his home for a time with a queer little fellow, Vasseur by name, in a rambling old backwoods house overlooking the beautiful water.

Vasseur was an enigma to the young adventurer and as such very interesting. He was very dark, could speak English, but brokenly, and in many ways his actions suggested a past life not above outlawry. Indeed, in those days it was safe to assume that every man in all that remote region, whose character and antecedents were not known, was a refugee from justice or a lurking predatory miscreant of one class or another.

All the furniture and belongings of Vasseur's house hinted at plunder; all of the man's actions had about them an atmosphere of furtiveness.

To pass suddenly from such surroundings into the charming circle of the Vernon household was a change which gave emphasis to the effect, and it caught the young man's imagination at once.

And how was it with Pauline?

A young girl under such circumstances does not analyze her feelings, and who shall do it for her?

She sat in the spacious room, and instinctively her chair was drawn close to her mother. Her heart was full of vague happiness, and any observer could have seen that she was quite unconscious of her beauty. Her expression was all attention, for every faculty of her nature had assumed a receptive attitude; and while Mr. Vernon and Burton Fairfax discussed the ancient social relations of the Vernons, the Fairfaxes and the Burtons, she found a most satisfying pleasure in the details, although it would have been quite impossible for to explain why.

Fairfax gladly accepted an invitation to take luncheon at Vernon Place; indeed, it required a little heroism on his part to refuse Mr. Vernon's urgent request that he remain in the house during the rest of his sojourn on the bay shore; especially hard was it to hold out against the hospitable insistence of the ladies, who, in the good old Southern style, joined in pressing him to stay. As it was, he took his departure late in the afternoon; but Vasseur's was not so far away that he could not come back every day if he saw fit.

If he saw fit! Did a young man ever fail to see fit to go back under such circumstances? Vernon Place was better in every way than Vasseur's; Mr. Vernon was a more interesting man than Vasseur;

Mrs. Vernon was a charming woman ; and Pauline —certainly Pauline was lovely, even if she did not talk much.

The young man left a very pleasant impression in the household. So pleasant, indeed, that it wiped out for the time all memory of the old wanderer who so lately had occupied almost their entire thought.

Pauline, after bidding good-by to Fairfax, ran to her own room and watched him go away. He had put on again his belt and pistols, his pouch of drawing-materials and his broad hat. The rifle across his shoulder gleamed bravely in the sunlight.

We could but laugh at such a display of weapons in our day ; but then it was different. The wonder is that a man could feel quite safe even when thus apparently over-armed.

To Pauline there was no suggestion of the bravado of mere outward pretense in the appearance of Fairfax, nor ought there to have been. The times were tragic enough. War between the United States and Great Britain was already progressing in the North and at any moment might be transferred to the Gulf coast. Not only this, but all the lawless men of the remote and to a degree unprotected regions were taking advantage of the disturbed state of things to redouble their defiance of local authority. The spirit of violence was in the air, and an unarmed man was an exception to a prevailing rule.

The vivid imagination of Pauline Vernon caught an impression from the young man's showy armament quite different from what such a vision would produce in the mind of a bright girl of our day. To her came a thrill of the romance in the midst of which she was living. She was not self-conscious enough or sufficiently trained in self-analysis to be aware of the source from which the glamour came; but she felt her right to enjoy to the full the deep and rich though elusive charm of the moment.

She watched the young man until he passed out of sight, then closed her eyes, the simple-hearted maiden that she was, as if she could thus shut in forever the fascinating picture.

CHAPTER II.

VASSEUR AND HIS JEWELS.

As Fairfax walked back toward Vasseur's, he was filled with a sense of indescribable satisfaction. The whole world just then was, so far as his feelings went, condensed so that all its essential delights were pressed together in this lonely nook, as flower petals are sometimes pressed into a *potpourri*.

He was old enough and certainly stalwart enough to be a man—his age was twenty-six—but just now he sauntered and smiled like a great pleased boy. His latest adventure had been of a sort to dash into his experience a good strong element of the tender strain of romance so dear to young men.

Who doesn't like mystery and lovely girls? Certainly Fairfax did not hesitate to acknowledge to himself that he was fascinated, not alone by the beauty and sweetness of Pauline, but as well by the air of mystery which seemed to envelop in a way the Vernon family.

How did Mr. Vernon know that he was the son of the late Col. Stirling Fairfax? Of course, our young friend was not aware of the means of knowledge sometimes possessed by a man whose wealth and peculiar influence control far-reaching and comprehensive combinations of force and intelligence.

From Mr. Vernon he had heard the story of old Burns, the preacher, and that, too, was adding its thrill of strangeness and pathos to his reflections.

But most of all, he thought of Pauline. Her beauty of form and face had captivated him, and the sound of her voice was yet echoing through his heart with a certain *timbre* which no other voice ever had. She had touched his hand, and that touch was there yet, continuing its delicate thrill. A breath of violet perfume, perhaps from a cluster of the blooms on her bosom, lingered in his nostrils. Moreover, he felt the exhiliration which comes but once in any lifetime—that waft of nameless and almost meaningless delight in oneself because of one's mere knowledge of another's existence.

It was past sundown when he reached Vasseur's, and he heard the mocking-birds fluting tenderly in the magnolias as he entered the low, oddly constructed house. A little way off, the sea was pounding on the beach with a heavy throbbing and swashing.

Vasseur himself met him at the door.

"*Mo'sieu* has had a good day, I hope," the little creole said, in his soft, insinuating voice. " It vare fine wetter zis day."

Fairfax looked down at him with a comprehensive smile, but only nodded a response. He flung aside his burden of implements and weapons.

"*Mo'sieu* is vare 'ungry, is it not? Suppaire it

come soon," Vasseur went on, rubbing his brown little hands together and grimacing violently.

"No; I dined late and well," said Fairfax, in French. "I am not at all hungry."

It was one of Vasseur's hobbies to speak English. He pretended to fancy himself quite at home in that language.

Fairfax had become sincerely fond of the little dark man, whose restless eyes, bushy, black hair and singularly mobile mouth in some way reminded him of the descriptions he had read of certain fascinating outlaws famous in Martinique—men of half or quarter breed, at once gentle, soft-voiced and murderous, who would die for you one day and rob you the next.

Vasseur looked no particular age. He was fifty, perhaps, though not a gray hair or a wrinkle proclaimed the years. A long, narrow forehead, slender black brows, deep-set black eyes, a high straight nose, a mouth small and expressive and a protruding chin made his face one to be remembered. In stature he was below the medium, but he was strong, tough, supple, restlessly active. It would seem contradictory to add that Vasseur's general air was that of extreme indolence, but such a contradiction existed in the man's make-up. He was not indolent, and yet his greatest activity was seen through an atmosphere of languor and indifference.

Fairfax found Vasseur's house a delightful lodge. It was built of pine logs and covered with long, rough boards; its rooms, large and airy, were yet huddled in appearance, and seemed to have no system in their arrangement. The floors—there was but one story—were of dried mortar, smooth and even, and the walls were hung with a great variety of dressed skins, while the chairs and tables, the bedsteads and the *armoires* were of every grade of finish, from a rude stool to the most exquisitely carved piece in mahogany. It was plain that this heterogeneous furniture had been obtained, piece by piece, in the course of a life devoted to snatching treasures from the sea; flotsam and jetsam had found their way into the house of the creole; and the mishaps of others had in this degree, at least, contributed to his enrichment. The reputation of having once been a pirate clung to Vasseur, though he stoutly denied it. But how came he by all the odd and valuable things in his possession, especially the precious stones? These latter he had shown to Fairfax—diamonds, rubies, emeralds, topazes, sapphires, opals, amethysts—hundreds of them, none of the more precious ones large or very valuable; but still, in the aggregate, the lot was worth quite a pretty sum. One amethyst, however, was remarkably large and beautiful, and had been cut to the form of a cross; the workmanship showed that a master hand had done it, and the color of the stone, almost a sapphire blue, was exquisite, clear as a summer sky and as transparent as the purest water.

If Vasseur loved anything with passionate steadfastness, it was this treasure of jewels, and above all, the amethyst cross was prized—nay, indeed it was worshiped. This he kept separate, inclosed in a much-soiled but sound old leather case, which he carried in an inside pocket of his waistcoat.

It amused Fairfax to encourage the man in his raptures over the beautiful stone cross; and, like any other man with a hobby, Vasseur was delighted to find an appreciative listener, while he expatiated on the merits of his property: but when Fairfax demanded the gem's history, its owner suddenly became confused for a moment and had some trouble to resume his air of half-jaunty indifference.

Of course, this was not surprising; it only led Fairfax to suspect that there was a good deal of truth in the rumor about Vasseur's antecedents. The man said that he bought the cross in Seville; but Fairfax thought he saw that it was not a very clear lie that he was telling.

That night something happened which caused Vasseur's jewels, and especially the amethyst cross, to enter as an important factor into the body of our story

CHAPTER III.

THE CAVALIERS.

At the time of which we write, there was a road, or, more correctly speaking, a trail, leading from the west shore of the bay of Saint Louis in a direction somewhat west of north through a wild country to the wilder region of the upper Pearl River. This trail, which was known as the Black-wolf Trail, had been a highway for the Indians as far back as tradition went—a road which led from their hunting-grounds to the breezy bluffs of the gulf, where they spent the hot season, like the philosophers that they were, in bathing, fishing, eating and smoking.

Since the coming of the white men, the Black-wolf Trail had been put to other uses. Soldiers, horses and cannon had followed it; caravans of settlers, with their oxen, their mules, their slaves and their household appliances, had made it the road to new homes and a life of hardy and lordly independence.

Large plantations were opened and comfortable, even spacious and, in a degree, luxurious houses built on the beautiful and fertile lands once tilled by the aborigines, whose descendants still skulked in the swamps and held the fastnesses of cane-brake and cypress-jungle all around the coast.

Many other trails, less distinct and more meandering, came into the Black-wolf Trail on its way from the highlands to the coast, and he was an alert and experienced woodman who could go among these crossing and apparently entangled paths without bewilderment.

In those days, all of the ways of the woods were ways of danger; for not only were the Indians treacherous and savage in the extreme, there were white men more to be feared than the red ones; reckless knights of adventure devoted to a life of utter lawlessness—bold riders whose dashing exploits would have been themes of song and story if done some centuries earlier—Claude Duvals, Robin Hoods, Wolfstanes of the new land, all seeking the excitement of desperate emprise, and all defying every word and letter of law, human or divine.

The wood-paths were know to these men as familiarly as the cow-paths of his father's farm are known to the country lad to-day in the same region. Singly or in small parties, these self-reliant freebooters rode beneath the pines and the wide-spreading oaks; the wary Indian heard their horses' feet beating the yellow sand and their careless songs echoing through the brakes. It was not for the red man to attack the outlaws; a sort of bond held between them, both being enemies to the settlers. Moreover, the Indians feared the "riders," as they named them, and were glad to slink away whenever those picturesque cavaliers made their appearance.

Most of the "riders" made pretense of being traders, buyers of cattle, furs, skins, cotton, negroes —anything, indeed; and sometimes they did buy, when buying seemed safer than taking by force; but robbery in one form or another was their main business.

Their operations extended over a wide area, and included all manner of theft and robbery, from the "holding up" of a traveller to the forcible seizure of slaves, cattle and other property on the plantations from Georgia to Louisiana.

Pearl River, as far up as Honey Island, afforded a waterway by which vessels of considerable draft could be used to bear the plunder of the cavaliers to New Orleans, by way of the Rigolets and Lake Pontchartrain; and the "traders" who managed these vessels shared in the rich profits. Indeed, no small part of the traffic of the city at that time came from this and somewhat similar sources. With the Lafittes, the de Jourdains and the Mascots on one side, and the *confrères* of Pierre Rameau on the other side, New Orleans was fed by constant streams of ill-gotten wealth.

As for Rameau and his immediate associates, they preferred, for prudential reasons, to do most of their boldest and most remunerative work at a long distance from their headquarters; wherefore, a greater part of the booty, especially stolen slaves, shipped down Pearl River came from Alabama, Georgia, Tennessee, and even as far away as the

Carolinas, while in the country round about Honey Island, within a radius of fifty or sixty miles, people and their property were not molested to any great degree. It was this policy, enforced by Rameau, which had so long protected him and his followers; for while common rumor established him as king of the island, and kept afloat startling stories of his prowess and daring, almost nothing had been done toward investigating the situation. The main fact was that wealthy and influential men in New Orleans, large sharers in the unholy revenues, were standing behind the outlaws and affording them the protection which it was so easy to give so long as the power of the civil and military government was almost paralyzed in Louisiana, and so long as these very citizens controlled directly or indirectly the government itself, either by corrupting the officials or by holding official positions themselves.

With a glance at the foregoing slight sketch of the situation of things in the Gulf-coast region, the readers of this story, which, in all its parts, is historically true, will be able to understand why a party of horsemen should be following the Black-wolf Trail in the direction of the bay of Saint Louis at a late hour in the night. The road in most places was wide enough for two of the cavaliers to go side by side, and four of them chatted as they rode, while the fifth, who evidently was the leader, held his way somewhat in advance, sitting on his horse like a statue, and maintaining a strict and apparently moody silence.

Seen in the deep gloom of the wood, the moving

figures were more like shadows than realities, and but for the heavy tramp of the horses and the occasional sharp jingle of a spur or the clink of a bridle-bit, they might have been regarded by a supersticious fancy as ghosts of the followers of De Soto or Bienville. Their voices, however, were evidently real, and what they were saying referred to the present.

"The king is breaking his own law to-night," said one to another, "and I don't expect anything out of it that'll pay for the trouble. What have these people down here got that 's worth going after? We can't take their niggers, for they'd be known, and I don't expect much money."

"You might wager your head," remarked the other, "that the king knows what he is about. When did he ever fail to do just what he wanted to? There 's more 'n we dream of at the end of this ride."

"Maybe so; I don't say there ain't; but it 's a queer move, you must say that."

"All of our moves are queer enough, for that matter."

"Yes, but—"

"But—but—what 's the use of yer 'buts?' Yer a constitutional grumbler, Tom Newkirk—a cronic, incurable growler."

"Mebbe so, but—"

"Oh, grumble at my foot, my head aches!"

At this point the last speaker burst forth singing in a low mellow voice an old and not very elegant ditty about a maid who—

"Went away, went a-wa-y—
With her love to a fair countrie."

He had reached what was perhaps the last stanza and was droning out the fact that—

"Her lover was false and cold was his heart,
And she died by his cruel hand,"

when the leader suddenly exclaimed in a tone that indicated irritation:

"I'm tired of that. Stop it! This is no time for your songs."

The singer obeyed promptly; but could not refrain from muttering under his breath:

"Devilish particular all at once; must be ailing!"

"Who's got the grumbles now?" said his companion, tauntingly. "Told you that something queer was at the bottom of this here move."

"Humph! I'll admit that when the king gets so particular that he won't let a fellow sing, there must be something kind o' bilious on hand."

The country through which the little cavalcade was passing is to-day almost as wild as ever; the forests have retaken many of the old-time plantations, and one may follow trials like that of the Black-wolf for miles in every direction under trim pines and moss-hung oaks apparently hoary with age. At that time, however, the trees were old in reality, and the way led through jungles where wolves yelled and snarled and panthers screamed back and forth to one another from thicket to thicket. Here and there the horses' feet plashed the darkling ponds and bayous, while the booming and the wallowing of the alligators made the night hideous. Overhead the giant tracery of gnarled and knotted boughs and the finer outlines of leaves, fronds and sprays seemed wrought by some dusky magic on the starry, cloudless blue of the sky. The boles of the great trees arose, solid and firmly buttressed, steadfast as columns of stone, and appeared to support the vast spangled arch of night. On high, a gentle breeze rustled; the dew, cool and fragrant, hung upon everything, and there was a suggestion of fruit in all the wandering perfumes that came from groves of haw and wild apple, tangled berry-vines and flowering festoons of grape.

At a certain place at the edge of a marsh, over which there came a sharp tingle of salt air and a far away boom of sea-water, the leader of the cavaliers drew up his horse and called the others around him, so that his strikingly tall and shapely figure made the center of a dark group sketched against the marsh rushes and the shining line of the bay.

"What is done to-night," he said, "is between us; not another soul upon earth is ever to know even a hint of it. I have chosen you four, as the best of my men, to join me in an affair of great importance to me. It may turn out profitable in itself; it may not; but, in any event, you four will be well paid."

The men drew closer, leaning toward him over their saddles, as he proceeded to describe his plan and its purpose. Like most leaders, he deceived his followers, while at the same time he told them the truth as far as he went.

He was going to rob Vasseur; that much was openly avowed. He had good reason to believe, he said, that Vasseur had in his house a treasure of precious stones, probably of great value, besides a large amount of gold coin. How this information had been obtained he did not say, nor did the men inquire; they were in the habit of taking his word without question and were ready now to follow him without fear.

"One thing is to be borne in mind," he went on: "There is to be no personal hurt done to the man or to any of his household. We are to gain our point by clever work."

It was soon disclosed, as he proceeded with his statement, that what he meant by clever work was a most atrocious method of procedure, involving the last degree of cruelty short of murder, provided that such cruelty should become necessary in order to insure success in the enterprise.

As soon as the council was ended, the leader resumed his course, which now followed the marsh for a short distance and then turned directly across it to a thinly timbered ridge beyond. The horses floundered through the deep, black ooze, their feet sinking so far down that it required desperate lunges to draw them out.

They soon reached a bluff overlooking the bay in a southeasterly direction; here a fairly good roadway ran parallel with the beach, following which for a mile southward, they came to Vasseur's house, hid away in the trees and vines like some great straggling bird-nest, dim and silent.

The cavaliers put on black cloth masks as soon as they reached the bluff. It was not usual for them to wear a disguise; but this was an extraordinary exploit; it called for every precaution. Indeed, a piece of treachery scarcely ever before heard of, even among robbers, was in this act now to be done by the King of Honey Island. No one of the riders knew of this peculiar phase of the matter, however, save the king himself.

There was no hesitation, therefore, and not a twinge of what a desperado might call conscience. The plan was carried out with promptness, precision and success.

Before Vasseur was fairly awake, he was bound hand and foot, and lay on the floor absolutely helpless, gazing wildly at his assailants.

Fairfax, too, was surprised in his bed. He made vigorous resistance; but it was of no use. Four men, each as strong or stronger than he, cast themselves upon him and quickly overpowered him, binding his arms and legs with brutal disregard for the torture inflicted, and thrusting a gag between his teeth.

"I know you! I know you!" screamed Vasseur, before his mouth was stopped. "I know you, Pierre Rameau. You might just as well take off that mask; it does not disguise you in the least. Ah, you treacherous, soulless, perjured villain!"

The gag went in before he could say more; but he lay on his back and cursed with his eyes.

Three of the cavaliers were now sent out to keep watch. Some of the slaves had been aroused, but

THE ROBBING OF VASSEUR.—See Page 32.

they were easily quieted; a word and the sight of a gun or a saber in the hand of a tall masked man sent them shivering and speechless into their cabins where they crouched like wild animals, scarcely breathing for fear they were to be dragged away and sold.

The work which the riders had come to do was accomplished in a very short space of time. Vasseur's money and his treasure of precious stones were soon found and taken; but when the chief had examined the latter he turned to Vasseur and said:

"The cross is not here. Where is it?"

The man, being gagged, of course there was no answer; but the curses were still flashing out of his eyes, while his small, compact frame shook with a passion that no cords could bind.

After gazing through his mask for a moment at the grimacing countenance of his victim, the chief of the riders stooped and began to search the fellow's clothes. Vasseur strained desperately trying to break the cords that bound him, his fury fairly blazing from his dark face. Very deliberately the robber continued his quest till with a little start of satisfaction he laid hands on the worn leather case containing the amethyst cross.

At this moment, Vasseur spit out the gag with a great breath which sent it across the room.

"Pierre Rameau, you dastard!" he screamed in French. "You faithless and honorless hound! I'll kill you for this—I'll track you—dog you—follow you forever, or kill you!"

The robber deliberately set his foot upon the helpless man's mouth and thus stopped his speech.

"Fetch here that gag," he said to one of his followers; but when he removed his foot and before the gag could be used, Vasseur managed to shriek:

"I will inform on you—I will lead government troops against you—I'll have vengeance—I'll—"

"Go out and mount; I'll come immediately," said the chief to his men. "Be ready to ride instantly."

He drew a pistol and leveled it at Vasseur, but checked himself almost in the act of firing.

The four cavaliers were mounted, one of them holding the chief's horse; they waited impatiently in the rather chill morning breeze, and saw that a faint touch of dawn was whitening the sky-line of the day.

When at last the chief came forth, he walked rapidly, and, mounting as if in a mighty hurry, spoke the one word: "Come!" and galloped away.

None of the cavaliers looked behind; but if one had, he might have seen a flicker of fire through the small window-holes of Vasseur's house, and a little later, the place was all aflame.

Doubtless, the chief, who was aware that both Vasseur and Fairfax had, by the accidental slipping aside of his mask, seen his face, was desirous of thus putting an end to them and to the possibility of any trouble from them thereafter. Certainly, there was no other reasonable explanation of his sudden change from the express purpose to leave Vasseur unharmed. At all events, no act of that desperate man's life was more representative of his absolute heartlessness or of his promptness in doing whatever seemed to him safest, without regard in the least to anything save his own personal success. He rode away from the burning house, leaving his two human victims to roast there, and the act did not even change a line in the expression of his dark, calm face.

One thing was photographed in the memory of Fairfax: The singular cold gleam of the robber's eyes, as they appeared to narrow and lengthen with a cat-like stare. He might forget the other features of that face, even the slender whitish scar slanting across the left cheek; but the shape and expression of the eyes could not be lost. He lay there thinking:

"If I ever see you again, I'll know you."

But the gag held back every effort to speak.

CHAPTER IV.

ECHOES FROM LAWLESS DAYS.

For a while it looked as if Vasseur and Fairfax would be roasted alive in the burning house, as the leader of the cavaliers had intended when he applied the fire; but the slaves rallied from their stupor of fright in time to come to the rescue.

The two men, still bound and gagged, were dragged forth without any ceremony and left lying at some distance from the building, while the excited blacks made heroic efforts to save first the house itself and then the furniture. Their work was quite in vain, however, for the dry, resinous pine logs and boards, yielded to the flames as if with delight, flinging out such heat that nothing less invulnerable than a salamander could have gone within the doors. They made a great hubbub as they rushed here and there through the black pitch-smoke and the increasing glare, their half-clad sable forms looking like veritable demons raging around some infernal center of torture.

Fairfax lay on his back under a fig-tree and watched helplessly and with what resignation he could command the rapid and weird changes of the scene. The negroes had deemed it best to leave the men tied, seeing at a glance that to unbind them would require great effort and much loss of valuable time, which had better be spent in efforts to save property. It was a strikingly characteristic fact that not one of them thought of cutting the cords! Both Fairfax and Vasseur tried to make them think of it; but the ludicrous grimaces, which under the circumstances were their only language, conveyed no such suggestion to the excited Africans, wherefore, as the conflagration proceeded, Vasseur raged in stifling silence, and Fairfax strove to deport himself with all the dignity becoming the last of a great Virginia family, considering the peculiarities of the situation.

Meanwhile, the five cavaliers were speeding on their way to Honey Island. Their ride back along the Black-wolf Trail was far brisker than was their pace when we saw them going down to the bay; indeed, by the time that full daylight was abroad in the woods, they were far up by the banks of Pearl River, galloping along single file, with a cane-brake on one hand and a wild jungle of live-oaks and tangled vines on the other. The chief had led them by a new route from Vasseur's to the trail, a crossway that ran past the humble home of Lapin, the overseer of Mr. Vernon's plantation. Day was beginning to shoot up its first faint shimmer as they rode near the little place, startling a pack of dogs from their slumbers under a low shed and drawing from them a broadside of discordant baying. Some domestic fowls, roosting on a rude grape trellis, cackled lustily.

Two savage-looking bloodhounds cleared the low yard fence at a bound and came tearing along after the horsemen, as if to drag them from their saddles.

"Don't shoot!" commanded the chief, as one of the cavaliers lifted his gun. "We are not niggers; they'll quit when they discover our scent. Hold your fire."

Sure enough it was so; the dogs turned about almost instantly, when they discovered that it was white men in the saddles, and trotted leisurely back the way they had come.

While this was going on, a singular incident added significance to what would have otherwise been scarcely worth our noting.

At the sound of the chief's voice, some one in the house leaped out of bed and ran to the little square window-hole that overlooked the path along which the cavaliers were cantering. A moment later, just as the chief was on the point of disappearing among the trees, a head covered with long, scattering, disheveled locks of white hair was thrust out, the face showing haggard and shrunken with intense excitement, and the sunken blue eyes followed in strange wise the horseman's movements.

The chief glanced back just at that point, but he did not see the face in the window-hole; if he had seen it and recognized it, the effect upon him would have been greater than a row of leveled guns could have produced.

Little note made the grim riders of this incident,

"DON'T SHOOT!" COMMANDED THE CHIEF.—See *Page* 38.

they did not note it at all, in fact, but galloped on in reckless mood, knowing that there was no force to pursue them, and that every bound their horses made bore them that much nearer to the land of their comrades, the almost impenetrable wilderness of Honey Island, where their chief was king, and where the division of spoils was the only evidence of law.

One came upon their track, however—a tall old man on foot and unarmed. He strode out from Lapin's cabin and followed the trail, stepping slowly and firmly, yet showing as if from within the window of his countenance a consuming eagerness and a great hope.

It was thus that Alexander Max Burns once more got a glimpse of the man who had stolen his child. That man's voice had startled him from his morning's sleep under Lapin's roof, and the hurried look through the window had photographed on his brain a picture of terrible significance to him. For the merest point of time his eyes had rested upon Kirk MacCollough. He muttered that name as he trudged deeper and deeper into the gloomy forest following the trail of the cavaliers.

What is it that makes our consciousness of an enemy's personal beauty something appealing and, in a way, distressing? An old duelist has been heard to say that he would rather stand before an ordinary-looking dead shot than before a handsome bungler. The glamour of a fine, magnetic presence is strangely confusing; and the effect seems more powerful when the face is an evil one, especially when the evil is not on the outside and shows only elusively and by subtle indirection from within. Max Burns felt the fascination that flashed from the robber-chief's face, and for a time it almost unnerved him; the beauty it wore, like some shining mask, did not suggest at all times the dark spirit of the desperate and lawless man. Long, curling yellow hair and a fine full beard of the same color; a straight nose; a good forehead; long, narrow, clear-gray eyes and a mouth indescribably haughty and stern in its expression, were supplemented by a frame of unusual statute and symmetry. This was Pierre Rameau, formerly Kirk MacCollough, now the King of Honey Island, as old Max Burns saw him in the gray morning light, an apparition of unspeakable meaning to him, gleam like a phantom of evil for a second and then fade, as it were, into the gloom of the moss-hung woods.

Certainly it was not the Kirk MacCollough of twelve years ago—not the slender, fair-faced youth who had stolen the girl—though the reckless half-smile still lingered and the old stamp of utter unrestraint was as plain as ever. No, not the boyish Kirk MacCollough, but the man, full-grown to his prime, masterful, commanding, a leader of men, and yet there was no mistaking his identity.

Max Burns was old, and for fifty years had been a preacher whose sermons had overflowed with sentimental tenderness; but he had a side to his nature which was as hard as Scotch granite. It was with this hard side out that he was pursuing Kirk MacCollough; and yet, even through this, the spell of the man's strong and beautiful face found its way to his heart.

The effect of it was but temporary, so far as checking his determination was concerned; but it never quite left him during the rest of the day as he slowly but steadily followed the trail into the main road and on toward the upper Pearl-River region.

Literally, the preacher had no scrip for his journey, no staff, no means of living; he depended, as the old-time minister of the backwoods was wont to do, upon the hand of Providence. Here and there a trapper's or a hunter's hut, here and yonder a settler's cabin offered him rest, food, shelter. He did not tell his story; but he prayed at the fireside of all, and he managed to leave behind him, wherever he went, a memorable something—sweet, strange and altogether welcome to the simple pioneer hearts. Sometimes he fell among desperate men, robbers themselves, or aiders and abettors of them, and even with these he was at home; for he bore with him the charm of childlike faith, combined with the touching appeal of unprotected old age.

What helped him most of all, perhaps, was his singing; for age had scarcely touched the deep, rich music of his voice, and his memory was stored with hymns and tunes that enthralled the hearts of his entertainers.

The strolling preachers of all denominations traversed our frontier regions in those days, and Max Burns was accepted as a member of the class without a question, without suspicion, and made freely welcome by every household as a privileged if not in every instance a venerated person. Curious enough does it appear when recorded, but it is, nevertheless, a historical fact, that the preacher found for some time a home with one Dick Becket, well known as the fighting fiddler, who was a red-headed man, very bow-legged, much freckled and badly scarred by an old knife-cut across the nose, and whose cabin was about three miles east of Pearl River, opposite the southern end of Honey Island.

This Dick Becket was a trapper and, to some extent, a trader with the Indians. His cabin was often the stopping-place of the freebooters, with whom he kept on good terms without having anything to do with their enterprises. He charged liberal prices for their board and lodging, and so his place became known far and near as Dick's. He lived to a great age, dying in 1867 on the banks of Pearl River, not far from where his first cabin stood. It was from him, at first hand, that many of the Honey Island legends came into circulation in their present form. He fiddled as long as he lived, and was a noted story-teller. He took Burns in and became greatly attached to him, ever afterward calling him Daddy or Parson Burns.

Thus established within a comparatively short distance of Pierre Rameau's base of operations, the old man felt that at last he was on the point of reaching the end of his long wanderings. There could be no doubt now that Pierre Rameau and MacCollough were one and the same man, nor did it look possible for the outlaw to prevent his approach, provided that he could avoid recognition.

The writer of this story has become the owner of a curious and singularly interesting collection of papers, labeled "The Pearl River Records," and it is from these and from Dick Becket's stories that he has obtained the main facts in connection with Rev. Max Burns's sojourn in the region of Honey Island. The information is meager enough touching the old man's motive; but this lack naturally came of his reticence and caution in communicating with the people who treated him so kindly. Supplementing the fiddler's reminiscences and the "Records"—most of which have to do with the exploits of various outlaws, from Rameau, Lafitte, Murrell and Copeland, down to Rube Burrow and Eugene Bunch—the recollections of Orlando Favre, a very old half-breed Indian, who died some fifteen years ago, have been relied upon; but, after all, the facts are meager and scattering. Indeed, what has already been told in the present chapter cannot be added to. The further adventures of Max Burns, in so far as they will be found of importance in this story, will be looked for at another stage of our progress.

We must now return to the bay of Saint Louis, where we left Vasseur and Fairfax enduring as best they could a situation at once awkward and trying in the extreme. To be bound and gagged could be borne after a fashion, so long as the evil was enforced by an irresistible enemy; moreover, since every moment added the torture of cruelly tight-drawn cords to wrists and ankles, the first part of the ordeal was much milder than the latter part; but when it came to lying prone, stiff and speechless while a great fire raged almost over them it was the unbearable that had to be borne; it was torture too exasperating for even the temper of Fairfax. He too gave way to violent "paroxysms of silence," as he afterward expressed it.

When Vasseur was at length released, he was too weak and benumbed by the pressure of the bonds and by the exhaustive wrath-passion that he had indulged in for his curses and cuffs to do much harm; but he distributed both with unstinted liberality as he limped and hopped wildly about amongst the negroes.

The house and nearly everything in if were burned to ashes in an incredibly short time. Fairfax could not repress a smile when he found that his travelling-bag containing his clothes had been saved, while his sketches and his weapons—his pistols and his gun, a rifle of great value—had been overlooked and left to be destroyed. As for Vasseur, his mind, what little of it was presently available, raged with the memory of his lost treasure of jewels. He screamed in French, he screeched in Italian, he cursed and swore without fear of confusion of tongues, and through it all ran something about having been betrayed and robbed by an individual who owed him an eternal debt of gratitude. All this, considering that the man was still in his night-clothes, of which a red night-cap was a most conspicuous garment, would have been highly amusing at any other time; and even now, at its worst, it was weirdly, almost demoniacally, comical.

Fairfax dressed himself forthwith, and then stood, with his hands in his pockets, staring at the scene, as one does when one feels especially perplexed and helpless in the midst of sudden disaster. He turned quickly, however, when Vasseur came near. The little fellow could scarcely speak intelligibly, and the froth of excitement was clotted on his lips.

"It was zat Pierre Rameau!" he cried, not forgetting to air his English even in this extremity. "Zat villaine, zat robbaire! He steal evareting! He burn my *maison;* he care off my propriety!"

Usually it was not hard for Fairfax to find words; but now he could frame no suitable comment on the occasion. He stood looking at his swarthy little host, and smiling half mechanically, without moving his lips to make him a response. There was pathos as well as comedy in the situation.

The negroes, men, women and children, gathered in awe-struck groups to gaze on the fire, making their remarks in undertones, the women crying and the half-naked little ones clinging to the coarse, scant skirts of their mothers.

"Ah! Ze villaine! Ze scoun'rel! Ze robbaire! Oh! Ah! Ah! Ah! My jewels! My pretty jewels!" still wailed Vasseur, after the house was white ashes and the sun had come up from the sea like a great round flower of flame. "My precious stones! My beautiful cross! My money! Zey are all gone—gone! He took zem! Oh! Ze perfide vagabone! Ze *scélérat!*"

When Fairfax had pulled himself together sufficiently to consider the situation calmly, his first effort was toward reducing Vasseur to a rational state of mind, a task by no means easy to accomplish. He succeeded in a measure at length, and when the poor little man had found some clothes and a pipe, the whole matter was talked over; and so it happened that Fairfax heard a strange story.

Eight years prior to the robbery at Vasseur's, the two men, Vasseur and Rameau, had been comrades and equal sharers in the dangers and the profits of a daring piece of piracy done in the far East. In dividing the spoils, Vasseur gladly accepted a large quantity of jewels, some of them the personal property of Rameau, in lieu of their value in money, his passion for precious stones controlling his greed for gold; but a goodly pile of money fell to his share also, and he abandoned the sea forthwith to settle himself, with a body of slaves, on a plantation in San Domingo, whence, when disturbances came, he fled to his present abode on the beautiful bluffs of the bay of Saint Louis.

Vasseur gave the details of his story without reserve. He was boiling over with indignation, and his passion made him recklessly communicative; indeed, he was almost crazed, and seemed to find vent for his overcharge of nervous excitement in laying bare the innermost secrets of his past experience.

Under ordinary circumstances and in a normal mood, Fairfax most probably would have refused to hear these terrible confessions; and yet they were of a kind to enthrall the imagination of a young man, himself passionately fond of adventure; and when he was told that the daring and villainous act just perpetrated by the riders from Honey Island had been directed by Pierre Rameau in person, he felt that, no matter what had been Vasseur's crimes, the little man was justifiable in considering himself atrociously betrayed and outraged by his former partner in felony.

It was a revelation to Fairfax thus to find himself the companion and comrade in misfortune of a whilom pirate; but, strange as it may seem, he did not recoil from the discovery. Doubtless he recognized it as a necessary part of the life around him, and found food for his fancy in regarding it as an incident of the slowly receding buccaneer days—a stray, lingering wave of the wild tide of lawlessness which formerly flowed from the Caribbean across the Gulf into the famous rendezvous of Bay Saint Louis; at all events, he found a certain exhilaration possessing him, and as he walked up to the Vernon place that same morning he could not cast off a sense of the link which connected him with some great chain of picturesque events past, present and to come.

When he neared the house he heard the noisy mocking-birds in the oaks and magnolias, and the first person he saw was Mlle. Pauline Vernon standing, tall, bright and beautiful, on the veranda under the vines. Something in her form and face sent a tender thrill through him, and in a moment he was strangely happy. Youth casts out the evil spirit of misfortune so easily in the worst case; and, after all, what had happened to Fairfax was no more than a stimulating bit of experience in the rougher current of the wild life into which he had voluntarily thrown himself. He had seen Pierre Rameau in one of his most picturesque attitudes, and the apparition was of itself worth all that he had paid for it in submitting to the gag and to imminent danger of being roasted alive. The artist within him was complacently happy over the whole affair. In truth, he could not have denied that the robber's face had its fascination. Some day he would paint it from memory, or mayhap he might yet see those strange, terrible, magnetic eyes again.

CHAPTER V.

A BREAKFAST AT VERNON PLACE.

As Fairfax approached the veranda, Mr. Vernon came out of the hall, booted as if for a ride; at the same time a servant led a horse around from the rear of the house. Father and daughter both smiled at sight of the young man, and Mr. Vernon welcomed him with a hearty, loud "Good-morning," his voice ringing out pleasantly:

"Glad to see you, my boy—glad to see you. Hope you slept well last night. It was a grand night for sound, refreshing sleep!"

Fairfax lifted his hat and shook hands with them both. For the single moment that his fingers closed over those of Mlle. Pauline he looked into her shy but friendly eyes and forgot all that had passed during the night.

"And how are they down at Vasseur's?" continued Mr. Vernon. "Is my little neighbor well?"

He always spoke of Vasseur in the diminutive.

The inquiry caused Fairfax to start perceptibly. It was a rude transition from the mood of the moment to a thought of what had come to pass during the night. At first he had no words ready. Like an abashed boy, he stood looking now at Mlle. Pauline and then at her father. There was little enough of shyness or hesitation in his nature; but somehow the questions threw him into confusion. Just then the subject called up was not welcome to him; it would have been so much pleasanter could he have been left alone with Mlle. Pauline to forget that there ever was a Vasseur. He hesitated but a moment, however, seeing that his change of countenance had stirred up some sort of uneasiness in the mind of Mr. Vernon, who had observed it.

"Vasseur was robbed last night," he bluntly said, "and his house was burned."

"Robbed! Burned!" exclaimed Mr. Vernon, whose turn it now was to be taken by surprise.

"What do you mean to say, Mr. Fairfax!"

Mlle. Pauline drew close to her stalwart, shaggy father, and put an arm over his immense shoulder. The blood had left her face, so that it was as white as a lily petal.

It did not give Fairfax any pleasure to tell the story. Perhaps, being a very young man, he was aware that his part in the affair had been neither heroic nor picturesque, and that he must at best appear to have been an easy victim to a bold assault. This was an exhilarating consciousness.

Mr. Vernon's brow grew dark as he listened, and he combed his beard with his fingers.

"I will ride down and see Vasseur," he said. "It may be that I can be of service to him. Go in, Mr. Fairfax; the ladies will ask you a thousand questions; I will return immediately."

"But it is dreadful! It is dangerous! You will be killed!" cried Pauline, clinging to him, nervously. "Don't go, father! Please, don't."

He kissed her, laughing meantime to pooh-pooh her fears, then went down the steps and vaulted with a superb show of muscular energy into the saddle. Before he rode away, he sat for a time stroking the glossy neck of his horse, while the groom fetched a pair of heavy holster pistols and hung them at the pommel of the saddle; then his gun was also handed to him.

Mrs. Vernon made her appearance at this point. She saw forthwith that something unusual had happened, and began to ask questions, growing excited as she proceeded. The groom stood listening with open mouth and rolling eyes.

"Mr. Fairfax will tell you everything," said Mr. Vernon; "it's nothing so terrible, after all. The danger is past, if there ever was any, and I'm only going down to console poor little Vasseur."

"And, say, dear," he turned and added to his wife, after he had ridden to some distance, "ask Mr. Fairfax to have some breakfast; I don't think he has taken any this morning. I may return in time to have coffee with you; but don't wait."

Mrs. Vernon made a gesture of despair and began to cry hysterically.

"I will not stay in this terrible place any longer!" she exclaimed with vehemence. "We must go back to the city at once. Oh, but this is unbearable! Robbers down there—only a mile or so away! What if—if—what if they had come here!"

This was addressed to Mr. Vernon, but he did not hear; his horse was already galloping briskly away. The three, Mrs. Vernon, Pauline and Fairfax, stood looking after him until he had passed out of sight amid the fringe of trees along the bluff of the bay shore. What to them was a reality, quite in keeping with the time and the place, must appear to us, at this distance and with our surroundings, like an illustration torn from some old novel. Even in that day, however, when every inhabitant of the gulf coast was more or less familiar with lawlessness and violence in their most picturesque forms, there was something startling in each new phase of the reckless life that throbbed along the old creole borders. It is impossible for men and women to live in the midst of romance and not realize it in some degree.

"He ought to have lived in the days of Richard the Lionheart," said Fairfax, turning his gaze from where Mr. Vernon had disappeared in the wood to the pale face of Pauline. "He would have been a knight of iron with that frame of his." He spoke lightly, more to break up the situation and call the ladies back to themselves than to give expression to the fancy of the moment, suggested by the superb horsemanship just witnessed.

"But the robbers! They will kill him!" insisted Mrs. Vernon. "He is going right to them!"

"Never fear, madam," said Fairfax with an assuring smile; "there isn't the slightest danger. Those gallant knights of the road are many miles from here at present. It appears they knew too much about Vasseur's treasure, and so planned a successful raid on it. There is no more danger from them; they are gone."

"But we have jewels, too," said Mrs. Vernon with a quick look at Pauline. "They might want our diamonds!"

Fairfax laughed outright, and the ladies joined him timidly, as if under protest.

"If I may speak of it," he said, "you are forgetting to make further mention of breakfast. I am preposterously hungry after my night's adventures."

"A thousand pardons!" exclaimed Mrs. Vernon. "We will go in at once."

The appeal to her hospitality was with her, as it has always been with the Southern hostess, sufficient to drive almost anything else from her mind.

Pauline led the way to the breakfast-room, where the table was spread near a rude alcove in the soft light of vine-colored windows. The wildness of the place was emphasized by woody perfumes, that strayed in along with brilliant song-phrases of the thrushes and mocking-birds. The air itself, as it rustled through open doors and windows, was a breath of the blooming virgin wilderness, and there was a note of remoteness and loneliness in the swash of the sea and the sough of the pines. It may have been the sense of isolation induced by the surroundings that made Fairfax enjoy in some indefinable way the indirect appeal to his protection, which he felt rather than saw or heard coming to him from Mrs. Vernon and her daughter.

Although he felt it necessary to hide from the

ladies every doubt he might have as to their perfect security, he found himself tingling with pleasure, to know that his presence gave them a sense of safety. It now seemed to him inexplicable that Mr. Vernon should have brought his wife and daughter to this lonely and exposed place. If the bay of Saint Louis is a secluded, dreamy, far-withdrawn spot even now, what was it at the beginning of our century?

"I shall insist on going back to our house in New Orleans at once," said Mrs. Vernon, as they took their places at the table, and she signaled for a servant. "I am not willing to live here any longer."

She shrugged her shoulders and shivered.

"It may be as you think, Mr. Fairfax, that there is no danger; but who wants to live where outlaws ride past one's window by night and rob and burn one's neighbor's house! And, besides, I'm heartily tired of this horrid place!"

Her vivacity gave a charming piquancy to her expression of discontent. She spoke of Vasseur as her neighbor, but, in fact, she had never seen the man or his house.

Fairfax could not have the heart to simulate opposition to the natural feeling of his hostess, especially since he was hoping and wishing that the departure of the Vernons for New Orleans would be hastened by every possible good fortune. He was ready to go with them at a moment's notice, and would have been glad to give the notice himself.

"Your experience here will be pleasant to remember," he said, "and I should think that such an outing would add an express charm to your enjoyment of the city. I am sure that even my unheroic adventures with the masked raiders from the wilderness will afford me most enjoyable recollections so soon as I can get them in the proper perspective. To be perfectly frank, I am myself quite willing to return to New Orleans."

"Father will be ready to go now," spoke up Pauline, for the first time; "he will not wish to keep us here any longer."

It was useless for Fairfax to try, he could not lead the conversation away from the robbers, and so they sat long at the table discussing the subject most unwelcome to him until Mr. Vernon returned just in time to take coffee with them.

The incoming of the bluff and cheery host changed the atmosphere of the room at once; Mrs. Vernon and Pauline were smiling and comparatively at ease again.

"I have sent a small boat with orders to my overseer at the Chandeleurs to bring up another large schooner; I'm going to take everything away from here." These were Mr. Vernon's first words. "My sloop is just in from New Orleans," he added, turning some papers in his hands. "The war between England and the United States is taking a new turn it seems, and this coast will not long be safe. We will return to New Orleans at once."

Mrs. Vernon and Pauline exchanged a glance of delight; evidently just then they were glad of anything, even war, that would drive them away from their wildwood home and back to the security and comfort of the city. They forgot Pierre Rameau and his cavaliers, they forgot Vasseur and his house in ashes, as on the instant the vision of the mansion on the narrow street in New Orleans, arose in their minds with the murmur of man's activities and the gleam of passing vehicles. Indeed, the thought of war was vague, remote, shrouded in the misty distance; even the United States seemed to them not the country in which they lived, but rather some far-off land in which they had but a nominal interest.

Fairfax had left New York just in advance of the beginning of war, and perhaps no better impression can be given of the wide, unconquered distances of our country before steam and electricity had compressed them, than to imagine that, although for some months the fighting had been going on, the news of it was just fairly reaching this nook of the gulf coast where he found himself so deeply and sweetly content that the thought of his country's peril or of his duty, as the son of a patriot soldier, calling him to arms had not once arisen in his mind. He had heard the war mentioned in New Orleans; but it had not impressed him as a matter of importance to himself.

"I am selfish enough to be glad when I hear you say that you are going back to the city," he said, "for I shall have to depend upon you to give me room in your vessel. I was just telling the ladies that last night's experiences have quite filled my cup f desire, and that I am willing to retire from this picturesque region."

Mr. Vernon laughed, but it was easy to see that behind his appearance of cheerfulness grave thoughts were pressing upon him. His heavy, bearded face showed unmistakable lines of trouble, and in his deep-set eyes a cloud was hovering. He sipped his coffee and made light remarks; but Pauline's quick sympathy discovered his real mood.

"Something has happened to disturb you, papa," she ventured. "There is something you dread for us to know."

The perfect frankness of her voice and manner and the outright sincerity of her words seemed to touch her father. A slight flush crept into his cheeks along the fringe of his ample white beard; he looked at her with a gleam of tenderness in his eyes.

"You are a very close observer," he said, in half-banter. "You read me as if my face were a book."

"He finds it hard to tear away from the freedom of this wild place," remarked Mrs. Vernon. "I wish we could take the whole estate along with us to the city."

"I wish I knew that we could be sure of safety, even in New Orleans," said Mr. Vernon. "It is better to be in the city than here; but what will become of it when an English fleet and army lay siege to it?"

"But they will never come away off there, will they?" inquired Pauline, with all the faith of a child in long distances.

Her father laughed.

"We will not borrow trouble," he said, as he folded the papers in his hand and bestowed them in a pocket of his ample jacket, meantime permitting Pauline to refill his cup. Then he changed his tone and said that they would sail for New Orleans to-morrow morning, if the breeze should be favorable.

Fairfax saw that something of more direct personal interest than news of the progress of the war was demanding Mr. Vernon's thought. A subtlety of insight, accidental and momentary, perhaps, gave him a half-glimpse of what it was, or, at least, engendered a suspicion of its origin, if not of its nature and substance.

"How did you find Vasseur?" he inquired. "Is he quieting down to a robbed man's best philosophy?"

"Poor little fellow!" Mr. Vernon answered. "He cries for his jewels as a mother cries for her lost children."

"What is he going to do?"

"I don't know; no more does he; but I should not like to be the man that robbed him. He is little, but he is as deadly as a viper and as persistent as time itself."

Something in Mr. Vernon's voice and manner, as he said this, suggested to Fairfax that there was a meaning between the words; but the truth was that Mr. Vernon's thoughts were not on Vasseur and his troubles. Uppermost in his mind was a shadow of what the war might bring to him and his. Not that he had any cowardly fears; but there had been matters connected with his early career which rendered the probabilities of his falling into the hands of the English a thing not to be regarded without unspeakable dread. He knew enough about military science to be well aware of the defenseless condition of New Orleans in the presence of such a fleet and such an army as the British government might be able to send there. Now the news that came to him from one in high connection with the government indicated that a strong fleet and an army overwhelming in numbers would probably soon be in front of New Orleans and under command of a distinguished British officer. What would be the result? It seemed to him that there could be but one answer: The city would fall, and the whole gulf coast would be ravaged.

He excused himself presently, with the plea that he had much to do in preparing for the departure for New Orleans, and went out.

Fairfax felt compelled, under the circumstances, to accept the hospitality of the Vernons during the rest of his stay, seeing that, since the burning of Vasseur's place, there was no other available alternative, and besides he could not muster up the slightest unwillingness in the matter. He was glad, indeed, with a genuine boyish gladness, and could not hide the pleasure his situation gave him.

Fairfax was bold to make the most of his surroundings; but Pauline when she found herself for a moment alone with him under the vines of the rude veranda, suddenly felt an access of shyness not in the least characteristic, and shrank away from him, in spirit at least, taking refuge within that impenetrable close which is walled by the reserve of unaffected girlhood. He, however, was too happy to desire more than to be near her and see her, to feel that he formed part of a picture with her, that they stood on the same plane and were outlined against the same romantic background; and to dream that perhaps they might go, side by side, through a long and happy future.

CHAPTER VI.

AN UNKNOWN SCHOONER.

With a favorable wind and with the temperature at the average degree for springtime, the voyage from the bay of Saint Louis to New Orleans, by way of Lake Borgne, the Rigolets and Lake Pontchartrain, is a charming experience. Passing out of the bay's mouth in a southeasterly direction, the course is over a shallow sound, set with sand-bars and dotted with low islands, some of them densely wooded, others covered with rushes and marshgrass. On the right for miles shine the white bluffs of the mainland, crowned at the time of our story with groves of live-oaks and magnolias, immense in size and bearing the unmistakable marks of great age. It was these beautiful headlands that cast their glamour over the imagination of the old French explorer as he sailed by in 1699, on his way to Pontchartrain and Maurepas. From then till now, the fascination of the coast as seen from the sea has held and strengthened, so that no person can pass it by without dreaming the dreams of eternal, breezy, balmy summer. The dusky oaks spread their arms so far, their leaves and their trailing moss shimmer so vaguely, they cast such dark, cool shadows below, and over them hovers a sheen so tender! Small wonder that even men like Iberville, Chateaugue and Bienville made fine plans for possessing a paradise so fair to see, and harbored the thought of peace and rest on the airy bluffs under the romantic groves where the red men held their summer feasts and worshiped the golden sun!

On the left, as the vessel's course curves westward toward Borgne, the crescent of the Chandeleurs bounds the horizon, while stretching away southward, swimming apparently against both sky and water, the outlying marshes of Louisiana waver and flicker like a bank of sunlit clouds.

This restless sheet of water, tumbling its short white-capped waves between the islands and the mainland, is Mississippi Sound, of which Lake Borgne is but a wider part that finds connection with Pontchartrain through a broad bayou, or series of bayous, called the Rigolets.

Pearl River falls into Lake Borgne some miles eastward from the Rigolets, and its mouth, joining with many little bayous, fills the grassy marshes on either side with a silvery net-work of water.

A glance at a good map of the region will show how perfectly adapted was this whole tangle of lakes, creeks, rivers, islands, marshes, swamps and densely timbered mainlands to the purposes of the outlaws, whose swift little vessels darted through the intricate water-ways like wild-fowl in their native haunt. What had the pirates to fear so long as there was no government properly so called in Louisiana? When their pockets were well filled with golden loot, they even ventured boldly into New Orleans or Mobile, and drank and gambled and held high carousal with jolly planters and reckless traders in the hotels and cafés. Men like Lafitte and Rameau had a way of making fair weather for themselves; indeed, they were not without influence in circles of society, the proudest and highest. From Barataria Lake, on one side, to Honey Island, on the other, New Orleans was hedged in, so to speak, with a cordon of outlaws, whose leaders dictated, in no small degree, the policy of the city in trade and commerce, law and politics.

Mr. Vernon was explaining all this to Fairfax as they sat smoking on the deck of the little vessel which was bearing them past Half-Moon Island into the tumbling little sea called Lake Borgne. Mrs. Vernon and Pauline were below, and a group of family servants, huddled forward, were lounging idly and enjoying the lazy swing of the waves. Three black men, short, gaunt, with muscles like iron bands on their sturdy limbs, were the vessel's crew. One, whose woolly head was grizzled with age, watched the tiller, and gave orders in a queer mincing patois.

"You do not mean to say, Mr. Vernon, that you are abandoning your place at Bay Saint Louis," remarked Fairfax, in the course of their conversation; "you surely are not going to leave it to go to ruin!"

"I cannot say for how long; but certainly I am

abandoning it," said Mr. Vernon. "It is no longer safe for myself or my slaves to stay there. Besides, if the war reach here everything will be destroyed, and even if that calamity be averted, there remains the general unsafe condition of society and government here."

Pauline just then came from below.

"But do you think the British are really likely to attack this coast?" inquired Fairfax

"It is not only likely but almost certain," was the reply.

"And with what result?"

"Disaster to us."

At this point Mr. Vernon arose and went to speak to the black man at the tiller. He was beginning to fear that with the breeze as it now set they were not going to be able to pass the Rigolets before nightfall, and that indeed they might be forced to anchor off the mouth of Pearl River to await a change of wind. The thought was anything but pleasant.

Already the sun was slipping down the west, and every minute the breeze became more unfavorable and also more fickle, puffing irregularly and at times threatening to cease altogether.

The negro sailors were working hard and with a great deal of adroitness to make the most of the situation; for they were not unaware of the danger to them in spending a night in the track of the Pearl River vessels. To them the thought of falling into the hands of pirates or slave-thieves had all the force of romantic terror possible to their savage imagination.

Fairfax, in blissful ignorance of any special significance attaching to the situation, abandoned himself to the pleasure of looking into Pauline's face and listening to her voice. In some sweet way the girl's grace and beauty, her smiles, her voice, her proud, yet unconscious air of security, her mobility and her indescribable shy boldness, so to call it, seemed to Fairfax to be the center of expression for the sea, the sky and the air; she was to him the interpretation of the great, mysterious dream of nature.

Pauline may have been quite as unconscious of the young man's admiration as she appeared to be; but, doubtless, some satisfying sense of her influence upon him stole through her mind, a waft from that wonderland of experience, toward which it is the blessed privilege of every maiden to drift, half expecting, half doubting.

They were both under the influence of a very tender and beautiful, yet indistinct, mood, which made it altogether delightful to sit or stand near each other and merely play with the outer fringe of sentiment, while the *Water-Bird* slipped gently along between the yellow marshes.

Suddenly a sail, shining as white as snow in the now almost level rays of the sun, separated itself from a clump of oaks on a distant hummock, and appeared to slip forth across a level, grassy marsh.

All hands on deck saw it at once. Mr. Vernon sent below for his glass. A moment later, Mrs.

Vernon came up. She watched her husband who, despite his age and bulk, was climbing with surprising nimbleness aloft in order to have a clear view of the approaching sail. It proved to be a schooner coming down Pearl River into Borgne; he could not make out its further description; but it appeared to be a fast little craft, well manned and admirably handled. Although the breeze was puffy, it favored the stranger and she seemed to be skimming along very briskly and steadily.

Mr. Vernon came down out of the rigging and gave some orders in an undertone to the man at the tiller, then he passed forward, speaking in the same tone to the other black sailors.

Fairfax caught at once the meaning of this quiet work, and when Mr. Vernon came to the ladies and said: "You had better go below for a while, we shall need all the deck-room to work the sails," there was more in his manner than his wife and daughter noticed.

Mrs. Vernon objected to being confined again in the stuffy little cabin just when she was beginning to enjoy the sweet fragrance of the open air; but Fairfax assisted her and Pauline to descend and then returned to the deck.

"I wanted to avoid a scene," said Mr. Vernon, "and I don't like the appearance of the fellow yonder," pointing at the sail. "It's no use for us to try to run away; you see that at a glance. Of course she may be all right; but I don't like her looks nor the place she is coming from. At any rate, we've got to take our chance."

"Do you mean to say that you suspect her of being a pirate?"

"It is safe to suspect everything that comes out of Pearl River of being in some way connected with wrongdoing; but still, this may be the exception."

"We'd better get ready to fight, then," said Fairfax. "Have you no arms on board?" At the same time his eyes sought the little swivel that stood nearly amidship. "Is that gun in condition?"

Mr. Vernon could not help laughing in his beard at the young man's prompt combativeness and his admirable coolness, and he felt a pang of regret when he had to say frankly that it would be sheer desperation to attempt resistance, should the schooner prove to be one of the Pearl-River pirates bent upon their capture.

"They are carrying at least three guns," he added, "and I counted ten men of their crew; besides, they could sail right up to us and board us."

A cloud passed over the young man's face, and a sudden realization of what might be at hand went down like a leaden load upon his heart. The first thought was what would befall Pauline. He stood for a few moments like one who had received an almost stunning blow. Mr. Vernon watched him narrowly and was inwardly delighted when presently he shook off his weakness and exclaimed:

"But what are we to do? Are we to let them take us, if they wish, without our making any resistance? For my part, sir, I do not consent to any such a thing. We can but add a very little fury to their manner of dealing with us by fighting them like men. Earnestly, sir, I insist on meeting this matter bravely."

"So do I," said Mr. Vernon, "but the question is: What course would, in reality, be true bravery? I have no shot on board for the swivel, and what could you and I do against a schooner's crew."

"You have done very wrong," said Fairfax, almost hotly, "to bring your family into this situation. It was a great oversight not to prepare for such an emergency."

Mr. Vernon eyed his young friend, but made no direct reply to his hasty words. He saw that he could depend upon him in desperate need, and this was the most and the best that he could ask just then.

"There will probably be a light fog at nightfall; if we can give them the slip till then we may be able to get away; it is our only chance, provided they are enemies. They have a long run to make yet before they get into the lake; meantime, if we can pass the point yonder and find the mouth of the Rigolets and the fog at the same time, we may escape."

It was a well laid plan; but the wind was refractory, shifting and growing more unreliable every moment.

Fairfax could not understand Mr. Vernon's apparent indifference; it was so opposed to what his own nature prompted under such a stress that it exasperated him, while, at the same time, he felt his own inability to suggest anything feasible.

Meantime, their little craft had been set as close to the wind as she could run, and was making fair speed in a northwesterly course toward a marsh point which, in those days, had a hummock clothed with low, spreading live-oaks. The fog was already beginning to fill the atmosphere with a thin, gray twilight effect, and the distant schooner's sails were softening into dimness; but the breeze slackened until it could be scarcely felt; moreover, as they crept behind the point, even this breath was shut off, and suddenly it was a dead calm.

Mr. Vernon ordered his men to cast anchor, and then, lighting his pipe, he went up to Fairfax, who was tramping back and forth, chafing helplessly.

"They can't reach us till morning, at all events," he said; "it will be all that they can do to get out of the river."

"And so all that we can hope for is to lie here and wait," Fairfax muttered, "and be done for in the morning. It seems to me a tame way for men who pretend to have any courage to choose. Surely, there is some—"

"Young man," Mr. Vernon's voice was very even and low, as he interrupted, but it had a certain savage *timbre*—"young man, you are on my vessel; it is your duty to obey my orders; you are going to obey them. If you have any suggestions to make I will give them consideration; but understand that I command here, and that you do not occupy any official position whatever."

Fairfax stood amazed; he looked at Mr. Vernon's almost giant bulk looming in the gray dusk; it appeared to dilate and take on the rugged outlines that his imagination would have given to some old buccaneer. The remote arrogance and the immediate authority with which the surprising words had been uttered seemed to come from a man not in the least like the Mr. Vernon of yesterday. It was as if the man's nature had suddenly reverted to a state once its normal one and stood ready to assert by sheer force an ancient supremacy. Fairfax felt the sting of the situation, and at the same time his judgment came to his aid. There could be no denying Mr. Vernon's right to command his own vessel.

"I beg your pardon, sir," he managed to say; "you are mistaken if you think me ungrateful enough to offer any impertinent objections to your method of conducting your own affairs. I did not mean anything of the kind."

He hated himself the next moment for having found no better way of expressing what, after all, was not very clear in his own mind; but his embarrassment was not in the least relieved when Mr. Vernon, with a gruff chuckle, turned abruptly away and went below.

Fairfax looked around him, half dazed.

Fairfax was not in a mood to doubt and accuse. His recent experiences had opened his eyes to the darkest possibilities of the life into which he had been suddenly drawn so deeply. The feeling that he had not managed himself in the least adroitly, and that probably he had shown his weakest side to Mr. Vernon, helped to irritate him; moreover, the danger, if danger it was, hovering so near to Pauline affected him strangely. This young girl had taken possession of him; he realized it now. And was he about to see her fall into the hands of men like Pierre Rameau?

Mr. Vernon did not come on deck for some hours; when he re-appeared a light breath of wind was beginning to blow, and he immediately ordered all hands to make ready to put the vessel under sail.

The fog, though not so dense as it had been, was still too heavy to permit any distinct view through it. When the little craft began to move, Mr. Vernon went forward. As he passed Fairfax, he said in a low voice:

"Stand by to pass my orders to the man at the tiller; we must not speak above our breath. If we can get through to the lake, we are safe."

By the lake, he meant Ponchartrain, and their way thither lay through the main channel of the Rigolets.

So gently did the vessel move that the ladies sleeping below did not wake; the only sounds to be heard were an occasional creak of cord or spar and the light ripple of the water at the prow.

Mr. Vernon was feeling his way toward the mouth of the channel with nothing to guide him save his sense of distances and directions. The wind was somewhat against him and there was not an object by which he could exactly fix his whereabouts. So weak was the breeze, moreover, that the vessel crept at but a snail's pace over the darkling water. It was near daylight; indeed, the pale influence of the morning was diffusing itself through the fog when the breeze began to freshen a little, sending a ripple over Borgne and quickening the movement of the vessel. The soft, gray vail wavered and lifted perceptibly, and Mr. Vernon had just made out the marsh-points at the mouth of the channel and was giving a low order, when suddenly a vessel, distant a stone's throw, showed itself through the fog directly ahead, and at the same instant "Ahoy, there!" came in a loud, clear voice from the stranger's deck.

CHAPTER VII.

LIEUTENANT BALLANCHE.

There was little space for action on the part of Mr. Vernon, between the moment when his vessel was hailed and that when it was necessary for him to answer. In shorter time than we take to write it, the two crafts were almost touching.

"Avast, or I'll blow you out of the water!" shouted a voice not in the least nautical, but full of determination; the voice of a landsman, who, if he could not readily find the phraseology of the sea, was evidently in no mood to be trifled with.

At the same time a twelve-pounder gun was turned so as to rake the deck of the *Water-Bird*.

"Blow away, Lieutenant Ballanche!" roared Mr. Vernon. "It would be a glorious thing to fire on me and my family! Ha! Ha! Ha! Blow away! Blow away!"

The little vessel was now passing astern of the schooner and not a half cable's length from it.

"Hello! Is that you, Mr. Vernon?" shouted the slim young officer who stood out most prominently on the schooner's deck. He spoke in French.

"Aye, that it is!" was the loud answer in the

same language. "I thought we should ram you amidship, but we missed, good luck to you and to us as well!"

"I wish to speak with you, sir," called out the young officer. "It is very important."

The two vessels were already going apart rapidly, their courses being different; but every word was heard, so favorable was everything to the conveyance of sounds.

Fairfax felt a load fall from his breast at this sudden turn in an adventure which but a moment before had filled him with such dismay as only youth and love and the thought of swift calamity to the one most dear to him could engender. In the stress of the apparent crisis he had thought only of the girl; and now that the strain was over, it seemed to him as if the same breath that had blown away his distress on Pauline's account had also lifted the fog; for the next moment the gray vail was so removed that the young officer on board the schooner came into clear relief against the tall marsh grass on the point beyond. His features could not be made out; but his form was tall, slender, graceful, and his attitude striking in the extreme. He wore the undress uniform of a lieutenant of infantry in the United States Army.

A half-hour later, the two vessels lay alongside of each other, and Lieutenant Ballanche came aboard of the *Water-Bird*. Fairfax watched him climb the rope from the gig to the deck; and at the request of Mr. Vernon went forward to be introduced to him.

The two young men shook hands and their eyes met steadily and frankly. Any shrewd observer would have said that they were mutually well impressed at first glance.

Edouard Ballanche was a creole from head to foot; that is, he was a Frenchman modified by the influences of American birth and experience. In his face burned the half-subdued fire of a passionate yet naturally gentle and tender nature, fortified and specialized by intimate acquaintance with almost every form of danger. You might have read in his eyes that he had seen duels; that life, though precious to him, was worn as a garment to be flung aside as lightly as a coat or glove; that honor was a word of unlimited significance to him. In speech he showed that deliberate facility which always suggests the cut and thrust and parry of a master swordsman. The impression he made was one of efficiency, courage and readiness, singularly blended with lightness, grace and superficial good humor.

He shook hands cordially with Mr. Vernon, and turned to acknowledge the introduction of Fairfax just as Pauline came from below.

"I took you for a pirate," said Mr. Vernon, "and was running away from you as fast as I could, I thought; but here we are, boarded by you, and at your mercy."

"The mistake was mutual, sir; I thought that you were on unlawful business of some sort, and have been all night afraid that you had got away from me. I am compelled to be vigilant now;

I hope, sir, that I have not troubled you too greatly.

"Your vigilance is something that no American patriot can grumble at," said Mr. Vernon. "Is there anything new from the seat of war? Anything about to turn up?"

"Nothing has been made public," replied the lieutenant, guardedly. "What may transpire at any moment is hard to foresee; doubtless we shall have our turn at the game of war down here in due time."

"You may speak freely in the presence of my friend here," remarked Mr. Vernon, with a smile at Ballanche's caution, concealed almost though it was; "he is one of us."

"I should trust him with my life," promptly responded the lieutenant, giving Fairfax again that straight frank look of perfect confidence. "What I wanted to say to you, Mr. Vernon, is that it is not safe to keep your family or your property any longer at Bay Saint Louis. The British may sail in upon us any day; indeed, we are expecting them soon."

It was hard for Lieutenant Ballanche, with all his politeness, to keep his gaze away from Pauline.

Fairfax was not aware that she had come on deck, else he would have noticed the suppressed enthusiasm of Ballanche's glances toward the hatchway.

As soon as Mr. Vernon discovered the presence of his daughter, he took Lieutenant Ballanche by the arm and led him toward her.

Fairfax turned in time to see the tall creole bowing low over her hand.

Mr. Vernon stood there like some grizzly giant of old, his shoulders and head looming heavily, while his daughter seemed to reflect upon him a suggestion of youthfulness blending with his show of years. Fairfax saw that Mr. Vernon regarded the young officer with emphatic interest and confidence, gave him distinguished consideration indeed, and that this marked attention seemed to be received quite as a matter of course. There was but a short conversation, and certainly nothing important was said; nevertheless, in some indirect way Fairfax caught from it a singularly vivid impression of being thrust far away and of passing out of consideration.

After a little while, however, Ballanche bowed to Pauline, and, taking Mr. Vernon's arm with a confidential touch, led him to a farther part of the deck where they could converse without being overheard.

Fairfax turned about, and with folded arms stood apart, scarcely thinking, but wrapped in a mood that filled the air about him with confused and indefinable apprehensions. He was not aware that Pauline had come near until she spoke, and then he started perceptibly (to himself, if not to her), and looked down at her as if from a great distance. We must remember that he had not slept during the night; this might, to a degree, account for the unnatural slowness with which he responded to the fresh, almost enthusiastic, manner of the girl, as she began to speak of the sun-glories that shimmered over the lonely marshes of the Rigolets.

Meantime, Lieutenant Ballanche was informing Mr. Vernon of the probability that a British fleet was at hand to co-operate with hostile Indians in the effort to devastate the whole country from Pensacola to New Orleans, and that in the latter city there was need of wise counsel and patriotic effort to counteract the influence which had been left over from the treasonable scheming of Aaron Burr and his Southern associates.

"Things are in a bad condition," he said, "and we need the work of men like you, Mr. Vernon, to bring order out of confusion, and to urge the citizens to a proper view of duty. At present, the most deplorable indifference as to the outcome of affairs prevails in New Orleans; nobody seems to realize our dreadful danger."

"The government seems to me most to blame," remarked Mr. Vernon. "Instead of building fortifications and fitting out such vessels as can be had for defense, it is spending most of its time and money searching for imaginary robbers and impossible pirates."

"It is true that our defenses are of no value, but you are wrong in thinking that our outlaws are imaginary. I have just been up Pearl River and to Honey Island, where robbers are more numerous than honest citizens. It is not of these, however, that we need to speak; bad as they are, they are less dangerous than those citizens, ostensibly respectable and worthy, who use their apparent social superiority as a cloak to hide the villainies they encourage."

Ballanche spoke with an earnestness amounting almost to vehemence, and by the half closing of his eyes and a certain immobility of all his features, his face took on an intensely resolute expression.

Mr. Vernon looked calmly at him, as if by a sort of masterful scrutiny he could read his inmost thoughts and draw from them a more comprehensive meaning than the speaker himself realized in them. Presently he said:

"You may be right, lieutenant; but, for my part, I see many sides to the question. New Orleans and Louisiana owe very little to any government, save that which they themselves represent. Understand, nevertheless, that I am for allegiance to the government at Washington, or at whatever other place the United States councils may meet, and that I am for a rigorous defense of New Orleans against any British force that may come; but I should advise careful speaking when it comes to characterizing our citizens as encouragers of villainies."

"But perhaps, sir, you do not know the condition of things in New Orleans."

"Lieutenant, I do know. How could I help knowing? I knew before you were born; I have know ever since; I know now."

Ballanche made a slight, quick movement and something like an almost invisible flush leaped into his olive-brown cheeks. Mr. Vernon's voice had been so deep and powerful and his attitude so suggestive of virile or leonine superiority that the young man had felt a shock, which for the moment confused him.

"What reliable word have you that a British fleet is near here?" Mr. Vernon continued, his manner changing to one of mere inquiry.

"None. The activity of the Indians and the presence of foreign emissaries among the tribes seem to indicate, however, that a strong movement is to be made."

"And what did you succeed in doing toward suppressing the Pearl-River robbers?" Mr. Vernon presently asked.

"Of course, I did nothing—nothing seems possible in the matter at present—but I found out a good deal about them, and have been thinking over a plan by which it might be possible to serve both them and the country."

"That would be a singular achievement, I should say."

"Yes, at first thought, it would appear so; but I believe it can be done."

Mr. Vernon stood waiting for the lieutenant to explain; but he did not urge him to proceed even by a look.

"If amnesty were tendered to all of the outlaws who should join our military forces and do service for the country, I believe that most of them would accept the offer in good faith. At all events, I am going to lay the matter before the governor."

Mr. Vernon made no remark; he stood in the attitude of a respectful listener whose mind had run ahead of what his companion had been saying; and when Lieutenant Bailanche looked into his strange, deep eyes, they were quite inscrutable.

"What do you think of the plan?" the young man inquired. "Is it not worth trying?"

"It may be; but what do you know of the feeling among the freebooters themselves on the subject?"

"I have some reason to believe that most of them would be glad to quit the life of outlaws. If the leaders can be reached the thing can be accomplished, I am almost sure."

"Who are the leaders?"

"It is not easy to find out. Of course Lafitte has all the Baratarian pirates under his thumb. But, although the mysterious Pierre Rameau is called King of Honey Island, I have found out to my satisfaction that there is one above him in command of the great Pearl River and inland organization; and that one lives in New Orleans, directing the proceedings from his safe position in the midst of the highest society of the city."

"And who is he?"

"I think that I know, but I cannot yet breathe his name in this connection; it would create a wild scene, I can assure you, sir."

Mr. Vernon folded his arms high upon his broad chest and appeared to lift himself until he showed taller than even the tall creole.

"If you begin to stir up records in New Orleans," he remarked, "you will soon have a heavy load on your hands. My own opinion is that nothing will be gained by any negotiations with pirates. The country can fight its battles without them."

"To do without outlaws of one sort or another," said Ballanche, " would be to enlist very few men in Louisiana."

" Perhaps."

"At all events, I shall make my report to the governor, and he may do as he shall see fit."

"Are you sure that the governor himself is entirely clear of entanglement with the powerful alliance of freebooters ?"

Again the eyes of the lieutenant became sharp and searching as he scanned Mr. Vernon's massive face, and said :

" Do you suspect him ?"

" Humph !" with a shrug, was the only answer Mr. Vernon gave. It was as if the ejaculation were meant to toss Ballanche aside.

A half-hour later the young officer took his leave.

" *Au revoir !*" he called from the gig as his crew pulled away toward the schooner. His farewell comprehended the whole group on the *Water-Bird's* deck ; and yet he was looking straight at Pauline. Fairfax noticed this, but seeing him going farther and farther away, while Pauline seemed quite content to stay where she was, the artist smiled very complacently.

Mr. Vernon ordered the vessel put under sail at once, speaking to his black men with an intonation that suggested impatience or great haste.

The most careless observer could have seen that something in the conversation between him and Lieutenant Ballanche had stimulated him ; but whether with anger or some other passion no one could have determined from his appearance or actions.

Up through the Rigolets the little vessel went, with a fair breeze and in as golden sunlight as ever drove away a fog. The channel, a broad and beautiful river connecting Lake Borgne with Lake Pontchartrain, flashed like silver between its grassy marsh meadows, over which the herons and wild geese, the pelicans and the plovers flew back and forth like shuttles through the warp of the dreamy weather. Here and there, scattered from distance to distance, picturesque clumps of live-oaks were set against the almost violet sky like orchards on a prairie.

CHAPTER VIII.

CHATEAU D'OR AND COLONEL LORING.

Mr. Vernon's house in New Orleans, was, perhaps, the most pretentious residence place in the city. Built of gray brick, it stood well back from the street, in the midst of old trees. Its broad varandas and high-hipped dormer-windows, showing but duskily forth through the foliage, which almost hid the balconies and oriels between, were solid and heavy. The whole structure was massive and solemn-looking, giving the general impression of exclusiveness and lofty loneliness. Under the live-oak and magnolia-boughs were long, crepuscular vistas, closed by clumps and clusters of orange-trees burdened with yellow fruit. Along the high brick wall that compassed the close grew masses of vines incomparably thick and rich, and everywhere the mocking-birds sang both by day and by night. It was a home typically Southern.

A carriage-way, closed by a double iron gate, passed between two stuccoed walls for a little distance and gave into a paved court, semicircular in shape, the chord of which was the irregular outline of one side of the house. Entrance to the close beyond this court was obtained by a door of wire lattice set in the street-wall directly in front of the steps leading up to the main hall, where two huge brick and stucco columns, heavily fluted, rose to support the roof of the veranda.

The grounds were large and everywhere showed that neither money nor care had been grudgingly spent to add beauty and comfort to the place. From base to roof, the house suggested in every angle and curve the wealth, pride and taste of its owner; but it also suggested more; the peculiar civilization grown out of the old Louisiana colonial life and out of the strange vicissitudes and exigencies of the development of New Orleans spoke through the architecture and surroundings. There were flowers everywhere, especially roses and cactuses, making the dusky air flash with colors—blended perfumes coming and going with the wind-pulses and all around and above the soft, satin rustle of leaves.

Mr. Vernon had named his place Chateau d'Or. He liked the name, he said, because a vessel that brought him good luck had borne it; but he never told what the good luck was or what had become of the vessel. It seemed to delight him no little when he was able to excite curiosity on this subject, only to leave it altogether unsatisfied. The name, in accordance with a custom still lingering in the creole country, was set in large letters over the gate, and still higher up was the sketch of a ship under full sail.

The Vernon household was well known to almost

everybody in the city; that is, the place and the
family name were familiar to the ears and eyes of
the people; but there were comparatively few persons who had gained anything like a "visiting
acquaintance" with the family. The circle of Mrs.
Vernon's friends was, however, as select as it was
small; and as for Pauline, she had but recently ventured into society without the formalities of a set
début. Mr. Vernon himself was, without being what
we call a public man, a leader of the people. His
influence was as powerful as it was general, and it
was exerted without effort and, apparently, without
ambition on his part. His long residence in Louisiana, his personal force and his great wealth had combined to give him this hold upon the people from
highest to lowest, and yet no one could say that he
was easily approached. He took no public part in
the affairs of the State or the city; but his influence
was always sought when matters of grave importance demanded the use of specially sound judgment,
or when the more unmanageable element of the
people had to be perfectly controlled. He seemed
to possess the confidence of all the races and clans
of men in the city and, by some power, was able to
command them.

When Mrs. Vernon and Pauline found themselves
once more in Chateau d'Or they were as happy as it
is ever possible for a mother and her daughter to be.
Their stay at Bay Saint Louis had (although they
were probably not aware of it) been a powerful tonic
and invigorator.

Pauline went about the house and grounds singing like a happy bird, her face radiant, her step light and her heart brimming with half-formed dreams. There was nothing in all her circle of vision to shade or to mar the golden promise that filled it like the soft splendor of springtime. She knew nothing of life's evils—not even the plethora so often attending unlimited access to the luxuries of wealth had ever come to her—and the abounding good in her experience only urged her into a rich development, a radiant blooming, so to call it, which made her beauty of face and of form come out like the blowing of a rose.

The city was very gay when the Vernons came back to it, and Pauline found herself caught in the whirl like a butterfly in a June breeze. There was the theatre, there were the balls, the receptions, the excursions to the country-seats of wealthy planters—nothing was wanting that would keep her spirits at full flood; and there was the library at Chateau d'Or, where the romances that she loved so dearly filled many a mahogany shelf.

Both Fairfax and Lieutenant Ballanche had called frequently within the first month, and she had seen them often at the theatres and at balls and receptions given by her friends. They had been very attentive and very interesting; each in his way bringing to her receptive mind fascinating impressions and obscure, haunting visions of a great world of experience lying quite outside of her horizon. The young men were so different in personal appearance, in address, in habit of thought, in temper and in everything that goes to build and project individual character, that one served as a foil to emphasize the other at almost every point.

Pauline, while she had had every advantage that wealth could bring to her within the narrow and isolated circle of environment, was still no more than a provincial girl; and her limitations, though they probably enhanced to a degree her attractiveness, restricted her vision and compressed her understanding in some measure. A society girl of to-day, seeing one like Pauline, would call her strangely unsophisticated; still she was not less delighted than most ladies would have been when her mother announced that it was her purpose to "give a party," as the phrase goes, limiting the invitations mostly to young people.

When the evening came, with the grounds and the stately house brilliantly lighted, the whole interior wreathed and festooned with flowers and the black servants all assigned to duty, it would have been hard to decide which was the more radiantly happy, Mrs. Vernon or Pauline.

All the windows and doors were open, so that the gentle May winds crept through to stir the rich curtains and to make the candles in the many-armed candlesticks wave their silvery flames. Some of these candles were made of myrtle-wax, taken from the wild berries, after a local custom of the time, and as they burned they sent out a faint, exquisitely pleasant perfume, at once wild and sweet.

The rather somber mansion was transformed by lights and flowers into something like a gorgeous palace; even the heavy, black-mahogany furniture caught a gleam and a glow.

Pauline hugged her mother, under the impulse of a swift joy, when the time approached for the guests to begin arriving.

"Isn't it all beautiful!" she exclaimed, almost strangling Mrs. Vernon with her snowy, plump arms. "And I'm so very happy! See how the pictures come out, and how the statuary gives effect to everything! And the stairway—how the festoons of flowers and moss have changed it! I wonder who will be the first guest to come!"

"Mercy, child! Do you wish to kill your poor mother! See how you are spoiling my lace and disarranging my hair! I shall not be presentable!"

But Mrs. Vernon's arm clasped her daughter's waist and gave caress for caress with genuine creole vehemence.

They walked from room to room, in a final round of review, hand in hand, and commenting vivaciously on the beauty of the decorations.

"But I wonder why papa doesn't come?" said Pauline; "he promised to be in by eight."

"Some affair or other has detained him," answered the mother; "you know he has had much to look after since we returned. We have scarcely had an hour with him for a month and more."

"I think he might lay aside affairs for this evening, at least, when it would be so very nice to have him."

"Oh, but he will be here in good time; he likes

such a thing as this; he's never so light and bright and engaging as when in the midst of a company."

"And you are so beautiful this evening, mamma. He will be very proud of you."

"Ah, if I were young like you, you might say that; but I'm not going to flatter you. Do you know, Pauline, that it is positively dangerous for a young woman to think herself beautiful?"

"Why, no! If she really is beautiful, why should she not be perfectly frank in acknowledging her good fortune?"

They were passing before a grand mirror set in a bronze frame; they both looked in and stood for a moment contemplating themselves as reflected there.

A momentary pensiveness passed over Mrs. Vernon's face; but Pauline blushed just a little and smiled with an expression of sincere delight as she glanced over the reflection of a slender, graceful girl dressed in a gown of clinging, dull-white brocaded silk with a fluff of delicate lace at the upper line of the modestly designed corsage. It was a radiant face that threw back her smile, and the white arms and throat with their curious bracelets and slender pearl necklace shimmered softly.

At this moment, Mr. Vernon came in, accompanied by a tall, swart man. The two went directly upstairs to the room prepared for the gentlemen's dressing-room, but returned almost immediately, when Mr. Vernon presented his guest to the ladies as Col. Philip Loring.

The gentleman's bearing was military, soldierly

in the extreme, and his form and face suited well
the air of studied dignity he wore. While not
strictly handsome, his features were strong and
well-formed, and his eyes had a singular power, as
if of concentration and steadiness. He was bronzed
by exposure to wind and sun until his face was
olive-brown, although it could be seen that it was
not naturally dark, and there was a white scar, a
saber-cut it appeared, running in a slender line
across a part of his left cheek and ear. His neck was
corded with muscles and his hands were shapely,
large and sinewy.

"You have a lovely home here, Mrs. Vernon," he
said, speaking French with a curious accent. " I
have been telling your husband that he lives like a
grand duke."

Mrs. Vernon had often heard her husband speak
of Colonel Loring as one of his most trusted friends;
but she had never before seen him.

His smile, as he looked down into her face, was
peculiarly attractive, albeit there was in it something remote and inexplicably unsatisfactory.

" And you, mademoiselle," he continued, turning
with a bow to Pauline, " must be as happy as you
look, in such a place of enchantment. You will not
charge a rough old saber like me with flattery if I
tell you that you look like an especially dangerous
fairy in a most alluring bower."

Pauline's cheeks showed the slightest access of
pink under his bold yet not unpleasant glance.

"Your father and I," he added, " have long been
great friends, and I account it one of my far-apart

pieces of good fortune to be here, even by mere change, to-night."

"My father's friend is my friend," Pauline said; and she could not have accounted for the embarrassment she felt in delivering this bit of formality.

"And mine," joined Mrs. Vernon. "We are glad to welcome you as a chance guest this time, and we shall be proud to greet you as a privileged one hereafter at all times."

The conversation could go no further than these stiff commonplaces characteristic of the period and the place. Guests were arriving, and Mrs. Vernon and Pauline had duties to meet at once. They both turned away, leaving Colonel Loring standing, tall, straight, grimly attractive, beside a magnificent flowering cactus as tall and strange as he. Somehow they took his face with them, clearly set in their minds, and the scar on the cheek and ear was as white and the features as dark and magnetic as in the original.

Among the early guests was Lieutenant Ballanche. He shook hands with Mrs. Vernon, and, after a few words, passed on to meet Pauline.

"You were my prisoner the other morning. I am yours this evening," he said, with a happy look and referring, of course, to the little adventure on Lake Borgne. "But you will be generous, I know."

He did not look so tall in his full-dress uniform as he had in undress, but the fine high-bred air seemed to be more pronounced.

Pauline had seen him frequently since their first meeting. At present, however, he impressed her as

THE PARTY AT CHATEAU D'OR.—*See Page 92.*

much handsomer than ever before. Not that she really took time to think this. It was the impression and nothing more.

Fairfax came rather late. He had been delayed on his way by a queer little adventure on the street —an adventure which, although at the time it appeared to have no connection with his future, introduced an active element into the drama of his life.

At the entrance to a dark alley, a struggle was going on between two persons, and Fairfax heard, through his open carriage-window, low cries of anger and distress. He signaled his driver to stop, and at once sprang out and ran to the spot. A burly man was choking and beating a small hunchback, who fought with tooth and nail like a tiger cat. Fairfax called to the big fellow to let go his hold of the dwarf's neck, and not being heeded, dealt him a heavy blow on the ear with his fist. A watchman appeared at this moment and reached the spot just as the ruffian was trying to rise from where the cuff had landed him. Some time was spent by Fairfax in explaining to the officer his connection with the matter.

The little deformed man declared that his powerful assailant was trying to rob him of a small amount of silver money, but the accused stoutly maintained that the money was his and that the other had stolen it from him.

The light of a distant lamp set at the gate of a private house permitted Fairfax to see the dwarf's features but dimly, yet they were so unusual, so hideous indeed, that they fixed themselves firmly in his memory. The watchman knew both of the combatants and, laying his hand on the little fellow's strangely distorted shoulder, called him Crapaud Crapousin.

"Crapaud Crapousin," he growled, as he shook him rudely, "you are always into mischief! How many times must I chuck you in jail?"

Of course Fairfax got away from this scene as soon as he could. The delay, however, was longer than this brief telling may make it appear.

When he reached Chateau d'Or his right hand, with which he had delivered the blow on the man's ear, was paining him greatly, and later he discovered that he had broken a finger on the fellow's skull.

"But you must have it attended to at once," said Mr. Vernon; "fortunately there is a skillful surgeon present," and forthwith he hurried Fairfax into a room apart from the company, and sent a servant to bring Colonel Loring.

"It's nothing," Fairfax insisted, as a matter of form; but his pain was by no means hidden, and his hand was beginning to swell.

"A gentleman should never strike with his unarmed hand," said Mr. Vernon. "Why didn't you shoot the scoundrel?"

"I shot him with the only weapon I chanced to have," replied Fairfax, with a grim half-smile.

The music was swelling merrily and rippling through the house; the dancers were flashing back and forth and in and out; and the breeze coming in at the open windows and doors gently fanned the flushed young faces as they whirled.

When Colonel Loring approached and Mr. Vernon was about to speak, Fairfax looked up and saw before him Pierre Rameau. He could not help showing his surprise and astonishment.

"Let me present my friend, Colonel Philip Loring, Mr Fairfax. Colonel Loring is an expert surgeon; he will deal cunningly with your hurt hand."

Fairfax was staring, glaring, his lips compressed, his chin thrust out, his face white and rigid. He did not hear a word that Mr. Vernon said.

"Don't offer me your hand, Pierre Rameau, you base and conscienceless villain!" he exclaimed in a low, measured tone of voice, husky with rage. He appeared about to spring upon Loring and throttle him.

Colonel Loring without changing countenance turned to Mr. Vernon and, with a simple inflection of inquiry, said:

"What does this man mean?"

The wrath and the insulting epithets seemed not to have affected him in any way. Not a line of his face had changed its expression. He turned his eyes slowly and with a peculiar steadiness from Fairfax to his host and stood in an erect but supremely indifferent attitude.

The indignation of Fairfax was irrepressible; he could not be still. Doubtless he would have made a memorable scene of it if he had been left free to act.

Mr. Vernon stepped between the two men and

made a gesture that meant a command for them to be silent, and when he spoke it was scarcely above his breath.

"This is my house, Mr. Fairfax; you are both my friends and my guests; if you are enemies to each other, let me beg you not to make a scene here."

"I never had the honor of seeing the gentleman before," said Loring, in a tone that gave no suggestion of feeling, unless it might have been that a hint of contempt rang in it.

"You are the robber, Pierre Rameau," Fairfax boldly declared. "You cannot put me aside with your cool effrontery. I have seen your face once before; I would know it twenty years hence at a glance. You are the very man who robbed Vasseur.

"How can you call this scoundrel your friend, Mr. Vernon?" he added, after a moment's intense gaze into Loring's face. "He's the very man—"

"But, my dear Mr. Fairfax, you are mistaken. Colonel Loring is not Pierre Rameau or any other robber. He is my friend, just returned from Mexico. I understand your feelings now," Mr. Vernon went on, rapidly and earnestly, "but I assure you that you are suffering an honest mistake and your excitement to lead you too far."

"But, Mr. Vernon, I cannot be mistaken in this matter. *You* are mistaken, sir, yourself. That face—that scar—that man, from head to foot—that villain, when his mask slipped aside—"

The melodramatic almost hysterical excitement

of Fairfax contrasted curiously with the perfectly cool and even deprecatory manner of Mr. Vernon and of Colonel Loring; and yet Fairfax was very steady—rigid, indeed—and his look was dangerous. The apparition of Pierre Rameau could not be counterfeit, and for the moment he felt that Mr. Vernon could not help being aware of it, so distinct and complete was the identification to himself. He felt so intensely, under the sudden strain of recognition, that his bearing was awkward and stagy in comparison with the grace and ease of the waving figures seen through the flower-draped doorway giving into the parlors where the dancers were in full career.

It was at this moment that Fairfax saw Pauline pass across the field of his vision. She was dancing with Lieutenant Ballanche, and her face was illuminated with pleasure.

CHAPTER IX.

SOME SYLVAN SURPRISES.

Vasseur gathered together his slaves and his other personal property and with them loaded two luggers and a small schooner. Mr. Vernon had warned him that it was no longer safe to remain on the exposed coast of Bay Saint Louis. To be sure, the warning was scarcely needed after the raid of the cavaliers; but Mr. Vernon did not refer to this danger; it was the British fleet that was expected to appear in the gulf waters.

As a matter of fact, the fleet did not come immediately; but the British were sending emissaries to the Indians all through Alabama and Mississippi, inciting them to war against the whites. General Jackson had defeated the savages, after bloody fighting, on the 27th of March, at Tohopeka, and was taking steps to organize an army with which to gain possession of the Spanish forts along the gulf coast.

Everywhere among the white settlements the rumor had gone forth that great military events were impending; that most probably an English force absolutely overwhelming was about to be thrown into the country, to ravage it far and wide.

The frontier people were mostly poor, uneducated and possessed of but limited knowledge of the current affairs of the world, and it was no more than natural that they should receive an exaggerated impression of the threatened danger.

They were as brave as lions, however, and their patriotism knew no limit. Indian haters from their cradles up, it needed no more perfect goad than the British coalition with the savages to make every man, woman and child in the Southern settlements an implacable foe of everything English. Even the outlaws of Barataria and of Pearl River, when at last the test came, took the side of the United States in the struggle, although justice had set a price upon their heads.

Vasseur betook himself, with all his movable belongings, to a plantation southwest of New Orleans, in the La Fourche country. He thought that his slaves would be safe in this wild, out-of-the-way place, and here, in the care of an overseer, he left them, while he, dreaming of nothing but the recovery of his jewels and revenge on Pierre Rameau, went back to dog the tracks of that intrepid and successful robber and pirate.

Mounted on a strong, spirited pony, he made his way into the Pearl River country and found little trouble in associating himself, under an assumed name, with some of the free-and-easy inhabitants, who were more at ease on account of crushing defeat that had befallen their enemies, the Indians.

Like most of that class of men who had sought the remote gulf-coast region to hide from justice, Vasseur did not have the least respect for the legal methods of righting wrongs or of bringing to punishment those who did him injury. His nature was revengeful, and the only law he dreamed of appealing to was that of which he could appoint himself sole executive.

Small as he was, his strength was great, and no wolf was more savage or untiring. Cunning and full of expedients, sly as a fox and quick as a cat, he passed from place to place, attracting little notice, but always managing to collect, little by little, information concerning the whereabouts and the doings of the cavaliers of Honey Island.

The main purpose of our history will not permit us at present to follow Vasseur in his pursuit of Rameau, but the reader will understand the state of society prevailing in the gulf coast at the time of which we write if we sketch here a scene or two in the by-play we are now in view of—a by-play fairly characteristic of the time and the place, and at the same time important as a foundation for some later developments of our drama.

Among the acquaintances made by Vasseur in the Pearl River region was the preacher Burns. These two men, after a casual meeting, held together as if by the force of some hidden, sympathetic attraction. The fact was that Vasseur's instinct discovered in Burns a trustworthy spirit as well as a valuable store of information touching the country, its topography and its inhabitants. Moreover, the little Frenchman quickly made out that the preacher was not all preacher—that the old man had some important object in view other than the comforting and saving of the souls of men.

Burns read more of Vasseur's true character than the latter suspected, but he did not reach his secret. Each man, indeed, kept his innermost purpose well shrouded.

They often rode together, Vasseur, on his stanch, muscular pony, and Burns astride of a large, bony animal, presented to him by a group of his rough but generous frontier admirers, who had agreed that his preaching was " wo'th a hoss, saddle an' bridle ;" and in these somewhat eccentric journeys they met many strangers whose movements and purposes were more or less mysterious, and many others whose open faces and frank speech proclaimed them honest men.

Vasseur quickly noticed that Burns made his way by the point of his piety and with the wedge of religious sentiment. The hint was not lost on the ready Frenchman. He, too, was, apparently very religious, very devoted to prayer and pious reflection. He even let it be understood that preaching was a part of his life-work. If Burns saw through this shrewd use of an impious sham, he did not appear to notice it.

In the rude but comfortable cabins of the settlers the itinerants were given welcome to shelter and food in return for their songs and prayers. Often enough the family would join in the hymn-singing ; always the members would kneel during prayers.

It was a persistent, universal element of the American pioneer life, this reverence for the simplest forms of Christian worship. Even among the most lawless and desperate classes the influence of religious sentiment went a long way, and the minister of the gospel was treated as a sort of privileged character, to go and come at will and to be protected and cared for by everybody. He was a variable yet potent factor, an elusive but inestimable quantity, in the growth of the strange civilization of the backwoods. Like John of old, he was a strong, rough, picturesque orator of the wilderness, bidding men repent and prepare for the kingdom of heaven.

One fine morning in April, as Vasseur and Burns rode along a bridle-path, a little way from the east bank of Pearl River, going in a direction that would intersect the Black-wolf Trail a mile or two farther on, they fell in with a short, well-built, black-eyed young man, who informed them that he was a Methodist preacher on his way to New Orleans.

This comely youth was indeed a typical fledgling minister in appearance and was rather showily dressed in clerical garb.

He was a pleasing conversationalist, soft-voiced, versatile in expression, of ready humor and apparently well acquainted with the country. His age could not have been much beyond twenty-one years, though something lurking in the lines of his mobile features suggested deep and perhaps impressive experiences.

The horse that he was riding was poor, apparently

old and certainly quite lame; but his saddle was a costly one, silver-mounted and beautifully finished; his bridle was likewise very fine. A pair of heavy, silver-mounted holster pistols hung at his saddle-bow.

"They were given to me along with the saddle," he explained, "and though I have not the slightest use for them, I could not well refuse them."

"I suppose," he added interrogatively, after a moment's reflection, "there would be no harm in selling the weapons and using the money when I arrive in New Orleans?"

Mr. Burns and Vasseur both said that they could see no impropriety.

The three then discussed the peculiar hardships, vexations and ludicrous adventures in the ministerial life of the frontier.

They rode slowly along, on account of the lameness of the young stranger's horse, their way leading them through a wild, semi-tropical forest. The dense foliage of the trees met over their heads and shut out the sky, while on either hand the giant trunks stood so thick that the eye could penetrate but the shortest distance from the irregular roadway, save where here and there little glades opened and let the sunshine in on crowded and bristling clumps of dwarf palmetto; and but for the soughing of a brisk breeze through the frondous boughs on high, the silence would have been unbroken by any sound of the wilderness.

"I presume that one or the other of you, brethren, will be glad to swap horses with me," said the stranger, with a humorous twinkle in his sharp, black eyes; "mine is, as you see, a most desirable beast, especially as to his gait."

"I am sure that if you consider him desirable you had better keep him," remarked Mr. Burns, his own grave and wrinkled face relaxing a little; "I should not wish to relieve you of him."

"Me, I no wish ze good 'orse at all; dis one suit me var' well," said Vasseur.

The young preacher chuckled and turned a quarter about in his saddle, so that his weight was all on his left stirrup.

Suddenly he let fall the bridle-reins and, with lightning celerity, snatched both the pistols from the saddle-bow.

Burns and Vasseur found themselves looking each into the yawning muzzle of a weapon held by a hand as steady as a stone wall.

"Dismount—both on the same side there, gentlemen," came the cold, determined order, "and hold up your hands, or I'll bore you, center through, before you can wink!"

Then and there the young preacher robbed Vasseur of his money, a dagger and his horse; and, after placing the fine bridle and saddle upon the latter, mounted, and, with a mocking laugh, a rakish bow and a kiss of the fingers, rode away. He had touched nothing belonging to Mr. Burns.

It is not known whether or not Mr. Burns was taken by surprise when Vasseur, as did the disciple of old, began to rage and swear and curse like a buccaneer, his expletives ranging through the scale of three or four languages; but that he stood quietly by, his face inscrutably mournful in its expression, his thin, bony hands hanging at his sides, is well authenticated.

Vasseur exhausted himself of profanity, and then was fain to put his own saddle and bridle on the stranger's lame horse in order to proceed on the journey.

Burns objected to this.

"Take my beast," he said, "it will serve your purpose better, brother. The lame one will be good enough for me."

Vasseur looked abashed, for the thought had flashed into his mind that very second to do for Burns what the other preacher had done for him.

"You need this strong beast of mine," Burns urged, "to carry out your plans. Do not hesitate; he is yours, take him and welcome. I can get on with the other."

The little Frenchman was inwardly startled. What did Burns know of his plans? Had he suddenly divined them?

"You have undertaken a difficult, an almost impossible thing, brother, and you cannot afford to be poorly mounted in case of need," went on the old man. "This is a good, strong horse, and, although he does not look so, is a very swift one. Take him; I give him to you."

It was while they were parleying on this subject, Vasseur pretending that he was objecting to Burns's generosity, that the old man stooped and picked up a folded letter, the seal of which had been broken.

He opened it without hesitation, and found it to be a short note addressed to John A. Murrell—a name which, a few years later, was that of the most desperate and enterprising outlaw ever known in America.

It would have been better for Vasseur had he accepted the proffered horse at once; then he might have escaped the unpleasant experience which soon followed.

Like many another pretender he lingered too long to accentuate and collaterally reinforce his assumed sincerity.

It may have been the steady, searching gaze that Burns bent upon him, it may have been the old man's singular expression of kindliness, or it may have been the peculiar turn of the adventure just passed through; at all events, influenced by some power, Vasseur stood hesitating and demurring until three galloping horsemen armed to the teeth were close upon them.

Burns saw the new-comers first and with a spasm-like movement he fixed his eyes upon the leader, his face shriveling and blanching in a startling manner.

Vasseur turned quickly as the sound of horses' feet behind him shook him out of his insincerity, and it was now his turn to show amazement, surprise and despair all condensed in a single stare.

The riders reined in their horses and halted a rod distant, forming a finely picturesque group set against the dull, gray trunks and dusky interspaces of the wood.

Pierre Rameau was in front, mounted on a bold, proud horse, whose nostrils breathed the air of the wilderness with savage delight.

Vasseur, with the air of a wild beast caught in a close place, looked this way and that and was on the point of running off among the trees as fast as his legs could carry him, when Rameau leveled a pistol on him and bade him stand.

"What are you, gentlemen, doing here?" inquired the cavalier; but neither Burns nor Vasseur could answer promptly, so dry were their throats and so stiffened their tongues. Not that either wanted courage. But the situation under the circumstances was absolutely overpowering.

"Are you deaf, you little half-nigger?" continued Rameau, as he recognized Vasseur. "Speak instantly or I'll—"

Evidently Rameau was astonished, although his face retained its calm, cold, almost indifferent expression. He had not expected ever to meet Vasseur again; taking it for a certainty that the little fellow had been burned to ashes in the fire of his own house. Here he was, however, evidently intent on revenge, Rameau felt sure, and a most dangerous man he was to be hunted by.

"I was hunting my lost cattle," quickly responded the little Frenchman in his own tongue; "a man robbed us just now."

"Don't lie to me, half-breed; I know what you are up to; I can read you as if your face were a book. You are up here dogging my tracks—I have heard of you prowling around for some time."

Rameau's look and voice were cold, hard, cruel and Vasseur well knew that it was not worth while to make any further attempt to deceive him.

Burns stood beside his horse in an attitude which betrayed his intense excitement as much as did the extreme gray pallor and the almost distorted contraction of his face; but Rameau was too much occupied with Vasseur to give the old man more than a passing glance.

"Tie that fellow to a tree, Newkirk," said the leader of the cavaliers to one of his followers. "Tie him up and give him forty with a good gad."

The man at once obeyed the order.

Vasseur began to whine and beg; he saw that resistance would be madness; but the thought of a whipping was torture itself. When a boy and—shall it be said here?—a slave, he had known, on a plantation in San Domingo, what the lash felt like, falling on the bare back. The recollection coming to him suddenly drew up his limbs as if with rheumatic agony.

He pleaded in the name of all the saints he could think of and prayed in polyglot profusion.

Newkirk, aided by one of his fellows, seized him and, despite his struggles, placed him in a hugging attitude against a tree, where they bound him securely.

"Now cut some switches and give him a sound basting," said Rameau. "After he has been thoroughly tickled, maybe he won't be so anxious to hunt lost cattle in these woods!"

Then, while the men were selecting their gads, he turned to Burns.

"And are you a cattle-hunter, too?" he inquired with sarcastic intonation. "What have you got to say for yourself?"

The old man made a great effort, but his lips moved without giving forth a sound. Three times he tried to speak, his parched tongue crisping in his mouth like a frost-dried leaf.

"Some cat has got your tongue, too, eh! Perhaps you would like a few lashes before speaking to a gentleman. Is that it?"

Rameau said these words while looking hard into the old man's writhing face. As he did so, he felt a vague uneasiness, as of something forgotten or of something strange about to happen, and he almost shrank from the flaring yet aged-dulled eyes that gazed so fixedly at him.

When, at last, Burns found his voice, he leaned forward, and in a hoarse, rasping half-whisper, that hissed strangely through the woods, exclaimed:

"At last, Kirk MacCollough, I have found you!"

CHAPTER X.

BURNS AND MAC COLLOUGH.

When the man Newkirk began to lay on blows with a long switch across Vasseur's back, the little fellow begged and screamed and swore indiscriminately; but all to no effect. The time had come for him to receive a sound basting, as Rameau had ordered, and it was delivered with right good will, the full forty lashes ringing out keen and loud.

"Who are you?" demanded Rameau, half recoiling from the name that Burns had spoken, though his face showed no signs of surprise. "What do you mean by your crazy words?"

At the same time he rode close up beside the old man and, leaning forward, looked searchingly into his face.

"Kirk MacCollough, where—where is my child?" came from the dry, withered lips.

"Ah, I see you are crazy, poor old man!" muttered the outlaw; but he did not deceive Burns, who knew that he was recognized.

"I might well be crazy, Kirk MacCollough, with all that I have borne from you; but I am not—I am not." He lifted his hands, shaking as if with a palsy. " Kirk MacCollough, take me to my child !" he quavered. " Take me to her ! Let me see her once more and die !"

There was no intimation of recognition in Rameau's eyes. He straightened up in his saddle and made an impatient gesture.

" Hold your tongue," he said, speaking in an undertone ; " I will listen to you presently."

Meantime, the scourging of Vasseur had been proceeding, evidently much to the amusement of the onlooking cavaliers, and now the dust was rising from the little victim's jacket in thin smoke-like puffs at every blow. Newkirk was a strong man ; he made the gad chirrup on its way through the air ; the jacket and undergarments were but slender protection against his vigorous strokes.

Rameau turned and coolly looked on until the punishment was ended.

" Untie the cow-hunter now and let him go !" he ordered.

Vasseur, trembling and apparently almost exhausted, when the halter-straps were removed, stood there looking about him like a worried and sorely wounded wild animal ; his eyes shot out a strange gaze of mingled fear and fury ; his teeth chattered.

" Go, now, you half-nigger thief," said Rameau ; " and if ever again I find you prowling in this part of the country, I'll have you hanged to the first limb that's strong enough to bear you ! Go !'

Like a race-horse promptly starting at the word, Vasseur bolted away, running nimbly, but with a certain feeble swaying of his body, and was quickly lost sight of in the gloomy thickets of undergrowth near by.

A grim half-smile showed itself in Rameau's face; it appeared to make the slender white scar across his cheek and ear flicker balefully.

"Ride on," he said to his men; "take the saddle and bridle. Leave the horse; it is not worth being troubled with. I'll join you at Dick's."

The orders were promptly obeyed, and, a few moments later, Burns and Rameau were left together in the silence and the gloom of the moss-hung woods.

Half gay, half melancholy was the snatch of song borne back to their ears—a bit of sentimental rhyme that one of the outlaws, in a fine tenor voice, trolled as he rode:

"' Her lover was false and cold was his heart,
  And she died by his cruel hand;
  And the lover off to the wars did go,
  To fight in a foreign land.'"

Burns was still standing beside his horse, and, half leaning on the saddle, kept his deep-set eyes fixed so that they seemed to burn right into those of Pierre Rameau.

When the men were quite out of sight and hearing Rameau said:

"Old man, what do you want?"

"You know what I want, Kirk MacCollough. Where is my child—where is Margaret?"

"What do I know about your child? Who are you, to put such a question to me?"

"You have not forgotten me. It is useless for you to dissimulate. I am here Kirk MacCollough, humbly begging to see Margaret once more before I am dead. You are a bad man, but you cannot refuse me this."

"You are evidently laboring under some strange mistake, sir. My name is not MacCollough. I don't know anything about your child."

"Don't lie to me, Kirk MacCollough! It can do you no good—serve you no turn whatever. I know you. You know me. I have followed you step by step, from place to place, from country to country. You could not and cannot escape me. Where is Margaret?"

This was said in a louder voice and with an intonation that in some way suggested the implacable spirit of righteous fate. It did not, however, produce the slightest visible effect on Rameau. His face was absolutely indifferent in its expression. He regarded the tall, emaciated old man before him as a satisfied beast of prey might have eyed with soulless and careless eyes an undesirable victim.

"If you, like the little black scoundrel whom you have seen me punish in a light way, are also dogging my steps—" He broke off, hesitated and seemed to be reflecting with his eyes cast down. Presently, he said: "You must be crazy, stranger. An old man like you ought not to be risking himself in this wild place."

Burns lifted one hand, as if in prayer, and a strange, hungry, longing expression passed his face. For some moments he was silent, his lips moving, his eyes upturned.

When again he spoke, he seemed to have better control of himself.

"Kirk," he said, very gently, "you well know that I would not harm a hair of your head if I could, and, moreover, you can see how utterly powerless I am."

"Don't call me 'Kirk' or any other of your fanciful names!" exclaimed Rameau, his voice for the first time ringing impatiently. "I am Pierre Rameau—you may have heard of him—and I do not deal gently with those who set themselves like hounds to follow on my track! Do you hear?"

The old man drew in a deep, long breath, and held it as one does who is helpless and hopeless at a moment when some mighty desire fills the whole of life. He made a gesture that signified both pity and utter distress.

'I will address you with any name you like," he presently said; "but a name is nothing. You cannot turn me back or put me off by this pretense of not knowing who I am. I am Max Burns; I have never had any cause to be ashamed of my name; I want to see my child, my Margaret, your wife. Where is she, Kirk—where is she, Pierre Rameau?"

"Haven't I said that I don't know you, never knew you, never saw you before, don't know anything whatever about you or your daughter? Old man, you had better go home and be taken care of;

this is no place for you. Come, mount your horse and be off with you, I've no further time to waste here."

The irritating manner and tone with which the outlaw spoke these sentences were edged and pointed with the look he assumed—a stare of absolute disregard for the situation or anything it might suggest. He seemed mailed in the flawless armor of indifference; he could not be touched at any point. The cold, soulless, yet in some way fascinating gleam of his long, narrow eyes re-inforced the chilling and irresistible influence of his voice to a pitch that was torturing.

Burns realized with terrible distinctness that now and forever his last hope was being ground in the dust under this man's heel. There was no relief, no appeal, no glimmer of any ray even of chance; all was lost, gone. He appeared to shrink and collapse under the pressure of the revelation.

Rameau saw this effect as he sat gazing somewhat aslant with a steady, unchanging expression of countenance.

"Come, come!" he repeated. "Mount your horse and be off! And let me advise you that you will fare badly if you are ever found here or anywhere near here again."

Slowly the old man sank upon his knees and covered his face with his hands. His horse turned and touched him with its nose. The silence of the great, dark wilderness seemed to center in the spot and add an awful solemnity to Burns's voice as he began to pray.

Uplifting his hands and turning his pallid yet bronzed face toward heaven, he wailed aloud:

"O my God, hast Thou forsaken me? This, O Heavenly Master, is my hour of extremity!"

Thus far he proceeded in a passionate strain; then, checking himself, he closed his lips and prayed inwardly, until he was gruffly interrupted by Rameau, who exclaimed:

"Here, stop that tomfoolery! I have said for you to mount your horse and move off, and now I mean for you to do it! Get up from there, instantly!"

Something infinitely brutal and relentless in the outlaw's voice closed the gate of prayer with a slam so to speak, and caused Burns to start and rise, almost with a spring, to his feet.

Instantly the manner of both men changed.

"You old fool," said Rameau, "do you hope to deceive me? I see through your game; but I am not so easily taken in. Very small will be the reward that you will ever get for capturing me."

"'Reward'—'Reward,'" Burns repeated, "I suppose that I never have deserved anything better than this."

"You and that little nigger Vasseur are chums, I imagine. Great detectives and sleuths of the law, are you two fellows! Set out to capture Pierre Rameau, eh? Ah, your little plan is all plain enough to me now."

He had drawn one of his heavy holster pistols and now cocked it with a slow deliberate motion, his eyes seeming to lengthen and narrow themselves like those of a cat.

"You choose to play a part, Kirk MacCollough," the old man said; "you choose to deny everything, to spurn your own name, to treat me as a stranger, to refuse me the one last hope of my ruined life; but I tell you now that you shall not escape me!"

His eyes were burning and his voice was deep and strong, with a decided Scotch accent. His long white hair and matted beard shook with the vehement force of his speech. He had straightened himself up so that his tall frame was firmly erect and one bony hand was quivering high above his head.

"You shall not escape me," he repeated, with awful emphasis, "even though you riddle my body with all your bullets! I never will die—I cannot die until—"

"You are going to die right now," said Rameau, interrupting him. "Old man, I leave no person alive who says what you have said. You have spoken your own death-warrant. I am your executioner."

"Kirk MacCollough, you cannot kill me—you cannot. Death is not for me so long as you live! I am in God's hands; He will not wholly desert me, now that He has at last led me to you."

"Oh, you think that, do you? And you consider yourself bullet-proof, eh? Well, the test is quite easy."

He raised his pistol; but instantly lowered it, as a devilish light leaped into his strangely handsome face.

"Let me tell you before you die that you have no child. Margaret is dead. You are her murderer, not I, although I killed her. If you had not interfered with our love I should have been a happy husband and Margaret my happy wife in old Scotland to-day. You chose to treat me like a dog. I took the girl and did my best for her. She proved untrue to me in Spain, and I killed her. Now I am going to kill you. Nothing can save you. I'm glad that you came here; it makes my revenge so easy."

Burns stood as if petrified by the outlaw's words. His lifted hand fell by his side, his features took on a stony expression.

Pierre Rameau spoke without any special emphasis; but his words came forth from his lips like bullets from a gun. The desperation of a sudden mood induced by the memories arising in his mind was not the frenzy of an ordinary man. Indeed, he was not an ordinary man. The history of his deeds makes him an unparalleled character. With him anger was no more than mirth; he seemed to be passionless in the ordinary sense of the word. Any mood was to him a mere phase of conscienceless existence at the core of which burned a steady, intense selfishness.

"You wish to find Margaret, do you? You shall find her, if there's anything in your Presbyterian tomfoolery, in hell, where you both belong. You forced her to desperation; you made an outlaw of me. I am going to make a dead man of you!"

By some such reasoning as this does the desperate criminal almost always seek to justify his attitude. Rarely, indeed, do we find a man, whose deeds have made him the horror of mankind, whose name is sufficient to send a shudder through the world, whose whole record is black with outrages against the most sacred rights of others—rarely do we find such a man putting upon himself the blame of his condition and attitude. Somebody, he fancies, or pretends to fancy, has driven him from the path of honesty and honor. Circumstances have conspired against him; ill-luck has dogged him. Never once will he look truth in the face and say: "I am a villian from my mother's womb; I was born an Ishmaelite!"

As Burns stood there facing the worker of all his misery, he presented the other side of the inscription of life. His had been a career of right-doing. From his youth to old age he had thought little of himself; his chief happiness had been derived from doing good to others and from performing the duties of his holy calling. Like most Scotch Presbyterians, he had placed his faith in God with a seriousness and a literalness that brushed aside doubt as the dust of death. From long habit of thought and work he had grown into the form of his religion, had shaped his physical and moral life to it, had set his whole intellect in its groove and had come to regard himself as the unworthy but specially chosen object of Divine care. Never in his life, till this moment, had he doubted that for every prayer his God would offer relief.

Now, as in this supreme moment, his thoughts ran back over the past, lighting up the strange route of toil, anxiety, distress, delay and defeat by which he had at last come into the presence of Kirk MacCollough, it seemed to him the very despair of all despairs that this man should be able to sit there, proud, vigorous, painless,—a superb specimen of the animal man—and from his silver-mounted saddle, as from a king's throne, fling the fiat of a merciless fate into his face. For the first time since his youthful days a sudden whirl of passion possessed him. His frame distended itself, his eyes shot out a wild light, a foam sprang to his lips and flew out in a fine, white spray as he exclaimed:

"Imp of Satan! Liar of Liars! Do your worst! If my God has indeed forsaken me, my manhood has not! I am not afraid to die! Shoot, you poor, pitiful lying coward, shoot!"

He tore open his coat and bared his shaggy, emaciated breast as he spoke. The attitude, the look, the whole presence of the man flashed out a spirit which, on the stage, is melodrama, but which in real life is desperate heroism. He was expanded and rigid with uncontrollable, ecstatic desperation. His chin was thrust far out, his hands were clenched, his arms stood akimbo. But for the awful stress and sincerity of his mood the whole thing must have been ludicrous. As it was, however, the magic circle of the heroic, the extraordinary, the picturesque was drawn around it, and it was set apart forever as one of the focal points of human passion wherein self-forgetfulness and courage merge into absolute fearlessness.

Pierre Rameau looked on without any change of expression; but he could not fail to recognize and, in his own way, honor the old man's spirit. The cool, alert, thoughtful outlaw felt, however, that this very courage made Burns a most dangerous enemy to be running at large. What might not such a spirit, goaded to desperation, find it possible to accomplish? Self-preservation demanded the death of this man, and with Pierre Rameau there was no such thing as hesitancy or faltering.

He raised his pistol, took deliberate aim and sent an ounce leaden ball straight for the heart of Max Burns.

The old man flung up his arms and fell without a groan.

When the loud report of the weapon had ceased to clatter its echoes in the hollows of the wood, Rameau gave the crumpled body of his poor old victim a steady, searching look till it ceased to quiver, then rode away in the direction taken by his men, leaving Burns's horse standing stock-still, with its nose against its master's shoulder.

A dark cloud had crept up the west meantime, and now a dull roar, heavy and ominous, jarred the air. Lightning twinkled across the chasms between great, tumbled masses of vapor.

When Rameau saw the approaching storm a change came over his face. A close observer could have discovered that this strong, crime-hardened heart was afraid of the spirit that rode the hurricane.

He urged his horse to a swift gallop along the

trail, reloading his pistol as he went. It was quite out of the question for him to reach any house before the coming-on of the wind and rain which he well knew the cloud was bringing; but he recollected that there was a low, cane-thatched shed a little way off the trail, which might serve to shelter him and his horse. It had been built by a man who had camped there with his negroes while passing through the country. Rameau reached it just as the first flurry of the wind went over the tree-tops.

Behind this advance ripple came the great, ocean-like body of the storm, and when it struck the wood there was a mighty, rending sound; the earth shook, the sky appeared to fall, giant trees were snapped like reeds, and the whole forest bowed down before the hurricane.

Along with the wind roared a level current of rain, beaten into white, whirling spray that swept the ground.

Bolt after bolt of lightning fell upon the forest, splintering the pines and carving spiral grooves down the tough boles of the oaks.

Rameau clung to his frightened horse, expecting death every moment.

The rain was a deluge, and it was driven with such force that it was like breasting a mountain-torrent to stand in it.

Some of the lithe, slender trees bent down and beat the ground with their tops. The noise was a tumult of the most awful sounds.

It rains on the just and the unjust, the living and

the dead. Burns's horse stood by the old man's body and trembled, but would not go, while the rain poured, the lightning crashed and the hurricane flung the trees together in heaps.

CHAPTER XI.

SOME SMILES AND SOME FROWNS.

The guests at Chateau d'Or were not disturbed by the dramatic scene going on in the room where Fairfax, Colonel Loring and Mr. Vernon were grouped together under such peculiar circumstances.

Mrs. Vernon and Pauline were alert and facile hostesses, and as the custom of the time permitted them a wide latitude in their method of entertaining, it was easy for them to make the most of the occasion.

Everybody felt the charm of the place, with its flowery vistas, its effect of amplitude, its surprises of light, shadow, color, perspective and its pervading air of generous wealth and hospitable welcome.

Lieutenant Ballanche could not have been altogether unaware that he was one of the chief attractions of the occasion, yet he showed no sign of such consciousness. Everywhere he was met with smiles and with words and looks of approval. This was probably due as much to his military reputation as to his fine form, his clear-cut face and his extreme ease and grace of manner.

When he danced with Mlle. Marie de Sezannes the thought flashed through the company that never had a handsomer couple been seen in New Orleans society.

Mademoiselle de Sezannes was a dark brunette, tall, stately and of superb form, with the perfect skin, teeth and eyes which have always made creole beauty so distinctive and emphatic. She was richly dressed, with just enough of dark scarlet showing in her gown to contrast excellently with her complexion. She was loaded with jewels till she glittered like a savage princess, but her manner was exquisitely refined and modest. Tall as Lieutenant Ballanche was, Mademoiselle de Sezannes's head rose above his shoulder as she leaned on his arm.

Pauline had been dancing with a short, dark-eyed young man, who was now telling her what a friend her father had been to him. The reader, being present, would have recognized this gentleman at a glance as one of our acquaintances of the Pearl River woods, known in history as John A. Murrell, but passing upon the present occasion as Wilfred Parker, son of a rich Tennessee farmer. They stood for a brief space near the festooned railing of the stairway, and Parker's quick restless eyes soon singled out Mademoiselle de Sezannes and Lieutenant Ballanche.

"Your pardon, but who is the young lady on the lieutenant's arm?" he inquired in his brusque but fairly modulated voice.

"It is one of my sweetest friends. It is Mademoiselle Marie de Sezannes."

"She is superbly beautiful."

"Yes, every one says so; and she is as good as she is lovely."

"Her face shows that. The lieutenant looks as if he were in love with her. Ah— What is the lieutenant's name?"

"Ballanche. He is the famous young Indian fighter. He was with General Jackson."

"These fighting men make their way easily with the young ladies. I wish I knew how to fight."

"Lieutenant Ballanche thinks that we may have fighting here."

"Not to-night."

"You choose to make light in a very serious subject, I fear. He says that the British are going to attack New Orleans."

"If that is the case, I shall set out for Tennessee in the morning. It makes me nervous to think of danger."

Pauline looked at him to see whether he was chaffing or speaking seriously. Although he met her eyes with a bold, almost boyishly frank gaze, there was something in his face that troubled her.

He laughed, and said that he did not think there was any danger of an attack being soon made.

The lieutenant came up with Mademoiselle de Sezannes on his arm. Both were evidently in high spirits. Pauline presented Wilfred Parker, and then some duty called her away.

When the eyes of the two men met, it was like

flint meeting steel, so cold did they appear and so sharply flew out the commonplaces of polite but meaningless intercourse. Parker very much desired a further acquaintance with Mademoiselle de Sezannes; for he understood at a glance that she was rich as well as beautiful. Ballanche had no thought of permitting the young lady to leave his side so long as he could hold her.

Parker saw this, or felt it, and at once drew upon his resources of boldness and enterprise. Self-reliance was inexhaustible in him, and he always had an expedient which just fitted an exigency. Mademoiselle de Sezannes was impressed with the remarkable personal charm of this handsome youth, and was caught by the lure of his original and forthright manner. Perhaps she discovered at a glance that he admired her, and that he would not be slow to fall at her feet. Sometimes a discovery of this sort is very fascinating to a young woman. It was much more apt to be so then than now. Parker would not be shaken off by the lieutenant's coldness, but stood close to the beautiful girl, looking boldly into her face, and speaking with fluency and engaging versatility.

Mademoiselle de Sezannes dropped her fan. In those days, young ladies sometimes did this very skillfully; it was a way of testing the promptness and gracefulness of her admirers. We must not say that Mademoiselle de Sezannes' fan fell in accordance with a design of this sort; certainly, she let it fall with a most innocent air and with a pretty little start and a step backward.

Lieutenant Ballanche was a quick man, a man whose every muscle acted with almost instantaneous promptness at need. He bent toward the jeweled toy at once; but Parker was already handing it to Mademoiselle de Sezannes with an exquisite bow. Such celerity astounded the lieutenant; indeed, it actually offended him, and his face showed it in spite of him.

"That is a remarkably fine ruby, mademoiselle, in the hilt of your fan," said Parker, after gracefully receiving her thanks. "Such a stone might have a history."

"Monsieur Parker, you have very quick eyes," she smilingly answered, "and you guess well. This stone has a romantic history. Rochon, the last of the buccaneers, gave it to my grandfather. It is known as the buccaneer or Caribbean ruby."

"That is very interesting. Will you kindly let me look at it. I have a passion for old gems."

"Oh, certainly, monsieur. Every one desires to look at it. It is a famous little pebble."

He took the fan and held it so that the light fell favorably upon the rosy-hued setting.

"Superb!" he exclaimed. "It glows like fire and has the color of a red cherry's juice. Thank you, mademoiselle; it is a great pleasure to have seen the beautiful thing."

Parker was exquisitely dressed, and upon his own hands and bosom sparkled diamonds of no mean size. His air at that moment was that of a connoiseur delighted to have been permitted to look at a marvel in his special field of knowledge. He lacked the peculiar air of ease and finish, so to speak, that made Lieutenant Ballanche so notable in company; but there were a self-sufficiency, a readiness and a sharp vigilance that even the famous lieutenant could not command. Just a hint of the devil-may-care played over his features. Evidently he was one to watch, if you would not have him beat you in any race.

He looked boldly into Mademoiselle de Sezannes' eyes, and said:

"Will Mademoiselle de Sezannes honor me with the next dance?"

Ballanche had been just on the point of asking the great pleasure; but the quick youth had forestalled him.

"Yes, monsieur, with pleasure," she answered, "but let us pass one dance, if you please, I am a trifle tired."

"Take my arm, I will find you a seat."

He stepped close to her and bowed. He was so prompt, so taking in some way, and withal so outright that there was no denying him.

A moment later Lieutenant Ballanche found himself standing there alone, while the tall girl was walking away leaning with superb grace on the arm of the spry little muscular stranger. A flush of anger mantled the usually cool cheek of the soldier, and he turned on his heel, as if to give an order to a company behind him. He came near upsetting an old gentleman of short but portly figure.

"Your pardon, sir."

"Ah, pardon."

Both men bowed and apologized.

The old gentleman was Madamoiselle de Sezannes father, Octave de Sezannes, the banker and slave-trader. He rubbed his hands together in a business-like way and smiled with that perfunctory readiness noticeable in men who make money by sharp turns. The seal of his watch was a maltese cross of gold set with diamonds.

"Pardon, monsieur, we heavy men move but slowly and awkwardly; we are in everybody's way."

"But it is I who am to blame, Monsieur de Sezannes; I sprang around as if I meant to run away. I was angry, however, and you know an angry man is a fool."

He spoke lightly, but the ring of his sudden creole fury was not yet out of his voice.

"I saw, I saw; I know what you mean," said De Sezannes, with the air of one from whom nothing escapes. "The young fellow swooped down like a hawk and took Marie right away from you. Ha, ha, ha!"

Lieutenant Ballanche joined the old gentleman but dryly in his little laugh.

Through a rift in the company and beyond a curtained doorway he could see Madamoiselle de Sezannes sitting in a tall, carved chair and Parker standing by her side. They appeared to be charmed with each other's company. A little later they were going through a dance together, while Ballanche was taking wine with Monsieur de Sezannes.

In the meantime, Mr. Vernon was laboring to

convince Fairfax that Colonel Loring was not Pierre Rameau. Loring himself stood by, apparently quite indifferent as to the outcome, holding his head high and turning his half-closed, inscrutable eyes toward the ceiling.

Fairfax found himself in a predicament very difficult for one of his temperament and disposition to control. He felt that he could not be mistaken; he recollected with absolute memory every feature of the face disclosed to him when the loose cloth mask of the robber fell partly away on that very noteworthy night in March over at Vasseur's place. The form of the man, the peculiar beauty of his hands (long, shapely, muscular) and then the ring on his least finger—that of itself was identification beyond doubt; for no other ring like that was, in all probability, ever made. Moreover, the voice was unmistakable and the peculiar, half-nonchalant, half-reckless air could belong to no other man.

Still, what was Fairfax to say when Mr. Vernon sturdily, even peremptorily, declared that the person before him was well known to him, intimately known to him, indeed, and was a valued and distinguished friend of his, just returned from a long sojourn in Mexico? It was strange beyond comprehension, and there was no disputing about it; for surely Mr. Vernon ought to know, and beyond question he would not have such a man as Pierre Rameau in his house as an honored guest.

Of course Fairfax had but a crude knowledge of the social, political and moral condition of New

Orleans at that time. He was too close to the scene for his vision to have a correct focus upon it, and he knew but little of the comparatively recent history of the city in which Wilkinson had schemed and toward which all of Burr's treasonable plans had gravitated, nor was it possible for him to imagine the extent to which the lawlessness had insinuated itself into the very life-tissues of New Orleans society.

"I am sorry that this little mistake has happened," said Mr. Vernon, turning from one to the other, and trying to make the whole thing appear of no consequence; "but it's quite an honor, Loring, to be taken for Pierre Rameau, who is reputed to be the handsomest man in the South. You know my friend Fairfax here had quite an adventure with that renowned robber—was robbed by him, in short, and holds a just grudge against him."

"Ah, I see," said Loring. "I understand now. He has taken me for a robber."

"You've heard of Rameau?"

"No; but you must recall that I have been in Mexico for nearly three years."

"Certainly. Well, gentlemen, this ought to be satisfactory. Now, then, the broken finger; let's look to that. Mr. Vernon bustled a little and produced some bandage-cloth that a servant had fetched.

Colonel Loring promptly set the fractured bone, and with great skill and rapidity applied the wrapping.

"There," he said; "you are all right, sir. You will have no trouble with it."

"Thank you, sir," responded Fairfax coldly enough, in spite of an effort to regain his lost temper and appear kindly polite.

"Now, gentlemen," remarked Mr. Vernon, laying a hand on the arm of each and smiling from one to the other in his large way, "you are my guests and my friends; be friends to each other. Forget this curious little mischance, this awkward mistake."

By this time Fairfax had shaken off the outer coating of his mood and with something like his habitual frankness began to apologize.

'I am quite sorry," he exclaimed, "and chagrined that I should have spoken so hastily, Colonel Loring. I hope you understand my embarrassment, sir, and will forgive my passionate words. I really thought you were Pierre Rameau."

"It's nothing at all," insisted the colonel. "I don't care a straw about it. Let it drop here, sir, and be forgotten."

Somehow in an instant Fairfax regretted his apology. Surely, this man was Pierre Rameau—it was he from head to foot.

Mr. Vernon, still inclined to be heavily impetuous, kept his hold on the arm of each. With his double muscles, not the least impaired by age, he propelled them to the dining-room, where he made them eulogize his wines and his brandy.

In the midst of a rapid and light conversation, Loring suddenly exclaimed:

"Please excuse me, gentlemen. I am losing a greater pleasure than even your company affords me. Miss Vernon promised to dance with me. Excuse me."

And he hastened to the drawing-rooms. Fairfax looked after him with gloomy eyes and flushed cheeks. The bare thought of Pauline's dancing with that man went like a leaden bullet to his heart. In fact, just then his heart was particularly sensitive in this regard, for it seemed to him that Lieutenant Ballanche had been doing nothing but dance with Pauline the whole evening; and that man, or boy, rather, Parker—she had been unnecessarily agreeable to him. These were not exactly the thoughts of Fairfax. We must acquit him of actual petty jealousy. But somehow he felt left out for the time being, or as if he had failed to seize opportunity with manly promptness.

He wandered into the conservatory, where many tropical plants were flourishing. Here the music reached him in subdued waves and throbs; the brisk phrases of the violins were softened and sentimentalized by the distance till they seemed to creep through his sense, trailing a nameless melancholy behind. He stroked his moustache and gazed vacantly about.

Pauline felt some vague but troublesome stir of excitement in her heart when Colonel Loring came to remind her of the promised dance. It was as if she feared him and yet felt drawn toward him; as if some mystery in his nature or character possessed a fascination, while at the same time it suggested dark doubts.

There is a lure in vailed and shadowy things; we

cannot resist the influence of those elusive elements which, in some way, like fine films of connection, set us in communication with the unusual, the strange, the romantic. It is especially dangerous for a young girl to come within the reach of such an influence when a strong-willed and handsome man is at the base of it. The snake and the bird, the fascination of a deadly thing—we all know how nature lends to fatal venom the tender glow of a precious elixir.

Colonel Loring was an interesting talker. He had travelled in many lands. His mind was stored with recollections of adventure, of perils by land and sea, and these he could set in contrast with pleasant experiences of social life in many a gay city of the old world. He was in the early prime of manhood, strong, in perfect health, and he had, when he wished, a way of sending his vigor through his firm, positive voice into every word he spoke.

In his presence, with his hand clasping hers now and again during the old-fashioned dance, Pauline felt that she was acting a part in a romance, and the sensation lifted the color into her cheeks and lips.

When the dance ended, Colonel Loring slipped her arm through his and led her through a broad, garlanded doorway into the conservatory.

"It is deliciously cool here. Let us take a turn or two up and down this charming aisle. This is like Mexico," he said, touching a vigorous cactus. "I can almost feel the winds of the plains."

"Life here must seem very dull and tame to you

after all your stirring adventures," she suggested, looking up with frank interest into his face.

"No. It is delightful. I am enjoying every moment of it. I wish I could forget my whole past and begin anew from this moment."

There was a ring of infinite regret in his words, along with something wistful, that thrilled Pauline's heart.

She was about to speak with all the outright sympathy of her impulsive nature; she was going to enter straightway into the spirit of his mood; her words were already at her lips, and her eyes were upturned to his with an expression of earnestness and deep interest, when, just at the angle of he way between some tall vases, they came upon Fairfax standing quite still with folded arms. His eyes met Pauline's as she turned them quickly from Loring's face. Then the two men exchanged glances which conveyed no sign of pleasure. A deadly hatred, indeed, which had been kept hidden by both, showed itself ominously, as Loring, with head high and a sinister smile on his lips, passed on, taking Pauline with him.

She felt in some indirect way the change that passed over the dark face of the man whose arm she was touching, and something in the manner of Fairfax affected her unpleasantly. At the moment she did not examine or in fact fully realize her impression; but later, when Lieutenant Ballanche was telling her that in a day or two he was going away to report to General Jackson at some place in the interior, and when she saw how piqued and almost savage he looked as he glanced at Parker who was dancing again with Mademoiselle de Sezannes, she suddenly understood or half understood what was happening, save that it was impossible to connect herself with it. These men, she surmised, were, all four of them, ready to quarrel about Mademoiselle de Sezannes, and the thought at once suggested a duel or two.

In those days duels were of almost daily and nightly occurrence in New Orleans and at the famous dueling grounds of the surrounding country. Consequently death on the sword's point or at the pistol's mouth was not so shocking to think of as it is now. The creole girl of our story's time could not fairly understand the philosophy of it, but still she recognized the importance of what was called "the only method by which insulted honor may be defended and purified," or as another old writer states it: "the swiftest, the fairest and the most satisfactory mode of settling matters of deadly concern between gentlemen."

The party at Chateau d'Or was likely to be pleasantly remembered; but it was also, as we shall see, the generating point for some disagreeable developments and some strange and sinister complications.

"It has been delightful, charming," exclaimed Mrs. Vernon, flinging herself into Pauline's arms after the last guest had gone. "Every one was happy—and how lovely the whole house was! And you were so beautiful, dear, so very, very beautiful!"

Pauline returned her mother's vehement embrace, and they were standing thus linked in each other's arms when Mr. Vernon approached and encircled both with his bear-like hug.

Standing there, the group was a striking one. It was a living tableau of love as intense as it was strange and beautiful. There were the effect of high refinement in it and a delicate tenderness; but there was also something if but a hint of the ungoverned and the untrained.

CHAPTER XII.

COLONEL LORING AND PAULINE.

Fairfax went home from the party at Chateau d'-Or feeling that it had been an unfortunate affair for him, and yet he could not have explained with any degree of exactitude why it had been so.

The adventure with the hunchback lingered in his memory as something picturesquely sinister and pathetic; then Colonel Loring arose before him whichever way he turned his mind, with the growing certainty that he was identical with Pierre Rameau, the robber; but above and beyond all, Fairfax was annoyed with himself, because he had let the evening go by without paying any special attention to Pauline.

He felt humiliated that he should have frittered

away so much time with the wound on his hand which, after all, seemed so small a thing, while men like Parker and Lieutenant Ballanche were boldly seizing upon every advantage offered them for cultivating the good will of Mrs. Vernon and her daughter. He recognized himself as one of those imaginative, self-conscious youths who dream that the smallest matter affecting them is of prime importance to the rest of mankind. He could not resist the impulse to laugh in a bitter way at the turn affairs had taken with him. Like a small boy, he had made faces over a sore finger, while the most important crisis (as he now felt) of his whole life had drawn past him.

Imaginative young men not unfrequently regard a love matter with a sense of its incomparable value to themselves, and they feel indirect but deep amazement when made aware that it is of little significance to any one else in the whole world.

The truth was, however, that Fairfax realized in a way how little right he had to connect Pauline with any love-dream of his own. He had never spoken a word of love to her, and this seemed inexplicable to him now. Why had he not? Perhaps he had been foolishly sure of his standing in her regard; he had taken too much for granted.

Reflections like these, while they made him uneasy, as is one who consciously walks upon treacherous ground, led him to resolve that Pauline should hear his plea and give him his answer at the first opportune moment. Young men often make these resolves and almost as frequently, perhaps, recede from them when the crucial moment comes. It is love that makes men brave, and it is love as well that makes them cowards.

The summer went by—as summers do in that beautiful gulf-coast climate—with days that burned through the noon and softened down to delicious coolness toward nightfall, and nights whose dreamy splendor made the creole city, with all its gayety, its intrigue, its excitements, a place of indescribable allurements.

In the autumn, the English fleet was making ready to swing round the gulf-coast. Colonel Nichols had arrived at Pensacola, and acting for the British government, had set on foot a scheme by which he hoped to stir up the Indians to renewed hostilities and at the same time induce the white population of Louisiana to revolt against the United States government.

Lieutenant Ballanche went away to join General Jackson, to whom he reported the situation in the New Orleans district, and did not return until about the first days in December.

Colonel Loring also disappeared, going, it was understood, on a mission connected with some scheme of his in Mississippi, while Parker, the shrewd and self-confident youth, had bidden his many friends in New Orleans good-bye and set out for his home in Tennessee about the first of August.

Fairfax had still another cause for discontent which he made the most of. Colonel Loring had rescued Pauline and Mrs. Vernon from imminent danger in the midst of a crowd of rioting sailors and boatmen. The ladies were in the Vernon carriage, and just as it turned a street-corner they found themselves surrounded by a mob of men who were fighting with staves, knives, pistols, cutlasses and whatever other weapons they could command.

Aside from the actual danger of the situation; the brutal fury of the combatants; the atrocious profanity and the sickening sounds of slashing and stabbing and shooting; the bewilderment and fright of the coachman, who presently abandoned his place to seek safety in flight, and the wild rearing and plunging of the horses in the midst of the crowding and heedless mass of rioters—the ladies had good cause to faint at the mere thought of what brutality the scene implied, if they had been of the temperament dear to old romance. They called loudly for help, but who was likely to hear or to heed?

Fairfax chanced to be near the outer fringe of the crowd and recognized Pauline's voice. He rushed to the spot, only to find that Colonel Loring had already rendered all the service that was needed—had sprung, indeed, to the coachman's seat and was turning the horses down a narrow side-street. The eyes of the two men met for an instant at this point, Loring giving to his glance an expression of triumph, as Fairfax thought, and Fairfax himself scowling so viciously that, although Pauline looked straight into his face, she did not recognize him at the time.

Colonel Loring's promptness and nerve doubtless

saved the ladies from death or great injury. He
drove the carriage to Chateau d'Or and received
such thanks and such looks of gratitude as Fairfax
would have fought around the earth to win.

"I don't see how you did it, and so easily, too!"
said Mrs. Vernon, after they had entered the parlor.
Loring was still standing, hat in hand. "Please sit
down, Colonel Loring, and tell us all about it.
Mercy, how my heart is still fluttering! How *did*
you manage to get to us and take us out of that
horrible place?"

"It was nothing," he said, with his cold, peculiar
smile. "I merely turned the horses and drove
away. Any little boy could have done the same."

"But, no; that were impossible, sir," Pauline
urged. "Nobody but you could have done what
you did. When that dark, little man sprang at your
throat with the knife I thought he had stabbed you;
but you struck him with your hand and he fell quite
as if he had been shot. Oh, it was dreadful, and
you did not appear to care for it at all!"

Loring's narrow, fascinating eyes gazed steadily
into her face as he said:

"I have been accustomed to dangers so much
greater than that little affair could possibly bring,
that I hardly count myself a hero, Miss Vernon, for
having piloted you out of a trifling annoyance.
Pray do not think of it as a matter of any importance whatever. I deem it a bit of good fortune for
me that I can be at Chateau d'Or once more before
I take my leave of New Orleans for a time."

"And you are going away?" Mrs. Vernon

inquired with quick interest, that shaded sharply into regret. "Going away from us?"

"Yes—the war. I cannot rest idle while the country needs soldiers."

Pauline thought he looked the very model of what a soldier ought to be.

"And where shall you join the army?" she asked.

"I do not know yet; my place has not yet been assigned to me; but that matters little. A soldier's business is to obey orders and have no preferences."

"Lieutenant Ballanche is gone already, I believe; at least he bade us good-bye, and was expecting to go to the interior the next day."

"Yes, the governor sent him to look after some outlaws over on the Mississippi border, I believe; he's likely to have some amusement before he accomplishes his errand, I should think."

"You gentlemen have strange ideas of amusement. What entertainment do you see in fighting robbers?" interposed Mrs. Vernon in a deprecatory tone, that yet had an admiration point in it. "Is it such great sport to kill and be killed?"

"I don't call it sport," he said, turning his gaze slowly from Pauline to her mother, "but the excitement is a mighty tonic. When a man is hunting a man, or is hunted by one, he feels, to the limit of possibility, the true meaning of self-reliance."

"But it is terrible!" exclaimed Pauline. "It makes men worse than beasts of prey!"

Loring laughed a slow, heavy laugh, his strong, mysterious face lighting up strangely.

Mrs. Vernon and Pauline were sitting side by side upon a dark-tapestried sofa. Pauline was toying with her mother's hand.

"Isn't the whole of life terrible?" Loring demanded. "What, after all, is there to relieve it of its dark significance?"

The ladies looked disturbed. What he had said was depressing enough under the circumstances; but his voice, his manner and his inscrutable face made an impression singularly startling. It was one of those moments that come to all of us, when hidden things of strange import are half revealed to what, for want of a better name, we call our inner consciousness.

Pauline was aware of a sudden sympathy for this dark, weather-stained, scarred veteran who seemed to take such a jaundiced view of life. Her girl's heart went out to him as it might have done to a beautiful wounded animal. She felt the weight of his vast experience with evil pressing upon her with the effect of infinite pathos. She recalled what he had said to her on the evening of the party, and now, as she looked at him sitting there upright, muscular, sun-tanned, the picture of resolute, defiant health and vigor, she recognized in some way the romance that must lie behind him along the way he had come.

"The business of a soldier must be sad and saddening," she said, "and I do not wonder at your view of life; only you might promise yourself rest and happiness when the war is ended."

Mrs. Vernon was called away just then to meet some friends whom a servant announced.

As she arose to go, she made an apologetic gesture.

"Excuse me, but pray do not go till I return," she said.

Why she had spoken thus she could not have explained, save by admitting that he was a fascinating man to whom she felt that she owed her life and her daughter's.

Pauline involuntarily made a movement to clutch her mother's hand and detain her.

A faint glow of feeling suffused Loring's face; but no person, however skilled in physiognomy, could have read its meaning. In some way, it might have reminded one of that flash of hope now and again seen in the face of a man on the eve of his execution.

"It is so seldom that I can sit in a beautiful room like this and converse with—" He checked himself; he was speaking as if half in soliloquy. "I shall never forget," he went on, with a slight effort, "how beautiful these rooms were the other evening."

"It is very kind of you to remember it. The house was lovely."

"And you, too, were as lovely as an angel. I shall never forget how you looked."

The color came quickly to Pauline's cheeks and lips; but flattery was tolerable in those days; and besides, when a man is serious and sincere, it is not in woman's nature to resent his admiration.

"My dress was one that my grandmother wore when she was a girl, only I had it done over," she replied, with a *naïve* show of interest in the subject. "Every one said that it was very quaint and becoming. I like those old things. Don't you?"

"It was you that became the dress; you made it beautiful; you charmed everybody. The dress was nothing."

Pauline felt a sudden desire to run away from him, and yet, perhaps, she would not have gone if she had been under no obligation to stay.

"The occasion was exhilarating," she managed to say, with the most indifferent air. "I am especially proud that every one enjoyed it; for, you know, it was the first party I ever gave. And didn't you think Mademoiselle de Sezannes beautiful? She captivated all the gentlemen; but, then, she always does with her superb way and—"

"She looks like a Spanish Jewess," said Loring, interrupting her.

"But she is not like one, Colonel Loring," replied Pauline.

"I beg pardon. I did not mean to imply criticism. Mademoiselle de Sezannes impressed me very pleasantly. It is not so bad to look like a Jewess."

He arose as if to take his leave.

"But you promised my mother to wait till she returned," said Pauline, arising also. "You have not forgotten?"

"No; I will wait. But I never sit long. I have

this way of getting on my feet almost involuntarily. I seem to be made for—to be upright."

He smiled and made a gesture to signify he was chaffing, then added :

"But keep your seat, Miss Vernon ; I will walk to and fro, if you will permit it, while we continue our conversation. Do you know this is more like happiness than anything that has come to me for years? I must make the most of it."

He pushed toward her the chair in which he had been sitting.

She sat down, and when she looked up with her bright smile, her dark, vivacious eyes seemed to dazzle him. He turned about and walked with a light, singularly springy step across the room and back.

"My father is restless in this way sometimes," she said, "and walks the floor like a tiger in a cage. When I ask him why he does it, he always says that he is thinking of the sea. You know he was a sailor a long time ago."

"I am more receptive when in motion ; can think more clearly, can shake off a fit of discontent more easily. I walk back and forth when I wish to remember and when I wish to forget. Did you ever wish to forget anything?"

He stopped in front of her, with his head high. His face irradiated a strange light, his attitude had a fine touch of the dramatic—almost the melodramatic—in it. What was it that he could not forget? What was he trying to fasten forever in his memory?

"I forget nearly everything that I ought to keep in mind," she said, scarcely knowing what her words were. "I wish I had a good memory."

"It is a bad wish. If I could forget everything —the whole past, the whole world, everything but the present moment as it passes—I could be happy. Some one has said that the past is a cemetery, a place in which we bury dead experiences. Memory is a ghoul; it digs up nothing but corpses."

He was walking back and forth again with his strong chin elevated, his muscular shoulders thrown back, while his thin, firm lips seemed to writhe around his words. The cords in his neck stood out as if they bore a great strain.

"My life has been so happy and so uneventful," said Pauline, speaking with the frankness of a child, her voice betraying the fascination that his words and actions were exerting over her, "and I have seen so little of life that I cannot—"

"Oh, no, you cannot—" he interrupted—"you cannot understand. Men's lives are so different from yours, so beset, so borne upon by evil, so stirred by devilish impulses."

He had increased his pace until his strides had the energy of some powerful excitement and his bronze features were pinched and bloodless. The stress of the moment added a strange, indescribable beauty to his face.

For some moments there was silence between them; meantime they could hear Mrs. Vernon giving her callers a most animated account of the street adventure and of Colonel Loring's gallant service.

"We owe our lives to him," she declared, with emphasis. "And he risked his own so bravely!"

Without realizing her own sense of the fascination that was holding her fast, Pauline sat gazing at the man as he strode to and fro. Her face was sweetly flushed and her eyes shone with a soft, dreamy expression that told how powerfully her sympathies had been stirred.

Mrs. Vernon returned as soon as her visitors had gone.

Colonel Loring confronted her hat in hand.

"I shall not see you again before you hear of fighting," he said, indicating that he was about to go. He stood looking back and forth from mother to daughter as if he had something he wished to say but could not.

Mrs. Vernon extended her hand.

"Our prayers will attend you," she said, with a subdued smile, "and we shall hope to see you back very soon, safe and well."

He went away abruptly, leaving behind him an impression that never in the least faded on the memory of the two imaginative women

Pauline went almost immediately to her room. She wished to be alone. In her heart a feeling of indescribable unrest was blending with a vague sense of tenderness, pity, longing and fear, as if some evil were about to befall some one she loved. Loring's face was before her inner vision. His expression of dark brooding and hopelessness had fastened itself upon her memory, like a strange, haunting picture, and his voice, with its peculiar restrained coldness and its undertone of passionate despair, seemed to echo mysteriously through every cell of her consciousness. She leaned back in a white-cushioned chair and clasped her hands above her head.

CHAPTER XIII.

COLONEL LORING MAKES HIMSELF FELT.

Although the possibility of New Orleans being attacked by a British force had been for a month or two the chief topic of conversation in all the homes and in every *salle* and *café* in the city, nobody was prepared to receive the news when at last the fleet was reported off the islands that rim the southern confine of Mississippi Sound. A panic seized the people; and, as for the army, there was none to speak of.

General Jackson made haste to occupy the city with such forces as he could readily pull together, and began at once to prepare for a vigorous, if apparently hopeless, defense. The first difficulty that presented itself to the iron-hearted Tennesseean was that of securing the confidence and co-operation of a class of men who in a large degree controlled both New Orleans and Louisiana. He found that a deep-seated prejudice already existed against him in official circles, and that a clash of authority was likely to come immediately. Governor Claiborne had many enemies in the State, and as soon as he became a stanch supporter of Jackson's policy, which was a strictly military and not a little despotic one, they began to attack both the general and the governor from a hundred directions with the most insidious abuse.

Although the masses were loyal to the United States, the loyalty was a provincial one. The creoles especially regarded anything like national interference with the local affairs of Louisiana with but little favor, and at first they did not admire the rough and imperious general, whose manners and language were foreign to their taste, and whose imperious disposition would brook no interference, even in the way of suggestion, with his quickly formed plans.

Jackson attached Lieutenant Ballanche to his staff as soon as he arrived in New Orleans. This was considered an insult by some influential persons, who desired to have Colonel Loring occupy that position, and who had made a special suggestion to that effect, fortified by the statement that Loring knew the whole country as a sailor-pilot knows his chart, and was, besides, an officer of varied and successful experience in the service. Mr. Vernon, too, had added the weight of his name and recommendation, which had heretofore been almost all-powerful in Colonel Loring's behalf.

As for the colonel himself, he returned to New Orleans from no one knew exactly where, just in time to be informed of General Jackson's peremptory refusal while the words were scarcely cold.

"I do not need more staff-officers or more officers of any kind," was the bluff statement made by the already over-worked commander. "I need fighting men who have guns and will shoot with them whenever a red-coat gets in sight. Let every man forget office and think of his country for a while. If Colonel Loring desires to fight for New Orleans, let him report to me at once with a gun."

Ernest Faval, a politician of some note, and Mr. Vernon met, soon after this, in a restaurant not far from Jackson's headquarters, on Royal Street, where they discussed the matter in a characteristic way over a bottle of Burgundy. It must be recorded that they cursed and swore like pirates, meantime coupling General Jackson's name with a good deal that was by no means flattering to it.

The restaurant was one of the best in the city, and situated, as already stated, only a few doors distant from the house in which the commanding officer had established his headquarters. Indeed, Faval and Mr. Vernon were fresh from the exasperating interview already mentioned. They were, perhaps, pleasurably surprised when on the moment Loring chanced to drop in and join them at the table.

"You are ordered, sir," said Faval, in a mock military manner, "to put on the uniform of a private soldier and report with gun and accouterments, to General Jackson."

Loring smiled coldly, tossed off a glass of wine and, resting his elbows on the table, turned inquiring glances from one to the other of his companions.

"Jackson flatly refuses to appoint you," said Mr. Vernon, setting a strong tone of vexation in his words. "He treated us as if we had been two old women."

"And told us," added Faval, "that everybody must forget office, though I took notice that he did not offer to resign his own office."

"It was quite unexpected," Mr. Vernon went on. "I thought he would appoint you without a word on such recommendations as we were able to offer; but he refused in terms almost unbearably offensive, as if the thought set him in a rage. He was dignified enough, too; but I saw anger in his eyes."

Loring did not change countenance, or, if he did, it was but to broaden his sardonic smile.

"I am not surprised," he remarked, breaking a biscuit with the most indifferent air; "it was a fool's errand from the beginning. Claiborne knows more than you imagine, and what Claiborne knows Jackson knows."

"What do you mean?" demanded Mr. Vernon, with peremptory suddenness. His eyes shot out almost fierce inquiry.

Faval gave Loring a quick, warning glance which the latter understood at once.

Without an instant's hesitation and emitting not a ray of expression to hint his swift change of mental attitude, Colonel Loring said:

"What I mean is that Claiborne knows very well that you and Faval distrust him, and, of course, he is making good time in poisoning Jackson against you, as I should do, if I were he, under all the circumstances. I know something of General Jackson; he is a contemptible, jealous tyrant!"

Mr. Vernon laughed, with his eyes fixed steadily on those of Loring. If there had been a flash of suspicion it came and went like the flash of a firefly.

"It's a high-handed beginning, to say the least," growled Faval, "and for my part I don't relish it; though, for that matter, I have a poor way of helping myself."

"General Jackson probably thinks he can get along without Louisianaians in defending Louisiana," said Mr. Vernon, with a mechanical show of lightness. "Ta! He will soon find out his mistake, I hope."

"He takes Lieutenant Ballanche instead of you," Faval remarked turning to Loring. "The boy seems to be cheek by jowl with him and Claiborne. I suppose that old Sezannes and his money bags are the power behind the throne."

"What interest has Sezannes in the affair?" inquired Mr. Vernon, lifting his big, shaggy head with a motion at once swift and heavy.

"Ballanche is to be his son-in-law, I understand."

"Ta! Love rules war, too, eh?"

"Perhaps—when love controls money."

There was a moment of silence, and then Mr. Vernon, leaning back in his chair and stroking his tumbled beard, added;

"It strikes me, in spite of myself, that General

Jackson is just the man for the place he has taken with such *aplomb*."

Fival winced, inwardly if not outwardly. There was a touch of resentment in his tone when he said :

"Oh, he will make us all bestir ourselves. He will pull the strings and, like puppets, we'll have to hop and kick as if we liked it. War brings strange masters."

"He has already been to every probable point of defense all around the city," continued Mr. Vernon, thoughtfully, as if in soliloquy ; "and the steps he is taking look to me more like genuine military work than anything that has ever been done in this district."

Faval, whose greatest desire had been to have General Wilkinson returned to the command at New Orleans, cleared his throat and took a glass of brandy as if to wash something down.

"He has the prestige of recent victories to make way for him," he remarked, evasively, "and I don't doubt his ability. Perhaps it is a mistake, however, for even General Jackson to openly insult a man like you."

Mr. Vernon arched his brows and made a gesture which implied absolute disclaimer of everything personal to himself.

"I shall report with a gun when the enemy appears," he said. "It is the business of us all to fight for our country."

Loring eyed him steadily for a moment and then in a peculiar, low voice exclaimed :

"I am thirty-seven years old, and I have not yet permitted any man to play master over me. I shall hardly begin now."

Then he twirled a wine-glass carelessly and added:

"General Jackson, like any other plebeian who has risen a trifle above his present associates, fancies himself a Cæsar. It would be good for him to have his nose pulled."

"I should not care to do that piece of pulling," said Faval, dryly; "the nose of Andrew Jackson has the pluck of the devil behind it."

Mr. Vernon laughed; that leonine, growling chuckle of his came forth with a suddenness and force that fairly jarred the table. He seemed to be reflecting upon something that amused him greatly. Presently he said:

"He dismissed us, Faval, as if he'd been a district school-teacher and we his rather stupid pupils!"

"'If Colonel Loring desires to fight for New Orleans,'" said Faval, mocking General Jackson's manner, "'let him report to me at once with a gun.'"

Loring poured a glass of wine and held it up before him. There was a sardonic, devil-may-care gleam in his half-closed eyes.

"When I report to General Jackson he'll be a very much surprised man," he drawled, with that emphatic slowness which sometimes means a great deal. "My report will make his head swim."

"Oh, come, now," said Faval, "don't go too far

with your resentment. Doubtless we shall all have to fight under the tyrant. We can't turn our backs."

At this moment a gaunt, rough-looking, stern-faced man strode into the restaurant, his boots sounding heavily on the floor.

"There's General Jackson now!" said Mr. Vernon, and the others turned to see.

The deep-set eyes of the commander fixed themselves quickly on Faval, and there flashed out of them a perceptible glow of displeasure, as if some sudden vexation had come at sight of him.

The three arose from the table. Mr. Vernon made a step forward and saluted.

With a curt but comprehensive bow, General Jackson acknowledged the attention of the group. His eyes, however, did not turn from Faval, though the displeasure vanished from them evidently by force of his will.

Colonel Loring stood with folded arms while he gazed steadily into General Jackson's eyes.

Mr. Vernon extended his hand, and the commander shook it perfunctorily.

"May I introduce Colonel Loring of whom we were speaking this morning?" Mr. Vernon went on, in a cordial tone.

"Humph!" grunted Jackson. "How do you do, sir?"

The manner and the words were more careless and indifferent than in any sense malicious or purposely contemptuous; but, to say the least, the ring of downright impoliteness was unmistakable. It was plain enough that Colonel Loring's presence had not affected the commander a whit more pleasantly than had the suggestions in his behalf by Faval and Mr. Vernon.

Faval made a step half around the corner of the table as he saw some movement on the part of Loring.

"I am quite sure, General Jackson," Mr. Vernon was going on to say, "that you and Colonel Loring will find if pleasant to—"

The thought in his mind vanished on the instant, and he stopped midway of the sentence; but it was too late to interpose himself, although he tried with great promptness and decision.

What followed was, perhaps, the most astounding incident in all the turbulent and checkered experiences of Andrew Jackson.

Loring made a quick step forward, reached forth his right hand and, grasping the commander's nose between his thumb and forefinger, tweaked it and wrung it savagely.

"Take that!" he sneered, and then slapped the astonished man's cheek. "I will report to you with a gun when I see fit, you conceited ruffian!"

While he was speaking, Loring had passed briskly along, and in less than five seconds he was out of the room. Indeed, General Jackson, quick and decided as he always was in an emergency, had not recovered from his consternation before his assailant was quite gone. Faval, who had a way, as most unscrupulous politicians have, of making fair weather for himself just at the most critical moment, came to the commander's defense, or rather to his aid, with a pistol which he snatched forth and fired toward Loring a little too late to hit him; the bullet creased the door-post.

Jackson wheeled and pursued the retreating man. But what was the use? He was gone. The irate commander immediately gave orders for Loring's arrest; but he was not to be found so easily.

Jackson, if he suspected that Mr. Vernon and Faval secretly enjoyed his discomfiture, did not betray it. The matter was hushed up in short order, and not till many days afterward did the rumor go out in New Orleans that "Old Hickory" had had his nose pulled and his cheek slapped without being able to fitly resent it. Doubtless the pressure, sudden and apparently irresistible, of the military situation forced Jackson to cast behind him, for the time at least, all personal considerations and turn his whole attention to preparing the defense of New Orleans. At all events, while Mr. Vernon and Ernest Faval were yet with him, endeavoring to quiet him, Lieutenant Ballanche came in great haste to bear him startling news from down the river. The British were coasting along the marshes and feeling their way toward the city, or trying to get possession of Pontchartrain. As yet, nothing certain could be known of their numbers or equipments, saving that they appeared to be strong, well supplied and confident. There were great difficulties in the way of watching their movements, and so far it was doubtful what were their real intentions as to the point of attack.

General Jackson received the young lieutenant respectfully, even cordially, and after a few words with him aside, took his arm, and bowing to Faval and Mr. Vernon, walked away with him towards headquarters.

Faval, in his creole volatility, could restrain his indignation no longer. He clenched his hands and swore ; but Mr. Vernon was quite calm and apparently not in the least in sympathy with his companion's bitter criticism of the commander's personal treatment of them.

On the evening of this same day, Colonel Loring further distinguished himself by appearing suddenly in the de Sezannes box at the leading theatre of the city and throttling Lieutenant Ballanche, who at the time was engaged in conversation with Mademoiselle de Sezannes and her mother. The onslaught was so precipitate and so quickly done with that the perpetrator was gone before any general understanding of the startling affair was had by the audience. Ballanche was seized by the throat in a grip of iron, lifted bodily and dashed down stunned and almost lifeless at the feet of Mademoiselle de Sezannes.

The play going forward on the stage was not half so strikingly dramatic as this spectacular performance in real life, and, although the people of New Orleans were well used to scenes of violence, those who witnessed it were horrified by the peculiar atrocity it exhibited. Loring's two muscular hands closed about the young man's neck with frightful force, and his cold, long, narrow eyes flickered balefully under his straight, dark brows.

Mademoiselle de Sezannes and her mother screamed; the old man's face grew livid with fright as he flung up his fat hands and sank back, helpless, in his seat.

At this distance it is difficult to understand a state of society like that in New Orleans at the time of which we write; but the temper of the people may be suggested by the fact that, while the city lay apparently open to an alien and presumably reckless enemy whose fleet and troops were preparing for capture and booty, the leaders of social life and the chief military officers, Jackson excepted, were at the theatre enjoying a light play. Moreover, the strange incident just recorded did not much inconvenience either players or audience after the first thrill of excitement passed by. It was a momentary wonder, nothing more.

Mr. Vernon and his wife and daughter were in a box almost opposite the one occupied by the de Sezannes, and it chanced that Fairfax was with them at the moment when Loring appeared.

Pauline did not see the daring and brutal act; but when she turned in the direction indicated by her father's sudden, excited stare, Loring was standing there facing the stage. He was erect and rigid with a passion not otherwise observable, while Ballanche lay crumpled and still at Mademoiselle de Sezannes' feet. Something in the man's calm, mysterious face sent through her a thrill of indescribable sympathy. As he turned almost instantly to retreat from the auditorium, his eyes met hers with a quick movement of recognition, and he smiled with a peculiar, subdued gleam in his dark face.

She clutched her mother's arm, and her cheeks and lips turned pale as death. She felt rather than saw the flash of excitement which passed over the faces of the audience all turned upon the tall form now passing rapidly along the aisle that led to the main entrance.

Nobody attempted to stop Loring; even the policeman at the door either did not understand what had happened or feared him; for they stood aside when he approached and let him pass untouched.

Mr. Vernon sat motionless during the scene.

"What is it? What has happened?" demanded his wife, as soon as she could command her voice. "Has there been a fight? Is Lieutenant Ballanche hurt? Who did it? Was it Colonel Loring?"

With the assistance of the excited M. de Sezannes, Lieutenant Ballanche was slowly rising. Evidently he was confused and unable to realize what had happened. Instinctively, however, he righted his disturbed collar and pulled himself together with a show of dignity and coolness which won the admiration of the onlookers.

On this very evening a courier brought the news to General Jackson that the British forces were approaching the river from Lake Borgne by way of Bayou Bienvenu. Lieutenant Ballanche had not yet fully recovered from his bewilderment, when an officer came to hand him an order from the commander to report immediately at headquarters.

The rumor that the city was on the point of being occupied by the enemy went, somehow, afloat through the theatre. This completed the distraction of the audience. People began to go, at first by individuals or family groups, then, as the excitement increased, there was a wild rush and a tumult of hysterical voices. They poured into the street with the cry:

"The English! The English! The city is to be plundered and burnt!"

Mr. Vernon and Fairfax, along with a respectable minority of the audience, kept cool and quietly remained in their seats; but the look that came into Mr. Vernon's face when he heard the shout and for a moment felt that the British army was entering the city, told how terrible the announcement was to him.

"Come," he said to Fairfax, "we must get the ladies to a place of safety."

"Be calm, dear," he added, laying hold on his wife's arm.

Pauline was already clinging tightly to him, but her thoughts were not on the coming of the English soldiery. Somehow she was impressed with the feeling that Colonel Loring had, as if by a touch of magic, caused all this excitement and tumult.

CHAPTER XIV.

MR. VERNON AND COLONEL LORING.

It is best for the reader to keep all the time well in mind, as he follows the thread of this story, the historical peculiarities that blend with the romance affecting the lives of the people in whom we are interested. The growth of Louisiana from a colony of reckless military adventurers up to the stature of a great State has been a singular instance of evolution. Iberville and Bienville planted the seed of a strange race on the gulf coast, and the civilization (as we may call it, for want of a better name) which developed in the course of time in the Latin colony was mongrel in every sense. French, Spanish, Indian, negro, all blended. The lonely knights of fortune, in the earlier days of the occupation, took them wives from among the comely squaws of the wild tribes—girls of the Chouacas, the Chickasaws, the Creeks and the Cherokees—or mated themselves with slave-women from Cuba or St. Domingo. Cargoes of young women from the prisons and public pens of Paris—real Manon Lescauts, but unattended by their lovers—were sent over to be the wives of men who had run the gamut of hardship and of hardening experience. Crozat came with his contract to demoralize and Law with his scheme to ruin the colony. Gold fever, the fever of conquest, the thirst for discovery, the longing for lawless power and romantic glory possessed the grim, fearless, conscienceless adventurers. Now the French held the government; now the Spaniards took it; again the French; anon the Spaniards. There were slave insurrections, massacres of blacks and Indians, massacres of whites, constant war, pillage, robbery on sea and on land. But the French and the Spaniards were not alone. Anglo-Americans came slipping into the colony, and most of these were restless, reckless, hungry fellows on the lookout for a chance of fortune. Wilkinson came and Burr came and Claiborne and a troop of their kind, all of them burning for power and the glory thereof, money and the glitter of it. Here, too, came many a man, under an assumed name, to throw off an old life of dishonor and take on a new life of crime. The Lafittes, the Murrels, the Rameaus and their like drifted in, drawn by the magnetism of organized lawlessness. Indeed, as the years went by, the influence of Louisiana over desperate men reached to the farthest parts of the civilized earth and drew to the colony the choicest criminals and desperadoes —the flower of the race of outlaws left over from the scattered descendants of buccaneers, slave-snatchers and pirates.

Men who had been political schemers, revolutionists, plotters of treason, assassination, usurpation, were self-exiled to Louisiana, to escape the rope, the ax, the guillotine. Deposed nobles and princes came here, and, in sheer desperation, took up the life of the gambler, of the thief, the smuggler or the pirate.

But there was the other side of the medal; for opposed to the dark and turbulent majority stood the "saving remnant," a strong minority of refined Christian people, whom the exigencies of life had stranded on this sweet, slumberous, flowery shore, between the warm gulf stream and the stately Mississippi. Some of this remnant were people who had fled from one or another European country for what would have been glorious patriotism if successful, although when colored with failure it looked like hideous crime. Wrecks of true greatness lay stranded along Royal Street and Bourbon and Carondolette, side by side with vulgar flotsam and jetsam of the great Sea of Chance. True, it was often hard to discern the rotten from the sound; for the conscienceless, red-handed culprit in exile was inclined to draw about him much the same cloak of reserve and mysterious dignity worn by the expatriated prince or general whose only offense was the exalted love of country.

It will be readily seen how circumstances tended to rivet the armor of recklessness and lawlessness on even well-disposed people who chanced to come within the circle of this remote and isolated community. Where there is not the wholesome quarantine of moral, social and political censorship, desire swiftly falls to the level of the average and crime becomes epidemic. It is only when backed by law rigidly enforced that the ethics of higher civilization can hold a hand against conscienceless greed, passion and lust of power, even under the most favorable surroundings.

When Gen. Andrew Jackson came to New Orleans, he came as a typical Anglo-American, as contradistinguished from the Latin creole. He was a man of iron, rough, resolute, imperious, even impetuous, with the training of an Indian fighter and border chieftain, who had never known defeat. But here in the far-famed city of romance, here in the warm, languorous South, he found to his surprise that these pleasure-loving creoles, these descendants of princes and of buccaneers, these vivacious, picturesquely handsome men with the soft voices and the courtly manners, did not particularly admire and certainly did not fear him. They rather looked upon him as an interloper who assumed importance with the air of a *cornichon*. The up-country men were not in good repute there, anyway. Burr and Wilkinson and Claiborne and a whole clan of lesser fellows had given these creoles a great deal of trouble while preparing the way to lift them into the great American Union, and now Jackson was looked upon as the arch interloper. But not a few of the inhabitants of New Orleans who called themselves French were in reality English, Irish, German, Scotch or Polish refugees; and at this particular juncture, when the British army was about to assault the gates of the city, there were those among them who were glad to have the adamant of Jackson's will and the prestige of his courage and generalship thrust between them and the coming foe. One of these was Mr. Vernon. To him the thought of an English commander getting control of New Orleans was the vision of absolute ruin. Not only would it be the end of all his wealth and influence, but there would swiftly follow a terrible visitation of so-called justice upon his head. But for this he might have been indifferent, as were many of the population, or he might have preferred British success to the domination of men like Jackson and Claiborne.

He left the theatre on the night of the alarm with a great burden of trouble oppressing him. Fairfax had observed before this that Colonel Loring seemed to exert a singular influence over Mr. Vernon, or rather, it looked as if Mr. Vernon had some deep interest in the welfare of that dark, saturnine man who was, as he still believed, Pierre Rameau, the robber. Both Mrs. Vernon and Pauline had noticed this remarkable intimacy and had more than once wondered together regarding it. On a certain occasion, Pauline had accidentally overheard her father, when conferring alone with Loring, address him with impatience and speak as though chiding him for some fault.

"By these rash acts," Mr. Vernon was saying to him, on the morning following the scenes recorded in our last chapter, "you have made it probably impossible for you to stay in this country."

They were sitting facing each other in the library; Loring had come into the house by a side entrance from a private alley.

"Oh, well," was the careless answer, "if I can't stay I can go. There is Mexico; I can return to my mines."

Mr. Vernon gazed steadily at him with eyes that burned half wistfully, half in anger.

"But," he presently said, "it is time for you to quit this roving life; get yourself under control, and make the most of your talents. You are still young, just coming into the prime of life."

"I know—I've been thinking of it."

"But what does thinking amount to if you keep on? No man ever did acts more absolutely unjustifiable or most desperately foolish than—"

"Oh, certainly, there's no use of telling me that; but I couldn't help it. The only wonder is that I didn't kill them both; I usually do."

Loring spoke with an indescribable expression; it was if he felt no special interest in what he was saying—as if it were hollow mockery for him to speak at all. His eyes, his lips, the lines of his face gave forth a hard, hopeless, unfeeling light which seemed to come out of a physical rather than a mental dilemma.

"I saw no excuse whatever for your treatment of Ballanche," said Mr. Vernon. "It looked like a piece of wanton viciousness."

The old man's face had grown as gray as his beard, and the wrinkles deepened strangely.

Loring sat upright, not rigidly, but with a certain animal elasticity of limb and body which suggested a surplus of vital force. He made no response in words, and appeared to throw off with some superficial effort the whole burden of the subject.

"Of course, it will be impossible for you to join Jackson now," Mr. Vernon added, after a long silence.

"I shall probably go to the other side," said Loring, with a smile.

"The other side!"

"Why not? It's my best way to make it even."

"But, in honor, you cannot do that."

"Humph!"

"Moreover you know that for the English to take New Orleans would be ruin to me."

"Oh, yes; I know," Loring said.

"And you—"

"You might not fare so badly. The English commander has offered fine terms to Lafitte, and—"

"Ta! I know. But even Lafitte will not accept. He has reported to Claiborne."

"Reported to Claiborne!"

"Yes," Vernon affirmed.

Loring turned his eyes toward the ceiling with a slow, thoughtful motion, as if revolving a new perplexity.

"Who told you this?" he presently demanded.

"Vasseur."

"Vasseur!"

"Yes, he is here. He acted as go-between in the matter. He brought Lafitte's message to the governor."

"And how came Vasseur here?"

"Ta! I hadn't told you about his being robbed?"

"No."

"Pierre Rameau and his gang robbed him of all his money and took his jewels."

Loring laughed reflectively.

"Poor little nigger!" he said. "That went hard with him, I know."

"Yes. But he'll have his revenge. He is laying his plans well. Rameau is in the city, he says, and the whole fraternity of freemen of color is sworn to kill him. They are drawing their lines close around him."

Loring threw up his head, and his eyes became as two long, gleaming slits, while the angles of his jaws protruded like a cat's.

"But what are you going to do? It is time to act," Mr. Vernon inquired.

"Not much of anything, probably—report to Jackson with a gun, muzzle foremost, maybe."

He arose as if to go, but stood awhile twirling his hat and looking straight into the old man's eyes. A touch of something like tenderness—such a gleam as you see in a dog's eyes when he gazes at his master—came into his impenetrable face, when, at last, he put forth his hand.

"Good-bye," he said.

Mr. Vernon clutched the hand and wrung it, but said nothing.

As Loring went forth from the house, he met Vasseur coming in.

The men glared at each other. Vasseur showed both terror and surprise, and was evidently glad that Loring was in the humor to pass him by.

The latter did not swerve a hair's breadth from his course, and the little mulatto had to shy aside quickly to avoid being trampled under foot.

"Is Pierre Rameau your friend?" cried Vasseur, in French, as soon as he came into Mr. Vernon's presence, his voice husky and rasping.

"Pierre Rameau! What do you mean, you little scamp?"

"Did you not see him? He came out of here this moment! I met him at the gate!"

"No?"

"But yes, yes, this minute—Pierre Rameau!"

Vasseur was trembling violently.

On the moment, there was a sudden whirl of thoughts in Mr. Vernon's brain. Could it be? He grabbed his beard with one hand and, with the other pressed hard upon his forehead, stood motionless, every feature straining and every limb rigid. He was reflecting with the power and intensity of a sudden conviction.

After a little while, however, he mastered himself and demanded Vasseur's business.

"I have not any business," faltered the little man. "I saw Pierre Rameau come in here and—"

"You are a liar!"

Mr. Vernon held him by the throat and made him stand on tiptoe.

"You call my—my friend Pierre Rameau again, and I'll kill you, you black dog!"

It was the first time in many years that he had given way to a rush of anger.

Vasseur, unable to stand when released, sank into a chair.

"Forgive me, Vasseur," said Mr. Vernon in the next breath. "I did not mean to hurt you. I was angry. That man was not Pierre Rameau. He was Colonel Loring."

"Then you did not see the man I speak of," insisted Vasseur, doggedly. "I met Pierre Rameau coming out as I came in. I had tracked him— followed him here. I saw him come in, and I waited long for him to come out. I—"

Mr. Vernon interrupted him with an impatient wave of the hand.

"There is some mistake!"

Vasseur's cunning would not let him be deceived, but he felt some dangerous mystery hovering close to him and did not care to take further risk in penetrating it. A mind like his is quick, nimble, shifty. It must be in order to give it a fair chance. Moreover, it cuts straight through some difficulties that would be baffling to a higher intellect. Just now he was living for but one object, and whatever did not bear upon his purpose was of no interest to him; but, in spite of this, there was something in Mr. Vernon's attitude that aroused strange and obscure doubts, suspicions, dreads in his mind, while at the same time he saw that there was a bond of sympathy and interest uniting Mr. Vernon and Pierre Rameau. He suspected, although the suspicion scarcely took full shape just then, that the two men had been connected, as he and Rameau had, in some wild transactions, and were still necessary to each other, or would be at the crisis now so near. Indeed, Vasseur knew more of Mr. Vernon's past than the latter would have believed—more than it would have been safe for the little fellow to acknowledge.

When Vasseur had taken his leave, Mr. Vernon walked the floor, to and fro, his hands locked behind him, his heavy head and shoulders drooping and his eyes bent upon the carpet. He looked ten years older than he had looked three days before. His lips now and again moved silently, and the muscles of his neck and face twitched nervously.

Presently he took his hat and his great-coat, for a drizzling rain was falling, and went out. He felt that he must see Loring once more before he left the city. To this end he bent his steps toward the club-room of the *Chats-Huants* which was over the back part of a low restaurant near the river.

Chats-Huants [screech-owls] was the name of a mysterious organization which fell to pieces when, some time after the War of 1812, the robbers of Honey Island were routed and their power destroyed.

What seems most strange to one who gains access to the records is the fact that the *Chats-Huants*, although their proceedings were vailed, did not pretend to evade the authorities of New Orleans. It was well known that they were in league with smugglers, so-called "privateers" and negro-stealers; but it was understood as well that they were "operated" outside of Louisiana, or, in other words, that they were "importers" of unlawful wares, and that all of their gains went to swell the wealth of the State and the city.

Mr. Vernon felt sure that, if Loring had been deceiving him, and had been all this time operating with the Honey Island outlaws instead of being in Mexico—if Colonel Loring and Pierre Rameau were indeed identical as both Fairfax and Vasseur had declared—then the room of the *Chats-Huants* would be the place in which to look for him.

On the way, as the rain softly fell over his slouched hat and high-collared topcoat, Mr. Vernon kept repeating the name, " Pierre Rameau," " Pierre Rameau," not aloud, not even by lip-movement, but inwardly ; and it rang and echoed in his consciousness, as a lonely voice sometimes wanders back and forth and around in a wild mountain hollow. He felt that he was going to solve within the next half-hour a question involving one of those climaxes of experience from which no period of life is exempt— experiences that shock the very centers of strength, and affect the deepest sources of feeling. The Master of Destinies rarely uses stage effects in thrusting us into these extremes ; but, yet, it is not often that we are in the least prepared for any of them. A stroke of the drum, a glare of red-light, or the sudden blare of horns at just the moment of disclosure, might relieve rather than aggravate the effect.

The streets were slimy, the gutters ran full of muddy water, and a wind from the east had an edge of ice, albeit the roses were abloom along the walls. Mr. Vernon met few people ; he was not aware of meeting any, until a hand was laid on his arm, and a well-remembered voice said :

"May I have a word with you? Do you not know me?"

He stopped short and faced the speaker. It was almost in front of the entrance to the grimy building in which the *Chats-Huants* had their meeting-place. Not far away on one hand rolled the great yellow river with some vessels at anchor; on the other hand the uneven houses zigzagged along, dripping and unsightly. Two or three reckless-looking fellows passed by and entered the restaurant. The *Chats-Huants* were meeting.

CHAPTER XV.

A SCENE ON A WOODLAND STAGE.

The reader will recollect the heavy rain and the hurricane that came on immediately after the shooting of Burns by Pierre Rameau. But for that cool deluge of water, the old man would have bled to death, notwithstanding the comparative slightness of the wound, which, owing to the bullet's striking a large old silver watch and glancing thence along a rib, was but a jagged rip in the flesh across the left slope of the chest. As it was, the rain stanched the bleeding, and Burns regained consciousness some time during the following night.

His Scotch vitality was not yet exhausted. He raised himself to a sitting posture; but the effort reminded him of his hurt and the blood broke forth afresh, while a dull pain griped his breast. A roaring sound came into his head as he sank back again and relapsed into insensibility. It was but a swoon, however, followed presently by a gradual recovery, during which his mind recalled, in a panoramic way, the whole of his long and fruitless struggle in search of Margaret. All the terrible route from Scotland, zigzagging over almost half the earth, lay under his eyes as if mapped out in the glare of a calcium light. He realized how very old he was, and the nature of his wound he well knew, having thrust his fingers into the gaping rent. Life shriveled under his gaze to the dimensions of a scorched leaf, and he saw his thousands of unanswered prayers lying like dead insects thereon. Some of the tense strings of his faith were snapping under this strain. Numbly, blindly, he groped about in the darkness, the soaked earth under him, the dripping, wind-stirred boughs overhead. His long, gray hair fell across his drawn and sunken face, and his tumbled beard was separated into clammy wisps. He thought he was walking, but he was only wallowing on the ground, reaching out his hands and feet.

There is a great reserve in the Scotch physique as there is in the Scotch character. Mr. Burns was an extreme example, else how could he have lain there on the wet soil of the woods for three days and nights without so much as a sip of water and with nothing to stay the bleeding of his wound? He was but half conscious most of the time, and yet he heard a panther screaming all through one night, and once a wolf barked and howled close by. There was nothing in these sounds to frighten him; they came to him as in a dream, appealing to no particular sense, touching no particular chord of consciousness, simply echoing through him. Slowly he sank away, weaker and weaker, down, down into darkness. Every thought faded out but one—the thought of failure—the thought that he was dying without hope.

On the third day, in the afternoon, some great black birds, evil-looking, with bare, congested heads and hungry eyes, came sailing low round and round above him. He saw them, and thought: "They will eat me as soon as I am dead!" But there was no horror connected with the vision, which went farther and displayed his scattered and clean-picked bones. What could it matter to him, old, defeated, abandoned, dying, if vultures began their work at once? Could their beaks add one pang to his torture?

With singular minuteness, for his leisure was ample, he reviewed his religious life, seeking for some justification of the act of Divine Providence in thus casting him aside like a bit of old rubbish after all this wearying and fruitless effort—after all his trust and prayer.

And little Margaret—what of her? Beautiful, young, pure, with every bud of tender promise just showing the pink—why should she have been made the plaything of an enormous wrong, the helpless victim of an atrocious fate? He saw her as she was when she left him, fair, bright, loving, the idol of his widowed heart, and he followed her, step by step, through the cruel descent, until she lay in her coffin, murdered by that man.

By some mysterious cerebral action, he was able to note the correlation of his own experience with the girl's, and to fix, as by a flash, the meeting of his prayers with the successive downward rushes of her miserable career.

At every point where he sought her with most confidence and besought heaven with greatest faith, there she had met calamity or taken some desperate step in infamy. And whose was the fault? Surely she had not been born with the taint of evil in her blood. True, her father had been a reckless man in a way—convivial, given to gambling and to other vices; but he had kept his honor, as men sometimes reckon it, in a fair condition. Her mother was a sweet, patient little doll. Both parents died young.

And Kirk MacCollough! The name rang through the old man's fevered brain, and the tall, dark outlaw stalked across his vision like an actor across the stage of melodrama. What health, what strength, what immunity from the physical effects of moral recklessness! And what defiance of heaven and hell! In the pursuit of this man, Burns had wasted himself, his fortune, his career, his prayers, his life, while not a drop of desire had been lost by the outlaw. It was bitter food of reflection for the aged preacher as he lay on the ground, his withered limbs outstretched and the weakness of death in his nerves. Slowly his mind worked its way down to that last scene and began to take up its details one by one, analyzing them with merciless exactness. Meantime, by that curious power of the brain which enables it when abnormally stimulated to follow two lines of thought at once, he was reviewing Kirk MacCollough's origin and accounting for his career by referring all his darker characteristics to inheritance from his father, Thomas MacCollough, who committed a great political crime and was transported therefor in the first prime of his manhood while Kirk was yet a mere boy. Burns had never seen Thomas MacCollough, nor had he known much of the family before Kirk began to pay attention to Margaret; but since then he had found out the history which now seemed to account fitly for the young man's unparalleled course of evil. From father to son had descended the curse of outlawry.

But it was natural that Burns' mind, even in the last extremity of despair, should turn with all its Scotch stubbornness and tenacity to take a religious survey, so to call it, of the situation. Perhaps it would be better to say that his thoughts were not driven at once, even by direst calamity, out of the groove in which they had been running since first he began to be a preacher. It had been his rule to measure everything by the standard disclosed to him in the Bible. "Thus saith the Word" had been his hobby, his guide, his comfort. Never during his long, absorbing chase after his child and her atrocious lover, had he forgotten the Sabbath or failed to keep it holy; never had he neglected the simple forms of worship and of prayer to which his austere conscience and the obligations of his church bound him. He had lived unspotted, and now death hovered over him in that lonely place, with none to lift his head, speak a word of comfort to him or to touch his lips with water. Upon his soul the bitterness of all this settled, as his brain drew it in and analyzed it.

Suddenly there was a revulsion, and it was as if the poles of his nature had been reversed on the instant. From some source he gathered strength to lift his head and shoulders; then, leaning on one arm, he gazed wildly around. There was a terrible look in his face. He almost bounded to his feet and stood swaying and trembling, his long legs far apart and one hand raised far above his disheveled head. A dying tiger might have glared as did he, and it was with a wild beast's voice that he cried aloud:

"I will not die—I will not die—I cannot die, Kirk MacCollough, while you live!"

It was a grand theatre in which to make such a speech. The dusky trees and the lurking wild things were fitting audience. The realism of the acting was superhuman, and it was also superhumanly romantic. The stage accessories were in perfect harmony with it. Loneliness, grimness, solemnity brooded there, and the wide silence was fitting applause. Two of the evil birds took wing with loud flapping and sailed away from the dead bough on which they had been sitting so patiently. Burns was indirectly aware of them, as he rolled his bloodshot eyes and shook his head till the tangled hair fell over his forehead and temples.

His strength was but spasmodic. The next moment he tumbled down motionless.

Slowly the sun passed on to the western slope of the sky. The hideous vultures returned to circle round and round, lower and lower; but they did not dare make the attack. They might have done it soon, however, had they been left to their will.

Once more the old man roused himself and struggled to his feet. The pallor of death flared out of his face, the frenzy of death glittered in his eyes. There were fragments of dead leaves and clots of earth in his hair and beard. Again he flung his hand on high and stood wavering and trembling, while his voice broke forth with awful sonorousness:

"Vengeance! 'Vengeance is mine, and I will repay!'"

This time the theatre held one human auditor, who stopped short in his walk and gazed with wide-open eyes at the towering actor in that wild scene. At first Burns looked almost twice his real stature, so dilated was the expression of his form as seen against the dusky spaces and gloomy trunks of the wood.

"Wall, take my hat for a soap-kittle!" exclaimed the observer, resting the butt of his long rifle on his foot.

"W'y, w'at's the matter, parson? W'at in all creation air ye a-doin' yer?"

Burns started at the sound of the voice, and half-turned to look. The effort lost him his balance, and down he fell again, his arm still outstretched.

"Hello! Hello!" shouted the man, running forward as rapidly as a crooked leg would permit, "air ye ailin', parson?"

He half recoiled at the sight of the blood on Burns's clothes, and his rough face showed surprise and quick sympathy. He had been accustomed to open-air tragedies, had, indeed, been a star performer in not a few; but here was a mystery as well as a catastrophe. For lack of other vent to relieve his feelings withal he began to swear disapprovingly, intimating through his oaths that it would please him to hew limb from limb the man who hurt Parsons Burns.

"Parson, parson!" he exclaimed, stooping over him and touching his shoulder. "W'at's the matter of ye, parson?"

Then, as he received no answer, he straightened himself up, leaned on his gun and scratched his head with an air of contemplative confusion. Just then, a horse gave forth one of those casual snorts characteristic of the genus. It was the animal that Burns had ridden. Not far away it was browsing dolefully, with a melancholy twist in its cadaverous neck and switching its tail this way and that more by force of habit than in response to the attack of one or two thriftless flies which were content to worry a skin too tough for their tiny spears.

"Yer, yer, parson! W'at's this mean?" he went on, blustering a trifle and shaking the old man's shoulder. "Can't ye speak to a feller? Air ye bad hurt?"

Burns writhed about, turning his grimy face full upon his interrogator. The stare he gave the man fairly chilled him.

"Pierre Rameau—that's your name, eh?" he gurgled harshly. "Pierre Rameau, I will kill you —ki-i-ill you!"

He tried with desperate energy to gain his feet, but he faltered and fell.

"Kill! Kill!" he moaned. "I cannot—I will not die till I have killed you!"

The incomparable strangeness of his voice and the awful expression of his countenance cannot be indicated; nor can mere words give any adequate impression of the man, old, withered, ill-clad, groveling in the wet, sandy soil, soaked in blood and panting forth intolerable passion. He looked scarcely human—more like a beast of prey, wounded to death, tearing madly, blindly at whatever he could feel. His words soon became indistinguishable and ran together into a harsh, guttural growl.

Dick Beckett (doubtless the reader has recognized him) was at first too much astonished to be at himself. As soon as he began to pull his wits together, however, the whole truth became more than a suspicion in his mind.

"Who hurt ye, Daddy Burns?" he demanded in his natural tone of voice. "War it that air devil, Pierre Rameau?"

Perhaps hearing Burns repeat the great robber's name had suggested the thought to Dick Beckett, or it may have risen out of the prevalent habit of laying everything cruel and otherwise unaccountable at the feet of Rameau.

Dick knelt down beside the old man, and, still holding his gun in one hand, felt of the wound, after pulling away the rent clothes from around it. In vain he tried to arouse him.

"Well,—well—tut, tut, tut!" he spluttered.

Rising again to his feet and standing with most of his weight on his crooked leg, he contemplated the situation, while with the fingers of his left hand he worried the frowzy red hair that hung under the brim of his battered cap.

"Poor ole daddy!" he exclaimed, after a while. "He do seem to be 'bout done for!"

Dick possessed executive ability of a sort, and when he got his faculties rightly put together there was no such a thing as his giving up to circumstances contrary to his wish. He examined Burns and found that he was not yet dying. The next thing was to save him. This looked like a forlorn hope, but he would try it at all events. So he caught the lingering horse and with its aid bore Burns through the wood to his cabin.

Here I insert a short paragraph from the "Honey Island Records." The reader will feel, in reading it, a waft from the old reckless life of the frontier:

"Dick Beckett," it goes on to say, "found the preacher in a sad condition when he reached home with him, which it was after dark at the time, and he struck a light. The wound was a tear in the side dug by a pistol bullet that had been amazingly flattened on a silver watch afore doing it. 'I will save him!' said Dick Beckett, who was a good nurse besides a distracting fiddler: and, belike, he had original medicine—strange roots and such. Some do say he did possess a root of the man-plant which he salved the hurt with. Sure enough, anyway, he cured him betimes. What they do say, also, is that Dick Beckett did fiddle and play profane musick unto the preacher what time he convalesced, even such tunes as 'Sugar in the Gourd' and 'Riding on a Rail,' not to make special mention of 'There's Whiskey in my heel.' No doubt, however, this matters not, seeing that the preacher survived and at last went on his way."

In the French version of the story there is a statement not to be found in the other accounts.

"It cannot be denied," runs this creole document, which appears to be a rough translation of some lost English writing—"It cannot be denied that Burns, the preacher, did swear vengeance on Pierre Rameau, the robber (*forban* is the French word used), and did express himself in language dreadful in its nature. Some think that this Dick Beckett hath fiddled all the piety and tenderness of religion out of the old man's soul, for, after this, he is mightily changed in his temper and disposition, and some desperate acts are set down to his credit."

Dick Beckett himself, in his extreme old age, when his mind ran mostly on things long since done, was sometimes ready to talk about Burns; but even the garrulity of nearly a century of years did not overcome a certain tantalizing discretion. The most that he would tell was to the effect that Burns seemed a little "onsettled in 'is upper story w'en 'e got well."

"Yes," he would remark, 'I 'member how 'e

looked w'en 'e up an' tole me good-bye an' went off to s'arch for Pierre Rameau. 'Twas ob a Thursday mornin' an' 'e said:

"'Farewell Dick. I go unto Honey Island an woe be upon that infernal darn rascal what stole my chile!'"

Doubtless this seemed to the aged fiddler the exact language of Burns; but it does not sound like him. If we cannot wholly believe that there could have been a change so sudden and so radical in the character of one who had been for so many years a sincere and singularly humble-minded preacher, we must, at least, give due weight to the evidence tending to prove it.

One thing is pretty conclusively settled: Burns did penetrate to the innermost fastnesses of Honey Island, and, not finding Pierre Rameau there, made his way, by what route is not known, to New Orleans, where for some time he attracted little attention, though he wandered about by night and by day, going into all sorts of places, his eyes full of a half-smoldering fire and glancing keenly into the face of every person he met.

He had no money, and how he lived has never been found out, though after a time he met Vasseur, who thenceforward took such care of him as circumstances permitted.

He had but one thought and that thought was Pierre Rameau.

CHAPTER XVI.

IN THE RAIN.

"Do you know me?"

"Ta! Yes, how do you do?"

It was evident that Mr. Vernon was trying hard to cast off surprise and appear quite at ease; but lately he had been finding this more difficult than he was willing to acknowledge. His mind had been disturbed, and one burning suspicion was falling deeper and deeper into his heart.

He could not just then fairly understand why to see Burns standing before him should startle him so. True, the old man's face and form were clothed upon with an indescribable suggestion of weirdness; but to a man like Mr. Vernon this could not be a source of mental disquiet; it was not specially observed on the moment.

"I hope that you and your family have been well and happy since the time of your great kindness to me," said Burns, offering his hand, which Mr. Vernon felt to be like ice when he touched it.

Not the chill wind nor yet the almost numbing rain could account for the singular shiver and repulse which came out of that hand-clasp into Mr. Vernon's blood. It was like touching the flesh of a corpse, only it was far colder. On the old wanderer's cheeks burned hectic spots.

"Yes—yes, we are all very well—yes, very well. I am glad to see you again, sir. The ladies will be proud to have you come. Why haven't you been to the house?"

"I have been often but could not get in. Your man thinks I'm a beggar."

"Ta! I'll teach him better."

Evidently, the presence of Burns, while not exactly an annoyance to Mr. Vernon was by no means a pleasure. Aside from any effect produced upon him by an apparition so unexpected, and taking no account of the startling expression of the old preacher's strangely emaciated face and concentrated gaze, there was something inopportune, out-of-place and unwelcome in the sudden meeting. We have moments when any index to our past is unbearable. Mr. Vernon was constrained; his manner and voice were unnatural.

Burns eyed him a moment, then said:

"No. Don't bother with it. I am a beggar, a tramp, and I do not wish to disturb a happy family. What I went is easily told."

"Speak it, my dear sir, speak it; it is already yours."

Mr. Vernon was still holding that clammy hand and looking firmly and kindly, albeit with a sort of artificial expression, into Burns's deep-sunken and inflamed eyes.

"No, that is a polite lie. Wait till I make my desire known, then see if you can be so generous."

"Ta! 1 see you are ill. Come in and have some wine."

"I drink nothing but water. I am not ill. I am well and strong and shall reach my goal soon."

"I am glad to hear it, sir—very glad, indeed."

Mr. Vernon wanted to shake him off for the present and go into the club-room of the *Chats-Huants*; he wanted to see Colonel Loring again; but Burns would not be abandoned.

"I am close on the track of Pierre Rameau," he said, "and I want your help. Turn your hand for me now, and I have him."

Mr. Vernon stood silent, and a peculiar shadow crept over his face.

"Ah, I see you are quite prompt, quite ready!" exclaimed Burns, after a mere moment. The irony was merciless.

"What do you mean, sir?" demanded Mr. Vernon. A gray film of passion or of some other deep feeling crept over his cheeks above the beard.

"Bah! Where were you going just now?" demanded Burns, as if with authority.

"Sir!"

"I can tell you. You were going upstairs, in there, to the room of the *Chats-Huants*, to meet Pierre Rameau, the robber."

"Sir!"

"You know that it is so."

"It is not true—it is—"

"Don't be angry. Stop and think. Stop and

turn about. I like you; I owe my life to you. I would save yours now. Don't go in there."

Two or three suspicious-looking fellows came near and acted as if they were trying to overhear what was being said. Perhaps they thought it was a quarrel that would end in a fight, the most interesting thing in the world to such characters.

Burns, like the Ancient Mariner, was holding his auditor with his glittering eye. The wedding-guest was not more enthralled than was Mr. Vernon, albeit the latter turned abruptly and would hear no more for the moment. He could not, however, tear himself loose from the old man, who followed him and stepped again in front of him, now laying his hand on his top-coat's lapel and thrusting his eager, cadaverous lips close to his ear.

"Come aside somewhere, only for a minute. Don't stay here—for heaven's sake, don't!" he exclaimed, in a shrill whisper. "The time is at hand! Vengeance is mine! Come! I hear them approaching."

While he spoke, he was fairly forcing Mr. Vernon along, leading him away from the door of the restaurant.

About this time, a young man rode down the street at a swift pace and, flinging himself from the saddle of his beautiful horse, ran into the place, leaving the animal standing unhitched and unattended. A little later Colonel Loring came out, mounted and rode away.

So intent was Burns in his effort to draw Mr. Vernon aside, he did not notice this incident. Out slipped the *Chats-Huants*, one by one, two by two, quickly, silently, scattering and disappearing as if by magic.

A little later, a company of mounted soldiers swept round a corner and deployed in front of the building. Of course, they were too late to make the capture they had intended, and when they leaped from their horses, pistols in hand, and rushed in, they discovered that their bird had flown.

The clatter of hoofs as they came up attracted Burns's attention. He let go his hold and turned.

"In there! In there!" he cried, leaping forward. "Up the stairway to the right! Follow me!"

He led the way with incredible nimbleness for one so old and frail-looking. A long, keen knife flashed in his hand.

The rush was over in a minute. Doors were dashed open or kicked off their hinges, and the rooms above and below were searched without ceremony.

Mr. Vernon stood looking on, apparently quite calm. He had seen Colonel Loring go, and now he comprehended the whole affair. It had been well planned and well executed, notwithstanding the outcome. But for the faithful spy at Jackson's headquarters and the swift courier sent in the very nick of time, Loring would have been taken.

"I said all the time that the old fool was crazy," growled the officer who had led the dash. "The whole story was absurd."

"Yes, sir," replied the subaltern whom he

addressed, " it was indeed a fool's errand. Storming a junk-shop and led by a ragamuffin!"

They were coming out of the building, disappointed and vexed, ashamed of the part they had been forced to play in a scene so like a farce.

"You'd better go home and soak your head, old man!" added one of them, turning with brutal severity and addressing Burns. "I s'pose you've been drunk for a month."

The old man paid no attention to the remark, did not even glance at the speaker, but walked forth into the street and away, with his chin on his breast and his knife in his hand.

He overtook Mr. Vernon, or rather they came together when the latter emerged from a side street a block or two distant from the scene just witnessed. The rain was still slanting along the wind in a fine drizzle; Burns looked pinched and blue. Without a word, Mr. Vernon drew off his top-coat and hung it over the old man's shoulders.

"Put away your knife," he said. "You will need it."

Burns obeyed mechanically, hiding it somewhere in his bosom. Evidently he was but vaguely aware of what he was doing. His vision was introverted, his feelings were numbed.

"You will come home with me now," Mr. Vernon added, taking him gently by the arm. "We will have dinner."

Burns looked up quickly with a glance of suspicion or, perhaps, of deeper meaning.

"No," he said, "I will not."

Further words on the subject were shut off by the peremptory tone and manner. They walked on a little way in silence, hearing the surface-water bubble in the gutter beside the *trottoir*. Few people were in the streets; but the gambling-rooms were full, the coffee-houses noisy.

Suddenly Mr. Vernon closed his grasp more firmly on Burns's arm and, looking into his face said with the force of a command:

"Tell me, is Colonel Loring Pierre Rameau?"

Burns started at the mention of the latter name.

"You know Pierre Rameau; I know you do," he answered, slowly drawing out his words. "He calls himself Colonel Loring here in the city; but you know that he is Kirk MacCollough, son of Jane MacCollough, whose husband was Thomas MacCollough, the traitor, who was banished nearly forty years ago."

There was a horrible leer in the old preacher's eyes. It was the same glare that had been in the eyes of the vultures when they sailed low over him during those dreadful days in the woods. Behind his words there stretched an infinitude of significance; it was as if each syllable echoed back to some far date and stirred up long buried sentiments. Mr. Vernon stopped short in the street and held him as in a vise.

"What are you saying?" he demanded, hoarsely. "What do you know about Thomas MacCollough and Jane MacCollough? Who are you?"

Burns did not speak forthwith.

"Ta! You are crazy!" Mr. Vernon added,

thrusting him away with such force that he almost fell into the gutter. But there was no anger in the act.

"Yes, I am crazy," the old man said, when he had regained his equilibrium, "and you ought to be."

At this moment came a curious exchange of glances between them. It was like a quick acknowledgment of a common thought, pang-burdened and unwelcome to one, a matter of hopeless indifference to the other.

Mr. Vernon picked up the top-coat, which had fallen from Burns's shoulders, and replaced it with gentle care.

"I knew Jane MacCollough," he said; "she was Jane Alexander before she was married."

"Yes."

"And you said she had a son?"

"Yes; Kirk—Colonel Loring—Pierre Rameau. These three are one."

"You know this?"

"You know it."

They stood there in the rain and searching wind, the water dripping from their hat-brims and their gray locks tossing about. Mr. Vernon combed his abundant beard with his fingers.

Burns came closer to him.

"I think I had best tell you," he said; "for, after all, you ought to know."

"I know already," Mr. Vernon calmly replied, "all that you can tell me, and more."

"No, not all. Kirk MacCollough's last—no not

exactly last, nor yet his worst, but one of his acts you have no account of. I will tell you."

Then the old man described his meeting with Pierre Rameau in the Pearl-River country and the cold-blooded event of it. He showed no senile garrulity in delivering himself. Indeed, the blunt thrust of his sentences gave an awful realism to his story.

"I felt that it was best to tell you," he added at the end, with something like a suggestion of regret or apology for the infliction.

"Oh, certainly!" said Mr. Vernon.

The coolness of this remark, not far removed from sheer indifference, seemed to excite Burns inordinately, and, as if in retaliation, he began at once to tell what Rameau had said regarding the fate of Margaret, and consciously with great cunning or unconsciously with supreme feeling he presented the absolute dramatic spirit of the terrible deed.

Mr. Vernon stood in an attitude of stark attention. The story was quickly told with few gestures and in a low tone.

"But—but—" Burns hesitated a moment as he was concluding, gazing fixedly the while—"though you saved my life, though I would all but die for you and yours, I cannot spare him—I cannot spare him, even for you!"

Mr. Vernon wrung water from his beard and stood silent. The rain was soaking his clothes, but he did not feel it.

A little later, the two old men parted, Burns

refusing to accompany the other any farther or to accept any aid from him. Unconsciously, however, he wore away Mr. Vernon's comfortable top-coat.

At Chateau d'Or, meantime, Pauline and her mother were discussing a subject which mothers and daughters have busied themselves with since the first day that love and marriage were lifted to a true sanctity in human households. Fairfax had just gone away; and Pauline, with true French impetuosity, an inheritance from Madame Vernon, ran to that warm-hearted woman and flung herself into her arms. The act interpreted itself, for the mother knew every movement of her child and its meaning. She had expected this and was glad of it, and yet she felt a thrill that was more than half a pang as she clasped the lithe, quivering form and began passionately to kiss the blooming lips and cheeks. She felt hot tears dropping from the girl's eyes.

"But he is going to the army!" Pauline sobbed. "Going right away to fight!"

"And your father, too, is going," said Mrs. Vernon, stroking her bright hair, soothingly. "We must be as brave as they."

In the midst of her distress, which was so largely joy, Pauline felt a distinct satisfaction in the parallel implied by her mother's remark. It was as if she had said: "My dearest one, too, is going to join the army. If I can let mine go, you can let yours go. We are quite on an equality in the matter." The comfort in this leveling and blending suggestion may have been remote and obscure to a degree; but it was nevertheless unmistakable.

"But they will be killed! They will be brought back dead!" Pauline continued, putting a hand on each side of her mother's face and gazing through her tears.

"We'll hope not. We'll pray for their safety, my dear. God takes care of us all. He keeps our beloved ones for us."

"Our beloved ones!" The phrase was like a sweet chime in Pauline's ears.

"But why must war come just now, mamma, dear? Just now—just now when we are so happy!"

"Men must fight, you know; it is their glory. And we poor women must wait and pray."

A servant announced Mademoiselle de Sezannes, who soon appeared, still muffled in her carriage-cloak, with a touch of the rain on her clothes. Her beauty was much heightened by her air of excitement. She had come to Pauline for comfort in her distress. Lieutenant Ballanche had been sent down the river in command of a scouting party detached by order of General Jackson.

"I couldn't stay at home!" she exclaimed, casting aside her cloak and rushing impetuously into Pauline's embrace. "I am so troubled, so nervous! Papa says that the enemy will be in the city before the week is past."

Pauline pulled her down into her lap with girlish tenderness and fondness, soothing herself by caressing her friend.

Mrs. Vernon took Mademoiselle de Sezannes's

hand and stroked it. The three were drawn close together in a striking group near the center of the room whose windows were festooned inside with almost priceless tapestry and outside with blooming vines. Despite the chill of the December air, with its searching dampness, the perfume of roses and violets was sweetly prevalent throughout the house.

"Why, you have lost the set of your ring!" Mrs. Vernon exclaimed, as her fingers touched the little circle of gold claws that had held a large diamond in place.

"No!"

"Yes. See!"

Mademoiselle looked down and turned pale.

"And it was the ring he gave me—my—"

"Your engagement ring!"

For the time they forgot war and its terrors in their consternation over a lost bauble; but, then, the bauble stood for so much! They sprang to their feet, and the diamond set rolled, flashing, on the carpet. All three stooped to pick it up, and so pressed and crushed themselves together in beautiful disorder, actually laughing and ejaculating gayly.

"Oh, I could not—I could not lose this!" cried Mademoiselle de Sezannes.

She kissed the stone and fondled it against her cheek.

"You know I lost the large ruby out of my fan on the night of your party," she went on to say. "I'm having bad luck with my jewels."

"Do you mean to say that you lost the Caribbean ruby, as you called it?" inquired Mrs. Vernon.

"Yes, the buccaneer. You recollect, Pauline, that Mr. Parker admired it so much that evening. I was nearly heartbroken when I found that it was gone. Though I would rather lose a hundred like it than this darling set." And again she showered kisses on the diamond.

It would have been a trifle startling to the ladies, could they have been informed just then that Parker, *alias* John A. Murrell, had sold the ruby in Memphis and made merry with crapulous friends in expending the money received for it.

Mr. Vernon came in presently, wet and chilled. He went directly to his own room to change his clothes and be rubbed by a servant.

When he appeared again, it was to inform his wife and his daughter that they were to be sent to the plantation to remain until after the impending battle had been fought. Preparations for the move would be made immediately. Lapin, the overseer, had been notified, and would come early on the morrow with the proper vehicles for taking such things as would be needed. The ladies would go in the family carriage.

So sudden an announcement, at such a time, added much to the feeling of dread and to the confused apprehensions with which Mrs. Vernon and Pauline were already oppressed. It had in it the terrible reality of immediate and dire urgency. A whiff of battle-smoke wafted through the house could not have been more startling.

"Oh, if I could go with you!" cried Mademoiselle de Sezannes. "It will be awful!"

"But, you can go with us," said Mrs. Vernon. "Why not? There is room in the carriage."

"My dear child, yes," added Mr. Vernon, with a serious smile. "It would be so good of you to go and be company for Pauline and Madame Vernon."

"But, papa and—"

"Oh, there's not such hurry. You can go home and confer with your father. It will be safest for you to be with my family, I am very sure. Tell your father that I advise it and insist upon it. The city will be no place for young girls if the English defeat Jackson and come in."

In some way, through a medium thought at the time to be sufficiently authentic, the story had come to New Orleans that the British officers had promised their men the freedom of conscienceless conquerors, should they capture the city. As the rumors of their approach and of the overwhelming numbers they could oppose to the little handful of Americans were coupled with a report of such dark significance, the invaders were regarded as savages worse in every respect than the red men who had been so recently conquered by Jackson. A thrill of intolerable apprehension shot through the heart of the wicked city; but the bedizened dens of vice and infamy abated not one line or point of their cupidity, ceased not by night or by day their hideous carousals. There seemed to be as much danger within as without, in the event of such disorder as would follow the defeat of Jackson. Everybody was aware of the volcanic evil which was burning under the crust of life all around in those teeming places where the refuse of the whole world was packed.

What aggravated the danger was the clash between Jackson and this very class, whose leaders were, in fact, the chief men of the State. The iron-hearted general, however, apparently paid not the slightest attention to any particular individuals of the would-be obstructionists, albeit his eye saw everything and his hand was heavy when it fell. He grasped the situation more intelligently than did Governor Claiborne or any of his associates, and when the moment came, he declared martial law and took charge of everything with a suddenness and vigor that were irresistible. Even the vilest of the *forbans* and cut-throats were touched by the magnetic influence of his indomitable spirit and courage. Here was a general who was the fit leader of desperate men, and all these outlaws were nothing if not willing fighters and scoffers at danger and death.

Mr. Vernon felt the doubtfulness of the outcome, and, moreover, in any event, the safer place for his wife and Pauline, he thought, would be at the secluded plantation house. As for himself, he had determined that he would report at once to General Jackson.

CHAPTER XVII.

THE JACKSONIAN TEMPER.

The plantation to which Mrs. Vernon and Pauline were sent lay near the Mississippi River, a few miles below New Orleans. It was a lonely place, and the house, a very plain and simple structure, stood close to the edge of a dreary swamp. Hard by ran a narrow ditch or canal, which was now bankful of muddy-looking water.

Mademoiselle de Sezannes, at the urgent request of the Vernons, accompanied them, although her own parents decided to remain in the city.

One who is in the least familiar with the topography of the region round about New Orleans and with the plan of attack determined upon by the British general will suspect that the refugees, in going to the plantation, were running almost directly toward the enemy instead of fleeing from him. This was so in fact, although Mr. Vernon did not for a moment suppose that the final advance could be from any other direction than Lake Pontchartrain, which lies north of New Orleans.

Lieutenant Ballanche had not yet returned from his reconnaissance of the Bayou-Bienvenu region, nor had there come any definite report of the enemy's movements on Borgne or up the Rigolets when Mr. Vernon took his long rifle and reported to General Jackson, desiring to fight as an independent private.

It is always so in the case of an impending advance of an army upon a city wholly unprepared for defense. The want of a sufficient force to keep all the avenues of approach well under observation results, generally speaking, in a total ignorance of just what it is most needful to know. Doubtless General Jackson was in possession of more facts regarding the whereabouts and purposes of the English than the circumstances seemed to indicate; still the lack of troops and munitions and the confusing number and intricacy of the waterways and the landways by which it was quite possible for his foes to reach him made everything like regular military preparation and action on his part well nigh impossible. His memory was good, and when Mr. Vernon presented himself and asked to be assigned at once to duty, he recollected everything in connection with their past interviews. Secretly he was glad to make amends for the brusqueness of those occasions, and he was quick to understand that here was a chance for him to secure, perhaps, the adhesion of a class of malcontents who he understood would accept Mr. Vernon as their leader. He grasped the burly old man's hand with diplomatic warmth (for Jackson, despite his willfulness, was a born politician) and pressed it.

"I am glad you have come, Mr. Vernon," he said, with a straight, strong gaze of confidence and pleasure, "for I need you. You can serve me and the country to great advantage just now, sir—to great advantage, indeed. I want a company of volunteers armed with rifles, or, for that matter, with guns of whatever kind can be had. You are just the man to raise and lead such a company."

The general was a magnetic man, and he knew how to direct his great personal power; but in an instant he felt the counter-thrust of an invulnerable individuality. Mr. Vernon's immense physical proportions seemed just then to fling out a spiritual and moral spell which, if it did not entangle Jackson's agile mind, wrought a singular effect upon his imagination.

The two men stood facing each other in silence for a moment.

"Sit down, sir," said Jackson, presently, pushing a chair toward his visitor.

The room was a large, plain one, and simply furnished in the main. The gaunt frame of the general, as roughly clad as if he had just arrived from the farm, bristled with angles, and a stubble of wiry beard stood out stiffly on his grim, sunburnt face.

"I prefer to fight as a private individual attached to any company that you may choose to assign me to," said Mr. Vernon, without appearing to notice the proffered seat. "I am not seeking an office, general."

"Of course, you are not. But the office seeks you, sir."

"No, there are officers, and to spare, as you said the other day; and, besides, I am not a military man."

"You are a leader of citizens, and that's better."

Jackson could not help admiring the old man, standing there like a Hercules, grown gray in doing miracles of powess. What limbs he had, what shoulders, what a large head and what bulging muscles! Some rumor of his past life, a vague but fascinating story of wanderings on the seas and of stormy but successful experiences in the wars of many lands, had come to the general's ears from this or that accidental source. Very few imaginations are proof against such a film of romance hovering over an individual who emphasizes its allurement with a personal appearance altogether extraordinary.

"I am too old, general, to think of taking command of even a company," said Mr. Vernon after a moment. He spoke with respectful thoughtfulness, but behind his words was a reserve of something like conscious superiority, or, at least, of absolute self-confidence. He folded his arms across his immense chest, his long rifle in the hollow of his left elbow, its butt on the floor between his feet. "No, I prefer to fight as an individual rifleman; and, although I am old, my eyes are still good—I shoot well."

"Now, what is the use, Mr. Vernon, of your speaking like this!" demanded Jackson, with a hint of his stormy impatience in his voice. It was not of his nature to brook resistance. "Are you not going ever to cease resenting my refusal to appoint Loring? I assure you, sir, that had he been a gentleman instead of a scoundrel, I still had no place for him."

"Ta! It is you who are fretted! Do you imagine that if I felt so greatly aggrieved I should be here now offering myself as a private soldier? If I desired office, General Jackson, do you feel that I could not have it without asking you?"

There was nothing beneath the most superb dignity in Mr. Vernon's way of saying this. It was propounded as a simple question without any ring of personal pique or of undue assumption, and yet there was a sudden cold, hard gleam in his eyes.

"Oh, well," said Jackson, rather haughtily and as if dismissing the matter once for all, "you must do as you please."

"I will do this:" Mr. Vernon responded, without taking any notice of the general's mood; "I will raise a company at my own expense and have it report to you, properly equipped and officered."

Before there could be any reply to his words, he saluted gravely and walked out of the room.

The entrance at this moment of Governor Claiborne, General Villeré and M. Tousard, the French consul, forced Jackson's attention into a new channel; but during the interview, which was important, his thought kept turning back to the singular conference with Mr. Vernon. And yet what had there really been in it that should impress him? Certainly, the mere fact that a citizen of New Orleans had offered himself as a soldier was nothing peculiar or impressive; men were doing this every day. Moreover, what Mr. Vernon had said was simple enough. Jackson found that it was the man's personality, the extraordinary presence, the suggestion of almost immeasurable experience and of incomparable dignity, reserve, self-repression that lingered in his brain and appealed to him in some obscure but wonderfully potent way. It is credible that Jackson, who was a man of penetrating insight, felt that Mr. Vernon was a type embodying the strange spirit of this romantic creole civilization—that in his stalwart, massive frame there dwelt the composite soul of all this wild, free, untamable swarm in whose midst the general now found himself, with no efficient means of reaching their natures and warming their sympathies.

"What did Vernon want?" Claiborne ventured, in his smooth way, to inquire, after the immediate business of the interview was over.

"He offered his services," said Jackson, evasively.

"He did? That is fortunate just at this juncture. Do you know, general, that he is the most important man in Louisiana?"

"I have been told that he has influence."

"It is unbounded," said the French consul.

"Yes," added General Villeré, with quick interest, lighting a cigar meantime, "we can count upon everything if his hearty support can be secured at once."

"I asked him to raise and lead a company," said General Jackson.

"Why, general," said Villeré, " I must say that you

have blundered—unwittingly, of course. Raise and lead a company! You should have taken him close to you at once and made him a confidential adviser."

"It was he who came with Faval, some time ago, and asked me to take that devil, Colonel Loring, on my staff," Jackson replied dryly and with a savage shrug of the shoulders.

"He asked that? He favored Loring!" exclaimed Villeré, in an astonished tone. "Incredible!"

In his excitement he spoke in French, and Jackson did not understand his words; but his gestures and expression told as much as his language.

"Oh, it was Faval's work, perhaps," said Claiborne. "You know that Vernon and Faval have always been great friends."

"Vernon proposes to raise and equip a company of riflemen at his own expense," remarked Jackson, "but he flatly refuses to command it."

"Of course, he would refuse that, general," said the governor. "You should not expect a man of his stamp to come to that. I see that you have not understood him. Plainly, you do not recognize his importance."

"Important or not important," exclaimed Jackson, permitting his natural irascibility to appear, "I do not need his advice or, for that matter, yours either!"

Claiborne, who was no mean diplomat, held his temper and smiled blandly. He had the utmost confidence in Jackson, and was determined not to have a rupture with him ; but he feared Mr. Vernon's influence, and knew that it was necessary to prevent, if possible, any further disagreement between him and the commanding general. Negotiations were in progress between the governor and Lafitte, by which the former hoped to bring a large number of the outlaws of Barataria and other resorts to the aid of the government. Jackson was favoring this scheme, knowing that freebooters were capable of doing most effective service as soldiers. He now asked for a private interview with the general, and when they had passed into an adjoining room, he said :

" I understand your feelings, general, and am far from wishing to aggravate them ; but let me say to you in deepest confidence that Mr. Vernon is just now an indispensable person to us. He alone can control the mass of the creoles and especially the lawless class. I tell you that we cannot do without him."

Claiborne spoke more from conjecture than from any definite knowledge. He did know, however, that Mr. Vernon's influence was as powerful as it was mysterious ; that his wealth, though great, and his liberality, though democratic, could not wholly account for the hold he certainly had upon the dangerous class of persons who constituted in reality the larger number of the effective fighting men of the State.

Jackson walked the floor. He had been terribly worried with reports of plots and combinations against him in the city. The legislature had not done as he wished, the courts were disposed to assert the superiority of the law, and certain of his injudicious friends had magnified to him the evidences of sedition among the creole population. Added to all this, reinforcements were slow in arriving, and such as had come were miserably deficient in equipment, without food and very inadequately clad against the unusual cold of the season.

He felt that patriotism as well as self-interest demanded of the people of New Orleans and of Louisiana the most enthusiastic and heroic self-devotion in behalf of his purposes. Knowing his own courage and genius and seeing with the absolute vision of the born general the supreme need of the hour, he could have no patience with anything or anybody that did not fall at once into line and obey his every command, execute his every suggestion and show the most active faith in his superiority.

"I despise and detest the whole crew of Frenchmen," he presently blurted out, "and I'll blow them to everlasting scraps, before long, if they persist in their disloyalty to the country. Claiborne, you go at once and tell that legislature to adjourn—tell them that I say so."

The governor stood for a moment confounded; but it did not take long for him to see that General Jackson meant to be obeyed.

"I have already suggested an adjournment," he replied, "but of course there is some opposition."

"From the infernal creoles? But I will not permit opposition from anybody, do you hear? This thing is coming to a point right shortly. I am in command here and, by the Eternal, I am going to be master! You go at once, governor, and tell that legislature to shut up shop, and if it doesn't do it I'll pitch it bodily into the river. They haven't got a Wilkinson to trifle with now."

Along with General Jackson's assumption of superiority there went an immense capacity for being just what he assumed to be. He overawed Claiborne from the moment of his arrival in New Orleans, and, to all intents and purposes, took charge of the State Government.

It will never be known just how far actual treason went in plotting the betrayal of Jackson and the delivery of the city to the British commander; but the movement was more than an incipient impulse. There were many men in New Orleans who dreaded to have the power of the United States government well fixed in Louisiana. Wilkinson had more than winked at a free and easy understanding with the *forbans*, robbers, negro-stealers and smugglers, and there can be little doubt that Claiborne, although he would have preferred law and order, was the sort of politician to turn his back and not see the worst that his supporters did. He knew Mr. Vernon's power, had more than once felt it in his favor when it was political salvation to have it on his side.

He knew but little of Colonel Loring; but since the incident of the nose-pulling he had heard a great deal about him. Rumor was having it everywhere that Loring and Pierre Rameau were one and the same man, and that now the far-reaching organization of which this redoubtable outlaw was king would be turned against Jackson.

Claiborne had already gone too far in his support of General Jackson to take any backward step, even if he had desired to do it, and it was absolutely necessary now that he should use the finest diplomacy, in order to avoid falling between two stools.

"I will go at once, general, and have a conference with Louallier and Roffignac," said he, in a tone of ready compliance, "and, if possible, I will have the adjournment declared."

"Governor, there can be no ifs or ands about it; the adjournment must come at once!" exclaimed Jackson, with overbearing sternness. "They will adjourn, or I will adjourn them!"

Claiborne's face paled with sudden anger, but he made no response; simply bowed and retired. As he went out he met Lieutenant Ballanche coming in. The young man looked fatigued and somewhat in a hurry, as if he had come from a distance in great haste and was bearing important news; he greeted Claiborne deferentially as he passed, but did not stop. The sandy mud showing in splashes all over him told of a long, hard ride.

The governor would have given a good deal to know what message Ballanche was bearing, and under any other circumstances he would have turned back into the room. He could not trust himself to do this now; he was too much wrought upon by Jackson's tyranny. There was something in the young officer's look and manner, however, that told a stirring story.

CHAPTER XVIII.

SEEKING REFUGE.

The journey to the plantation was a comparatively short one, and the three women at first found it not so tiresome and uninteresting as they had feared, although it was depressing to a degree.

They set out early in the morning through a country somewhat gloomy, and in places covered with water. The rain fell at intervals, but the sun flashed warmly out between the showers, as the winter sun does in that fickle, April-like climate, giving them now and then a golden gleam while they were trundled slowly along under the moss-hung trees. The spacious carriage with its easy springs and luxurious cushions afforded ample room for its fair occupants to rest at ease.

Mademoiselle de Sezannes, who had never been much in the country and whose volatile spirits were easily set to effervescing, found a good deal to interest her on the way; but Mrs. Vernon and Pauline could not pull their minds away from the fact that they were once more leaving Chateau d'Or for an indefinite sojourn in a lonely plantation house. Their former experience of country life in a remote place, as they now involuntarily recalled it, did not present to their minds its more pleasing associations, but turned persistently to view those closing incidents which were coupled with the coming of Burns and the robbing of Vasseur. To be sure, Pauline remembered, with a girl's vivid faithfulness, every look, every word, every movement of Fairfax during those dawn-hours of her love; but the darker things would insist on taking precedence, and her mind dwelt upon all that she had heard of Pierre Rameau and his crimes. She and her mother had both strenuously objected to leaving the city, and having set out under protest, they woman-like, made the whole journey in a state of mind averse to any sentiments of wayfaring appreciation.

The venerable coachman, muffled in his broad-caped great-coat, hummed many a negro melody in a soft falsetto voice, and between snatches grumbled at the horses because they did not keep well in the rather vague roadway.

"It seems too bad," said Mademoiselle de Sezannes, after she had somewhat exhausted herself in making inquiries touching the natural objects new to her eyes as they passed them by in the strange old forest—"It seems too bad that this dreadful war should break up all our delightful winter enjoyments and send us away into exile to dream of slaughter and all manner of dreadful evils. Isn't it so, Pauline?"

"Do not speak of it! It rends my heart!" spoke up Mrs. Vernon. "I shall not see a moment's peace, asleep or awake, till it is all over."

"And how are we to be any safer away out here in the woods, I should like to know?" demanded Pauline, with more genuine petulance than her mother had ever before known her to indulge. "I know that I should feel better at home in the city."

"But if I were a man," exclaimed Mademoiselle de Sezannes, shrugging her fine shoulders and emphasizing her words with quick French gestures, "I would stay at home with my family and protect it instead of—"

"Oh, no," Mrs. Vernon interrupted. "How could you protect them single-handed? The men are behaving heroically, dear."

"And what of us? What shall we do when they have been killed? I think it more heroic to stay with those you love and lead them out of danger and keep yourself alive for them than to fight all the battles in the world and die."

"If the men felt in that way, dear, the English would burn New Orleans before the week's end. It would be unmitigated cowardice. Don't you know it would, dear?"

"I don't care! I don't care! So there!" exclaimed the excitable girl, beginning to cry. "I want to go back home. Tell the coachman to turn around. I can't go on! I can't! I can't!"

Pauline joined her friend in shedding tears freely. She, too, felt a sudden, uncontrollable desire to fly back to the city. The two clasped each other and nestled their young heads together, sobbing hysterically, while the carriage rolled softly along over the slushy sand or bumped against the palmetto roots.

Mrs. Vernon understood the unexpressed thoughts of the girls, and felt that fine sympathy which makes the true mother so clear and tender a critic of her daughter's love. She beat back, though she could not forget her own distress in her desire to console and inspirit those budding hearts upon which the first rude wind of trouble was blowing.

It was while she was using her best endeavors to distract their attention from the subject of the war that the carriage suddenly stopped, and she heard some one speaking to the coachman in a sharp, nasal voice.

"Kem all the way f'om town, hev ye?" the man was saying. "An' w'at air folks a-doin'up thar'?"

"I cayn' say, seh," answered the coachman, whose English was of the thin, mincing, creole kind. "I cayn' say vat zey do."

"An' who ye got inter the car'ge thar'?"

"I hev' ze madame an' ze ma'm'zelles, seh."

"Oh, weeming, air they? An' whar' air ye a-takin' 'em to?"

"To ze plantaseeon, seh."

"What pertic'ler plantation air ye a-takin' 'em to?"

"It ees Mess'u Vernon's, seh."

"Humph! Let me take er squint inter thet air vehicle."

Mrs. Vernon recoiled from the wizened, wrinkled

old face that was just then thrust close to the carriage window. Mademoiselle de Sezannes screamed shrilly.

"Beg parding, weeming, beg yer marciful parding!" exclaimed the queer looking old fellow, touching his 'coon-skin cap. "Don't ye be uneasy or afeared; Enos Peevy ain't agoin' to do ye no harm."

He shifted the long, heavy rifle by a quick, deft movement, so as to let it rest more easily in the hollow of his bony shoulder, at the same time a huge quid of tobacco was rolled from one side of his mouth to the other.

"Oh, no, no, weeming folks, I air your friend; don't ye git sceert. Hit air my jooty, ye know, bein' a scout fer Giner'l Jackson, ter kinder squint inter car'ges an' things ter see w'at's in 'em; but I don't hurt nobody ner nothin'."

He looked very kindly into the faces of the ladies and chewed his tobacco with great complacency.

Mademoiselle de Sezannes began to speak volubly to him in French; but he only grinned and scratched his head.

"'T ain't no use a-flingin' thet air sort er stuff at me, young 'oman. Up in Tennessee we jes' talks thet same ole lang'age w'at we allus did."

"You say you are scouting for Jackson?" suavely inquired Mrs. Vernon, merely to collect herself.

"Yas, mum; the gin'ral an' me runs together. Wharsomever ye fin' him ye'll stagger on to me pooty clost 'roun' thar'. He calls me Ole Eyes; but my name air nothin' but Enos Peevy."

"Thank you, sir. Good morning. Drive on, Catulle." Mrs. Vernon smiled and bowed to the man as graciously as if he had been a courtier.

The coachman, obedient to the order of his mistress, started the horses on at a brisk gait.

"What a queer person!" exclaimed Mademoiselle de Sezannes, when they were well away from the spot. "Tennessee must be a strange country if it is inhabited by that sort of people."

"But he had a kind face and an engaging way despite his odd dress and comical dialect," said Mrs. Vernon, "and I should be ready to trust him at a time of danger."

"Oh, but he's so hideously ugly."

"No, not ugly, dear; only outlandish-looking. I noted his features carefully and found them of almost Grecian regularity. Old age and exposure have wrinked and bronzed him; but he has clear, honest eyes and a good face, on the whole."

Mrs. Vernon urged the discussion in order to draw the minds of the girls away from the recent channel of thought. Pauline was inclined to side with Mademoiselle de Sezannes and say that the scout did not strike her as a person to be implicitly believed in. He must have had some ulterior design in stopping the carriage. It was very easy for a man to call himself a scout; he might be a robber or even an English spy. Certainly he had found out by most adroit work who they were, where they were going and what they had in their carriage. Perhaps he would come that very night and rob them of their money and jewels.

"Oh, I know that's just what he will do!" cried Mademoiselle de Sezannes, relapsing again into hysterical weeping and beginning to wring her hands. "Oh, please, Madame Vernon, tell the coachman to take us back! We shall all be murdered this very night!"

The suggestion was infectious. Pauline caught the chill of fear, and Mrs. Vernon lost control of herself at an unguarded moment.

The carriage rumbled on through the forest, and, if there had been any person to hear, the voices of the women crying in discord must have sounded strange indeed under the circumstances.

The coachman must also have been affected, for he urged his horses impatiently and kept increasing their speed until they were making a rather reckless dash of it along the road within view of a broad grassy marsh stretching away to a shining sheet of water.

Mrs. Vernon drew all the curtains close over the windows, as soon as she could command herself, and began to chide Mademoiselle de Sezannes and Pauline for their foolish excitement.

Just then there was the sound of a horse galloping by in an opposite course to that of the carriage. Pauline looked out of the little rear window, her eyes still streaming tears.

"Why, it is Lieutenant Ballanche!" she exclaimed. "Why didn't he stop and speak to us?"

Mademoiselle de Sezannes almost thrust her from the pane in her eagerness to look out.

"It is! It is!" she quavered. "Call to him! Stop him! Oh—"

She clasped her hands and gazed while the vigorous bounds of the horse bore the young officer farther and farther back along the meandering road between the trees, and presently lost him behind a fringe of bay bushes in the distance.

"Oh, he never looked back or made even a sign; and he must have known us!" cried Mademoiselle de Sezannes.

In a few minutes the carriage was drawn up in front of the plantation house, which was a one-story, wooden structure set upon a high foundation of oak posts connected by a lattice-work of slender boards. An orange grove, dark and rich, stood in the background, and over a squat, broad veranda grew a closely matted jasmine vine. In the distance were rows of negro cabins built under the shade of immense moss-draped live-oaks.

The coachman dismounted and opened the carriage-door for the ladies, and little Lizette, Lapin's daughter, ran out of the house to greet them. A sharp, salt breath from the marshes not far off was blowing merrily.

Mrs. Vernon descended first, followed by Mademoiselle de Sezannes, and then Pauline precipitated herself upon Lizette, whose dark, pretty face was all dimples and smiles.

The sun came out, too, as if to clear away with a flood of golden light all the gloom that had attended the little journey.

"Well, weeming folks, I air mighty much erbleeged ter ye for this yar ride w'at ye let me hev'," remarked the well-remembered voice of Enos Peevy, the scout. The old fellow had found a seat between the curved suspension springs behind the carriage, where he had ridden unobserved, and now he stepped forth, gun in hand, evidently well satisfied with himself and every person present.

"Ef ye 'd er knowed 'at I 's thar', I s'pec' ye 'd a' cried more 'n ye did. He-he-he! Ha-ha-ha! But ye didn't know it, did ye?" He chuckled and grimaced comically. "Well, weeming folks," he added presently, shouldering his long rifle and adjusting his otter-skin bullet-pouch and his transparent powder-horn, "I mus' be a-goin'. Ef ever I kin do ye a sarvice I'll do it. Good-bye, weeming folks."

He turned about and walked away, as straight as an arrow and as brisk as a boy; but before he had gone far he looked back, stopped, appeared to reflect a moment and then called back to them:

"Say, weeming folks, I'll tell ye what: Ef I see any sign o' Britishers eroun' yar, w'y, I'll jes' step in an' tell ye, so 's ye kin git up an' skin out afore they cotch ye."

There was something honest and earnest in the ring of his voice, and the gleam from his steel-blue eyes, if not warm, was steadfast and friendly. When he was gone, Mrs. Vernon remembered this and wondered why she had not thanked him for his proffered kindness; but the mention of British soldiers, coupled with the suggested probability that they might visit the place, so alarmed her, that she could not think of anything else for the moment that he was speaking.

They found the house most comfortably prepared for them, and when Lapin arrived later in the day, with such of the servants from Chateau d'Or as Mr. Vernon had thought best to send, there came such a sense of homelike security that they could not help looking at one another complacently in silent acknowledgment of what, it now seemed, had been a mood of undue nervousness.

Lizette had brought in from the flower-garden great bouquets of roses and violets (for, despite the unusual cold weather, the vines and tangled beds were still a mass of bloom), and with these she had deftly decorated the airy and fresh-smelling rooms. Moreover, a delicate luncheon was awaiting them, set in a cozy alcove where low, broad windows let in a soft light which was first filtered through a screen of magnolia-boughs and a gray fringe of Spanish moss.

Under the circumstances, it was quite impossible for three women, all of them French, to be otherwise than enthusiastic, even if their enthusiasm did consciously root itself back in a heavy sense of but half-suppressed dread.

Mademoiselle de Sezannes was, perhaps, the most cheerful one. She even tried to be gay over the conduct of Lieutenant Ballanche, whom she persisted in accusing of willfully passing her by unnoticed.

It is due to the young man to say, however, that he was scarcely aware of the carriage as he rode past it. His head was down, and his thoughts were fixed on a most important duty; for he was flying to General Jackson with news from within the enemy's lines. A fleet of barges, heavily manned with finely equipped soldiers, was on Bayou Bienvenu, and in a few hours the English would have an army safely landed below the city. The information this time was authentic, for with his own eyes he had seen what he was to report.

Naturally earnest and intense in his disposition, he felt to the fullest measure the responsibility resting upon him. He would not trust any courier to bear the message which might hold the fate of New Orleans and the country. So he rode all the way as fast as he dared urge his horse, and on his nerves lay the strain of an all-absorbing excitement. The carriage whisked past him as a mere formless, colorless incident of his flight to headquarters. He remembered afterward well enough when he would have given his life to know that he had halted just long enough to bid the coachman turn back and drive at once to New Orleans. Everything and every person visible about the carriage came out strong and clear, like a suddenly developed photograph, in his mind. The horses, the round-faced, snowy-wooled coachman, the closely drawn curtains, the wheels flecked with sandy mud —even the old man riding on the projection between the high-curved springs—he could see all so plainly and yet through what a film of horrible mystery! And in that closed vehicle, though unseen by him, the girl he loved, the girl who had so lately promised to be his wife was going on all unhindered to disappear as completely and mysteriously as if caught up by the spirits of the air.

Mrs. Vernon and the young ladies passed the rest of the day in comparative comfort of mind. Lapin was there with a score or more of strong colored men to protect them; everything look peaceful and sweet. Why should they be afraid? They would not be afraid, they declared they would not; they would be brave women worthy of strong-hearted patriotic men. They vowed it in their inmost hearts.

So long as daylight lasted, they held well to their determination and kept up a fine show of it; but even when dinner came, served so faultlessly by Lizette, their hearts began to sink a little, and they felt the chill creeping over them again.

Mrs. Vernon struggled vigorously against what she knew was the worst thing for them, but what could she do when a dense fog blew in from Borgne and the night became an encircling wall of blackness, through which the low moaning of some tall pine-trees crept with infinite sadness?

She looked for a book to read aloud and chanced upon an old edition of "*La Princesse de Cleves*," by Madame LaFayette. The girls huddled close to her, and she tried to make them interested in the story, taking care not to go too far into its sentimentalities. Her voice, however, sounded unnatural, she thought, and the volume was soon thrown aside.

"I can never, never go to sleep to-night!" cried

Mademoiselle de Sezannes. "Oh, why did I ever come here!"

Lapin was in the kitchen; they heard him singing a *patois* ditty between his pipes. Lizette had gone to bed.

"We shall be ashamed of ourselves in the morning," said Mrs. Vernon. "The sun will come up, and everything will be so bright and cheerful that it will seem like sinful folly to have been afraid."

"And think what they—what the men who are in the camps to-night may soon have to meet!" Pauline found courage to say. "It is they who have the right to be wretched; and yet I dare say they never think of complaining."

"I know I am heartless and selfish," Mademoiselle de Sezannes half sobbed, "but I can't help it—it's dreadful! Why did they send us away off out here alone in the dark? And then to think that he would ride right past like that!"

Mrs. Vernon smiled wretchedly.

"How could he know, dear, that you were in the carriage? All of the curtains were closely drawn, you remember, and he could not have seen any of us."

"He might have stopped us—he didn't look—he—"

Just then there arose a trampling sound, as of men crossing the veranda. Some one knocked on the door, and they heard voices.

Mrs. Vernon sprang to her feet, the girls clinging tightly and breathlessly to her.

Lapin came in from the kitchen when he heard

the knocking and stood irresolute. He still held his pipe in one hand, while with the other he was aimlessly fumbling in the pocket of his jacket.

"Go to see who it is," Mrs. Vernon managed to say.

Lapin went gingerly to the door and called out in a weak voice:

"Who's there?"

"A friend," was the prompt answer.

Pauline and her mother started and looked at each other.

It was the voice of Colonel Loring.

"Open the door immediately!" he commanded gruffly. "There's no time for ceremony!"

Lapin, in a very ague of fear, fumbled at the bars and bolts. His hands shook so that he made slow work of it, and when at last he quakingly pulled open the heavy wooden shutter, he fell back aghast before the tall form of the incomer and gasped hoarsely:

"Pierre Rameau!"

CHAPTER XIX.

THE SHADOWS OF DARK DAYS.

When Lieutenant Ballanche returned from his reconnaissance in the direction of the mouth of Bayou Bienvenu, he brought a report which caused General Jackson to issue orders immediately for the doubling of all the outpost pickets and for all the troops to hold themselves ready to march at the tap of the drum.

As yet the reinforcements so long and so anxiously waited for had not arrived, and the situation was most perplexing. From a hundred sources came the information, doubtless exaggerated and over-colored, that the creoles of the city were concocting an uprising in favor of the English. Thus to the commanding general it appeared that, with an overwhelming alien enemy before him, he should have to move his little army down the river and leave behind him a horde of traitors, who were but waiting for an opportunity to fall upon the supplies in the rear and so render defeat inevitable.

It was at this point that Mr. Vernon came to his aid with three hundred men well armed and equipped. They were not a soldierly looking battalion, measured by the ordinary standard of military taste, but there was fight in them; and Jackson, who read men at a glance, felt their efficiency, as he looked them over in a hasty review.

Mr. Vernon had acted with amazing energy in the matter, sending out runners to call a meeting in one of the public squares. Singularly enough these couriers did not seem to notify the better class of people; but entered the gambling dens, the low *cafés*, the haunts of the *Chats-Haunts*, the huts of the river rats and the garrets of the quadroon quarters. And out of these places poured men and youths of all colors, a motley crowd, speaking a half-dozen languages, strangely picturesque, ready for anything, and especially ready and willing to go and do whatever Jules Vernon might ask of them. Their coming together was reported to Jackson who, at first supposing them a mob of his enemies, thought of marching a force to disperse them; but he was restrained after much persuasion by Claiborne, Edward Livingston and Commodore Patterson.

Upon so small an event hung the fate of New Orleans. Had that meeting of the lawless ones been interfered with in the slightest by the military, the city would have been burned to the ground, with the result of a fatal panic in the already suffering American army.

Mr. Vernon had caused a small platform to be erected in the square; from this he addressed his motley assembly in English, in French, in Spanish and in German. He knew just what to say to them and just how to say it. His huge frame and powerfully magnetic face were stong auxiliaries to his eloquent words and richly sonorous voice. Almost immediately the vast crowd beneath him was wild with enthusiasm; their shouts were heard at Jackson's headquarters, whither word was quickly brought that a popular movement was being successfully agitated in his favor by Mr. Vernon.

The iron chieftain's face lit up with hope and pleasure. Ordering his horse, he at once rode to the scene, coming up at the time when the crowd was at its highest pitch of excitement.

Mr. Vernon took quick advantage of the incident.

Pointing to the general as he sat like a grim statue in his saddle, he thundered forth:

"Behold, citizens! Yonder rides your leader—your unconquerable general!"

Every face was turned, and every eye was riveted upon the gaunt form and implacable face of Jackson. He lifted his hat and waved it with a slow sweep around his head. For a moment they saw the shock of bristling hair, the stern brows and the firm lips—they saw the steely eyes gleam as with a vision of victory.

"Live the Republic!" roared Mr. Vernon, with the voice of a lion. "Live the brave general who has come to save New Orleans and Louisiana!"

He spoke in French, and his words were the signal for a very tempest of vehement applause. The excitable rabble took up the cry:

"Live the American Republic! Live the brave general!" And added thereto: "Down with the English!"

Claiborne, Louallier and other members of the State government chanced to be in the street, and when they heard the shouts paused to hearken.

"*Vive la république des Etas-Unis!*" arose clear and loud, above the general din.

"There!" exclaimed Clairborne. "What did I tell Jackson? That is Vernon warming up the slums. It means everything, everything!"

"If Vernon tells them to fetch him coals from the devil's oven, they will go after them!" said Louallier.

"And bring them in their bare hands," added Claiborne.

That very night three companies were formed and armed by Mr. Vernon, and the next day they reported for duty.

General Jackson was delighted, and when Mr. Vernon called at his headquarters, he seized his hand and wrung it savagely.

"You are the kind of a man that I like!" he exclaimed, his face lighting up and its hard lines softening into cordial enthusiasm of expression. "You are the noblest man of this noble State!"

There was no mistaking the general's feelings, and Mr. Vernon could not repel them; indeed the fire of the old days, when he fought by sea and land, was burning high now; he had fanned it with his own oratory in stirring up the embers in the breasts of that reckless crowd.

"I know, general, that the safety of New Orleans depends upon the courage and patriotism of her own children," was all the reply that he made; but his manner and voice told how deeply he felt.

"True, sir; true as Gospel!" said Jackson, still holding on to his hand. "And you will lead them, and those English dogs will yelp and cringe before you. You are the mainstay of everything now; we cannot do without you."

It was as if a son were speaking to a father. Jackson was in the full prime of life, and, though worn by sickness, still stalwart and rugged; but Mr. Vernon looked the master who could enforce his will, even with the stubborn and relentless commander. He smiled a strange, illuminating smile, and his deep-set eyes glowed out from under his grizzled and shaggy brows with a power that was irresistible

"I am at your command, general—I and these men. Where you say go, there we will go or die."

When Lieutenant Ballanche came in with the report from Bayou Bienvenu, Jackson sent immediately for Mr. Vernon, but was unable to see him till the next morning, when he told him of the advance of the English.

The old man's face blanched.

"But my wife and my daughter!" he hurriedly said. "They have just gone out to my plantation near the Bayou. I sent them there but yesterday."

"Then you had better go get them and bring them back," was Jackson's blunt rejoinder. "We march down the river immediately."

"Mademoiselle Marie de Sezannes is with my family," said Mr. Vernon, turning to Lieutenant Ballanche.

It was now that young officer's turn to grow a trifle pale.

"'Mademoiselle de Sezannes!'" he echoed quickly.

"Yes. She accompanied my wife and daughter."

"General," said the lieutenant, "I ask for a small detachment and leave to go after the ladies."

"You cannot go. I cannot spare you," was Jackson's brusque answer.

Then Mr. Vernon rose to his feet and fixed his eyes upon the general.

"General," he exclaimed, "the young lady is the lieutenant's promised wife! He must go!"

And he went.

There had been good reason for the failure of General Jackson's messenger to find Mr. Vernon on the day before. Indeed, if he had found him, his message must have been delayed; for Mr. Vernon was in no mood to be interrupted. He and Colonel Loring were having a memorable interview.

Loring came to Chateau d'Or, where the master of the place was superintending some hasty final touches in the way of securing it against intrusions, late in the afternoon. Mr. Vernon was astonished to see him.

"Why, what upon earth! What are you doing here?" he ejaculated, frowning darkly and speaking with infinite impatience. "You told me that you would not come back here again."

"I never keep my word," remarked Loring; "it's too inconvenient. I always do just what I happen to wish to do. What are you up to now?"

Mr. Vernon looked at him in a hopeless way; but he did not answer his question.

"You'll stay here, I suppose, and let the English soldiers show such mercy as they may to your family and you," continued Loring, half-sneeringly.

"I have sent my wife and daughter to Lapin at the plantation.

"At Bay Saint Louis?"

"No; on Bayou Bienvenu."

"Oh, out there! What did you send those defenseless women out there for?"

"For safety, in case—"

"Safety, indeed! Don't you know that right up Bayou Bienvenu the English army will come first?"

"No."

Mr. Vernon looked uneasily at Loring.

"Well," said the latter, "I know it, and you had better go fetch them back at once."

"How do you know?"

Loring laughed, and his laugh was like an open sneer.

"Oh, to be exact, I expect to lead those jolly redcoats in by that route."

"Ta! It is a nasty jest. Be serious if you can. You have something on your mind to say to me. Say it, please."

"Well, then, I need some money."

"Certainly—you always do; but how much?"

"Ten thousand dollars will do."

Mr. Vernon, who had been sitting, rose slowly and stood up before Loring.

"I will not give you one cent," he said, with the accent of finality.

"Yes, you will, when you know that I do not mean to gamble with it and that I am going straight to the British, who will send me out of this country."

"Ta!" ejaculated Mr. Vernon.

"You do not believe me? Well, on the whole, I do not wonder. But you must trust me this time, at all hazards."

"I have said no."

"To be sure, but that was before you knew that you owed me a hundred-fold the amount."

"Ta!"

Loring leaped to his feet like a tiger suddenly aroused to fury; but there was no particular change in the expression of his face. His eyelids may have drooped a trifle, so that the openings through which the cold gleam of his eyes shot out were narrowed to mere slits under his handsome brows.

"Do you dream who I am?"

The question was put with a sort of grinding intonation, and the speaker snapped his thumb and forefinger impatiently.

"Ta!"

"I am Pierre Rameau, and I want ten thousand dollars!"

"I am Jules Vernon, and—"

"Say, rather," interrupted Loring, "that you are Thomas MacCollough. I like accuracy in business matters."

Mr. Vernon glared and stood speechless.

"I know your whole past life, Thomas MacCollough, as well as I know my own. You need not become excited in the least. I have known it all these years of our acquaintance."

"I know your life, too, from your cradle to this moment," Mr. Vernon presently said in a dismal voice; "I have been told that your name is MacCollough, too—Kirk MacCollough."

"We seem to be pretty well acquainted, then, and possibly we are kinsmen."

Mr. Vernon lifted his hands as if to ward off the suggestion, and stepped backward a pace.

"I do not place my demand for the money on that ground, however," Loring went on with a measured, merciless manner of speech; "but wholly on the ground that you are my debtor. You have grown rich in dealing with Pierre Rameau, and now that you know who that mysterious man is, you cannot object to his demand for money, can you?"

Mr. Vernon tottered to a chair and sank into it with the air of one who collapses under a deadly stroke; his face withered; his eyes were dull and sunken. At that moment his age seemed doubled.

"I have no time. I am followed, hounded. Two dogs scent every track I make," Loring continued. "If you cannot give me money, why, of course, I must go without it. I have been a fool, played in hard luck, lost everything, and this infernal war has blocked every channel of my operations. You can feel my condition."

"What do I care for money!" cried Mr. Vernon, springing up again. "Take all I have—it is nothing—so you go and never return!"

"Oh, I promise that. I think you can depend upon that."

Mr. Vernon gazed at him with a look curiously searching, wistful, hopeless. The cold drops of a powerful excitement were beading the old man's forehead. He lifted his hand and wiped them away mechanically.

"Tell me one thing and tell me truly," he demanded, a husky tremor in his deep voice. "Tell me on your life: Are you the son of Thomas MacCollough?"

"There's no time now for explanations," said Loring, evasively. His face seemed to soften in some strange way. "It doesn't matter who I am. I am pressed. My life is at stake. I cannot parley."

Mr. Vernon stepped forward and laid a powerful grasp on the younger man's shoulder.. His fingers were like mighty hooks of steel; they closed over the hard, deltoid muscles with an almost paralyzing power.

"Speak to me! Tell me! You shall not go till you do!" he exclaimed, with the emphasis of desperation.

Loring tried to shake him off, not roughly but firmly. He might as well have tried to push out a wall of the house. The other hand closed upon him, and he felt how unequal would be the struggle with the grizzly giant before him. Indeed, his arms were as if pinioned to his sides.

"If you are indeed Thomas MacCullough's son," continued Mr. Vernon, in that deep, hoarse growl, "you will not lie or evade or hesitate now. Speak, I command you!"

"I seem to be rather helpless in your hold," said Loring. "When you get tired, let go of me, please."

Mr. Vernon's hand fell away, and he stepped back, drawing a deep breath as one does who controls passion by sheer force.

"Loring," he said slowly, "or Pierre Rameau, or Kirk MacCollough, whoever you are, it is—"

"Stop!" interrupted Loring. "Can you give me the money or not?"

A man-servant at the door was parleying with some one whose voice barely reached the room. Mr. Vernon had given orders to admit no person.

"If you are Kirk MacCollough I will give you the money," the old man almost whispered.

"I could lie to you," said Loring.

"If you could, you are not he."

Mr. Vernon spoke with a tone which seemed to have years of reflection and multitudes of memories in it.

Loring was fumbling in the breast of his vest as it trying to find something stowed away in deepest security there.

"A knife or a pistol will not serve you," said Mr Vernon, with calm dignity.

"I'm not so slow when I reach for a weapon," remarked the other indifferently. "Here, will that be a sufficient pledge for what money you can let me have?"

As he spoke he drew forth a small worn leather case and handed it to Mr. Vernon, open. It was the amethyst cross.

"That argues more forcibly than knife or pistol, doesn't it?"

The old man answered not a word; but an intense feeling seemed to rush into his face. His mouth twitched under his heavy, rimpled, gray beard.

At this moment there was some sort of disturbance at the hall-door; the servant was trying to keep the visitor from entering.

"Stand aside!" panted the voice of Burns.

The negro stood aside.

Loring turned about, and quicker than the gleam of an eye was the drawing of his pistol.

Burns came into the room, gliding like a serpent.

Mr. Vernon was ready for the emergency, and he was prompt and certain rather than quick. A stroke of his left hand sent Loring's pistol spinning across the floor; a sweep of his right caught Burns's arm as it flourished a long knife.

Loring did not hesitate a second, but, while Burns was struggling to free his arm, walked straightway out of the house.

In the effort to wring the knife from Burns's hand, Mr. Vernon let fall the amethyst cross, and it tumbled on the floor, where it lay, flashing a fine purple light.

―――◆―――

CHAPTER XX.

DESOLATION.

Mr. Vernon and Lieutenant Ballanche had no sooner received General Jackson's permission to take a detachment of men and go than they set out at full speed, riding down to the plantation house on Bayou Bienvenu.

Of course, Mr. Vernon's mind was crowded with the incidents of the interview with Loring, and almost as much was he affected by the conversation which had followed when he was left alone with old man Burns. The latter, balked in his effort to stab Loring, and seeing that Mr. Vernon would not let him go at once in further pursuit, gave up and stood pathetically helpless, gazing in blank, despairing inquiry at the powerful old man who had handled him as if he had been a child.

"You assassin!" exclaimed Mr. Vernon, quite out of patience and temper. "You attempt to do murder in my house!"

"'Murder?' No! That man's life belongs to any one who can take it! That was Pierre Rameau, I tell you!" Burns replied, with but little show of spirit.

He stood gazing into Mr. Vernon's eyes for a moment and then added:

"Did I not tell you what he did to me? I bore everything. What would you do if you were in my place—if he had killed your daughter—if he had wrecked your life—if he had murdered you in the woods?"

"Ta, man!" said Mr. Vernon. "You are excited and nervous. Sit down."

Then seeing the cross on the floor, he stooped and picked it up. Turning it over in his fingers, he was replacing it in the worn case, when Burns reached for it.

"Where did you get that?" demanded he, with sudden, breathless haste. "Did he have that?

That is Margaret's! His mother gave that to Margaret! Let me hold it! Let me touch it! Let me kiss it! Oh, it must have been on her bosom when—"

"Be still, man. You are wild," said Mr. Vernon. "You do not know what you are saying. This thing has been in my family for a century."

"Ah, well, I thought—forgive me—it is so like it."

The old man held his forehead in his hands as if recovering from dizziness. He reeled, and Mr. Vernon helped him into a chair and brought some wine.

"No, I never drink it," he said, putting aside the proffered glass.

After a little he appeared to shake off his weakness to a degree. Rising slowly, he said not another word, but picked up his great knife, which lay where it had fallen on the floor, and went out.

Mr. Vernon did not try to hinder him. The whole thing seemed unreal, and the old man's going had no significance beyond its connection with that sense of inevitable doom which impended shapeless, vague and altogether terrible, somewhere in the cloud on Mr. Vernon's life.

And so, as they went riding down through the solemn woods in the fine, gray rain that began to fall, Mr. Vernon scarcely spoke or lifted his gaze from the ground until they came near to the bank of Bayou Bienvenu; and, even then, it was the young man who broke the silence.

They were side by side, a short way in advance of their little troop, and the rain was blowing in their faces, when a man stepped into the road in front of them, not fifty paces distant. Ballanche drew up his horse, at the same time touching Mr. Vernon's arm.

"Hold!" he exclaimed, in a low voice, as he reached for his pistol. "Whom have we here!"

The man held up his hand and made a friendly sign.

"Ah, it's Peevy," said the lieutenant; "one of our special scouts. The English are not far away, I judge, else he would not be here. We will ride on and see what he is up to."

Mr. Vernon was all attention now; the suggestion of proximity to the British army made him think at once of his wife and daughter. The house was still two miles farther on.

"How now, Peevy?" called Ballanche, as soon as they came up to the scout. "What do you know by this time?"

Peevy saluted awkwardly and gazed off into the woods as if with utmost concern, chewing his quid meantime and delivering the brown juice at short intervals.

"I hev' seed some sign o' the enemy down yar a piece," he said.

"Some sign? What like? Where?" demanded Ballanche.

"They air jist over yar on the marsh. I counted nigh onter two hundred of 'em jes' at daylight this mornin'."

"But how far from here?"

"Ez the crow flies, hit air three miles mebbe to whar' they 's as thick ez birds in er pea-fiel'."

"Three miles! In what direction?"

Peevy jerked his thumb backward over his shoulder to indicate the point.

"And are they moving?"

"They moved las' night some."

"Which way? Up the bayou?"

"No, jes' er foolin' eround like. Some of 'em war down yar ter this yar house below yar."

"What house?"

"My house do you mean?"

Mr. Vernon and the lieutenant spoke together, both of them leaning forward as if about to throttle Peevy, whose dry, withered countenance did not change its expression.

"What did they do?" stormed forth Mr. Vernon right in the man's face.

"Cut up Jack, they did; kinder cleaned out the place, weeming folks an' all the likes. Lef' nothin' thar' 'cepting a lot o' scared niggers an' er couple o' lame mules."

Mr. Vernon did not wait to hear more, but drove his spurs into his horse. The nervous animal rushed away like a bolt from some powerful engine, tumbling Peevy flat on his back in the road.

"Golly mussy! Land o' Canaan! Better jes' onj'nt a feller's mortal frame an' tangle 'is bone etarnally!" cried the surprised scout, scrambling to his feet and examining his gun to see if it was injured. "Guess Mary Ann air not hurt—air ye, Mary Ann?" He patted the long, heavy weapon as he spoke to it. "Ef Mary Ann air all right, it don't mek' no diff'rence 'bout me."

Lieutenant Ballanche was, first of all, a good soldier, and although Peevy's communication had sent horror through his soul he kept his head.

The detachment headed by a sergeant reached the spot at this moment, and he ordered a halt while he hastily plied the scout with a few more questions.

"Do you mean the house right ahead on this road, two miles from here?" he demanded.

Peevy was busily wiping some dirt from Mary Ann's barrel and stock. Without looking up, he answered:

"Thet's jes' w'at I said ter ye."

The lieutenant motioned the troop to follow him, and set off almost as rapidly as Mr. Vernon had; but the scout took care to keep out of the way this time and stood looking after the riders till they passed out of sight.

"Well of all etarnal fools them's the beatenest 'at I ever seed!" he exclaimed, still rubbing Mary Ann. "Ef they don't watch out, them air Britishers 'll twist thar necks for 'em 'fore they know w'at's happened. W'y they mek's more noise 'an er Pennsylvany wagon on er rocky road. Hum! Well, Mary Ann, we'll look eroun' er leetle bit more."

He shouldered his rifle after repriming it and trudged away through the woods.

Mr. Vernon urged his horse on without one thought of what danger he might be speeding to. His whole life was centered in his wife and daughter. It was for them that all his wealth had been hoarded, all his plans laid, all his schemes wrought out. For years he had dealt with the mysterious Pierre Rameau, not personally and directly, but through an intermediate agent, and in the meantime had formed a close friendship for Colonel Loring, whose vast operations in Mexican mines he had shared, furnishing a large amount of money and receiving good returns upon the investments. Lately the truth had been coming into his mind and he now knew there was no Colonel Loring, no Mexican mines and no investments at all upon which his receipts had ostensibly been based. In fact it appeared that Pierre Rameau had been all this time deceiving him and roistering in gaming-houses and other places of iniquity at his expense, simply paying him interest on the amounts squandered. He now saw to what his years of illegal operations had brought him, and he reviewed with a sickening at heart the whole dark, hidden life that he had been living; but what was all this to another thought which since his several interviews with old man Burns had shaped itself to such proportions, that now it filled the whole vault of consciousness as with a nebulous horror? This Colonel Loring, this mysterious Pierre Rameau, this man whom all the world of the southwest knew of and trembled at but had never been able to see, had suddenly become to him the embodiment of conscience and retribution.

And what was to be the end? Mr. Vernon heard this question echoing about in his inmost heart where he kept his wife and daughter shrined?

What was to be the end? Would they soon know what he knew? Must his whole past life be unmasked to them?

But they? They were in danger this moment! In danger! Had not the scout said that they were carried away by a British detachment? He could not realize the situation; nothing came to his mind with distinctness, so blurring was the cloud of his distress.

Ballanche and his men followed Mr. Vernon as fast as they could ride; but did not overtake him till the plantation was reached. There they found it just as Peevy had said. The house was empty and silent. A body of the enemy had been there, both horse and foot, as they could see by the prints in the sandy soil all around. Most of the negroes were hiding in the swamp or in the tall grass of the salt marsh to the eastward.

Mr. Vernon leaped from his horse and ran into the building; but there was nothing to greet him save the sound of his own heavy footfalls.

When Lieutenant Ballanche came up, he too rushed into the house and gazed eagerly around as he hastened from room to room.

An old negro woman was found hiding in a corner of the kitchen pantry, whither she had run on hearing their approach. From her they managed to get a pretty complete account of what had happened. It was, in substance, the same story as that told by Enos Peevy. The ladies, including little Lizette Lapin, had been carried away by a band of soldiers. The poor old soul was still so frightened that her eyes rolled white and wild, and she stammered so that she could hardly speak.

The rain was still drizzling, blown along by a wind from Borgne and the marshes. In every direction, gray and dim, the country stretched out, with not a moving thing in sight save the tossing tree-tops, the waving horse-tail grass and the water-fowl beating along the shore-lines of bayou and lake. It was a landscape which might have well served the artist of loneliness.

Mr. Vernon and Lieutenant Ballanche went out of that desolate house and remounted their horses. There was nothing left for them to do but to go back to their duty in the army of Jackson.

It was just as they passed through the gate of the close that a shot rang out sharp and short down in the woods beyond the road.

Lieutenant Ballanche was all attention at once; he ordered his men to fall into line. Another shot, and then a scattering sputter of musketry followed. A moment later, Enos Peevy skulked into view among the moss-draped trees some hundred yards away. He was stooping low, trailing his long rifle and running rapidly toward them.

Ballanche understood the situation at a glance, and formed his men in open order behind the fence that flanked the road on one side.

Peevy soon came up and stopped behind a tree to ram home a bullet in his gun. They saw him unstop the power horn with his teeth and carefully fill the priming-pan. Ballanche rode close to him and spoke in a low tone:

"Where are they, Peevy?"
"Don't ye see 'em yonder?"
"How many?"
"Twenty, mebbe."

English uniforms glimmered between the trees in the direction of the bayou.

"I plugged one o' 'em," Peevy added, "an' ef ye 'll watch ye 'll see me flummix another 'n' purty quick."

"Don't shoot!" ordered the lieutenant. "Come back here with me. Let them come on."

The scout obeyed with bad grace, for he deemed it a shame not to shoot when an enemy offered a fair mark.

He walked beside the lieutenant's horse and kept his keen eyes turned back to scan the movements of the scattered line of redcoats.

It was evident to Ballanche that if his little detachment remained but a few moments longer where it now was, its way to New Orleans would be cut off. He ordered Peevy to mount behind him, a thing which the scout was very much opposed to.

"I feels better an' safer onter my feet," he urged, "an' 'en, besides, them air silk-stocking fellers can't ketch me, nohow."

But the lieutenant made his order peremptory, and the lean, skinny rifleman effected the mount from the fence-top.

In the shortest possible time the little band was in motion, going at a brisk pace along the road. But the enemy had seen them, and already the thin red line over-lapped the way.

There was nothing to do but to make a dash.

Mr. Vernon was at the lieutenant's side when the order was given. Down they rode together, Peevy sticking on as best he could, grasping the saddle with one hand and swinging Mary Ann free in the other.

A rattling volley and a chorus of shouts greeted them as they got well under way, and the bullets whistled about their ears.

Mr. Vernon's horse was the fleetest of all, and so he at once became their leader. He dashed upon and almost over a group of three red-coats in the middle of the road. One of them, after firing unsuccessfully at him, seized his horse's bridle and was dragged down for his pains.

Ballanche, encumbered with the scout, was not so successful; Mr. Vernon looked back and saw him trying to use his sword, while his horse was rearing and plunging. Wheeling about and drawing a long, heavy knife, his only weapon besides his holsters, he dashed to the young officer's rescue.

"Punch 'is etarnal eye out!" Peevy was screeching. "Whack 'im on the nose! Jag 'im inter the ribs!"

One of the English, a stalwart fellow, who was unaware of Mr. Vernon's approach, turned just in time to have his neck almost severed by a slash of that terrible Southern knife. And just then the rest of the little detachment reached the spot and all broke through together without the loss of a man.

"Golly mussy!" cried Peevy. "This yar's no

decent way o' fightin'! I can't do nothin' wi' Mary Ann an' hol' on ter this yar kickin' an' callyvortin' annymil at the same time! Blame sich etarnal foolishness! Le' 's go back an' try 'em over ag'in a-stan'in' onter the solid yarth."

But Lieutenant Ballanche gave no heed to his grumbling. He knew that Jackson's army was moving and that his place was in the van. His military experience told him that the English detachment through which they had broken was a party of reconnaisance and that the enemy's army was moving up the bayou in force.

"Ye can't shoot off'n a hoss nohow," Peevy continued to snarl. "How kin ye squint through the sights on er gun bar'l, when the annymil air a hi'kin' ye up an' er drappin' ye down an' er jigglin' ye ever so which way, I'd like ter know? They's jes' not er bit o' sense in the whole business! Ef I'd er been onto my legs, 'stid er flummixin' eround on this yar eternal annymil, I'd a got erbout four o' them air fellers shore es Mary Ann hedn't er snapped!"

When they reached New Orleans, Jackson was massing most of his available forces at a point some miles down the river, and all was excitement in the streets.

Mr. Vernon met Fairfax on a corner of Royal Street, and without a moment's hesitation told him the terrible news of the fate that had befallen Mrs. Vernon, Pauline and Mademoiselle de Sezannes. It was like a blow in the face to the young man; he actually staggered back as if hard hit.

"Gone! Taken away! Pauline in the hands of those brutal soldiers!" he faltered forth, gazing half doubtingly, half wildly at Mr. Vernon. "It can't be true! It isn't so, is it? Oh, sir, you are not in earnest!"

But he knew by the old man's look that it was all true.

"Yes, they are gone—gone," said Mr. Vernon, "and the English army lies between us and them!"

Fairfax was as pale as if dead, and his dry lips would not move when he tried to speak. In that moment of intense concentration of feeling he reviewed every happy hour that he had ever spent with Pauline and recalled every sweet word that she had ever spoken to him. It seemed as if by some sudden movement she had passed from him just now, away to the farthest bounds of the world.

"Vernon," he cried, giving way for a brief space to a burst of grief boyish in its intensity, "what can be done?"

Mr. Vernon looked at him very calmly and said: "There is fighting to be done."

"But what—what will become—what will those brutes do in the meantime? Are you sure, Mr. Vernon, that they were not there, hidden somewhere —or—"

"Calm yourself," said the old man, interrupting his passionate, almost incoherent words. "It is as I say. There is no hope but in fighting."

Fairfax felt a chill like death creep throughout his body, numbing and dazing him. There was nothing to say. He groaned as one does who is not conscious of anything save an unbearable agony of soul.

Mr. Vernon laid a heavy hand on the young man's shoulder, and they stood in silence, while the excited people went past them to and fro. The rain had ceased and the western sun flashed out fitfully between scudding clouds.

"Where were you going?" Mr. Vernon presently asked.

"To General Jackson's headquarters," he answered. "The army is moving."

"We will go together."

And arm in arm they went.

CHAPTER XXI.

RECOGNITION BY FIRE-LIGHT AND GUN-FLASH.

It was the afternoon of the 23d of December, 1814. Lieutenant Ballanche and Mr. Vernon were not the only friends of the American cause who had seen the British soldiery feeling their way toward New Orleans. Major Gabriel Villeré, by a most daring dash, had escaped from the enemy after they had captured him at his father's plantation-house. He brought news which, added to what the scout and Ballanche reported, confirmed Jackson in the belief that a large army was, indeed, immediately before him.

All was hurry and excitement. Orders had been sent to the officers of the various little divisions of the army to move their forces at once down the east bank of the river and take position in the vicinity of the Rodrigues Canal, a small flume or ditch stretching from the river to the swamp, an hour's ride below the city.

General Jackson, swarthy and bilious, rode out to Fort St. Charles to review the moving troops. Mr. Vernon joined him there and watched, grim and silent, while his own dusky riflemen filed past, their picturesque equipments and vivacious features showing in marked contrast to the stalwart Tennesseean backwoodsmen's copperas clothes and lean, unkempt faces. The reckless *forbans* flung up their *chapeaux* with jaunty grace and saluted the general with loud cheering, and then, catching sight of Mr. Vernon, they took up his name and redoubled the shout. The old man lifted his hat, and they saw a flash of battle in his eyes.

"By the Eternal," exclaimed Jackson, "we will make those redcoats feel us before morning! Mr. Vernon, your men look like bad fellows to face in a fight. I'd risk my head on them, sir—risk my head!"

"You shall not be deceived in them," said Mr. Vernon, preparing to join them in their march. "They will do whatever I tell them to."

"Then tell them, sir, to make mincemeat of those infernal invaders!"

Mr. Vernon extended his hand, and Jackson grasped it with hearty good-will.

RECOGNITION BY FIRE-LIGHT AND GUN-FLASH. 255

Near by, on a tall, gray horse, sat that strange genius, Edward Livingston, looking on with keen interest. He was Jackson's other self, his untiring and all-seeing friend and counselor. It was he who said to the commander, as Mr. Vernon rode away:

"There goes the king of all the outlaws, the master of the Barratarians, the *Chats-Huants* and the pirates of Honey Island. But for him they would have all been against us."

"King or devil," said Jackson, following with his eyes the grand figure of the old man as he galloped along the marching column to its head, "he is superb. He is magnetic. He fascinates me. There is something great in him."

Livingston smiled thoughtfully; for he himself was a friend of Lafittes and the defender of the freebooters. He had had great trouble at first getting Jackson's consent to permit any of them to join the army; but what was his influence, or even that of Lafitte, in comparison with Mr. Vernon's? He knew far more than he dared to tell the general; but at this moment of enthusiasm he could not forbear remarking, as Dacquin's colored men and Dominique's clouted smugglers from the waterhuts of Barrataria went dashing by:

"I told you this, general. Set devils to fight the devil."

"But that man Vernon is a gentleman, sir!" exclaimed Jackson impetuously, "he's no pirate!"

"Oh, of course not. You are right," replied the diplomatic Livingston, whose memory held on its leaves the inscriptions of Burr and Rameau and all the other great criminals who had made New Orleans their home or their calling-point. "You read men like print, general."

Somehow, flattery, no matter how bald and obvious, was welcome to Jackson when it came from the lips of this brilliant and engaging citizen whom he had attached to his staff.

Fairfax had been assigned to duty with General Coffee, and was already far on the way to the Rodrigues Canal.

When all the troop had passed, Jackson turned to Davezac, another of his citizen aids, and said, while his sunken, jaundiced face glowed with almost startling passion:

"We are invincible, sir, absolutely invincible! We will drive those redcoats into the gulf!"

And now he signaled to all the group and said:

"Come on! Come on! We will smash them!"

Away they went at a gallop, following the well-beaten road taken by the troops.

Mr. Vernon reached the neighborhood of the Villeré plantation before sundown, and by the time that General Jackson and his staff had arrived, he had formed a plan for a reconnaissance of the enemy's lines; a plan which, when presented to the commander, was accepted at once. He was allowed to choose fifty mounted men, some of them well acquainted with the country, and make a bold ride right down through the British pickets.

He was successful; and what he did had in it a fine smack of the old time and the knightly. The invaders had flung out a weak line of pickets, and upon one of these the horsemen cast themselves at headlong speed. Close by Mr. Vernon's side rode Vasseur, mounted on a wiry little creole pony. There, too, young Louis Livingston, son of Edward, smooth-faced and boyish, dashed along eager for the most dangerous adventure.

It was growing dark, and a thin fog was creeping across from the marshes of Borgne; the lights of the British camp-fires flared and flickered in a zigzag line from the river on the west to the dark swamp on the east. Mr. Vernon was familiar with every feature of the country, and there was one with him who knew just how to find the rustic bridges over the ditches and how to avoid the many miry sloughs wherein the horses would have stuck fast. So they rode in a line which was a parabola, the longer part of the curve skirting the swamp while the shorter touched the river levee.

The pony was shot dead under Vasseur, but this scarcely caused a pause in the rush. Mr. Vernon stooped and swung the little man up behind him. A little farther on, down went Louis Livingston's horse. The nimble youth was taken care of by one of his fellows in imitation of the leader.

At about the point where they reached the deepest swing of their charge they dashed almost over a party of officers taking tea by a fire. Mr. Vernon was still ahead of all the rest and Vasseur was clinging to him like a leech.

The group of surprised and startled Englishmen at the fire sprang up and reached wildly for their arms; but galloping over the soft, sandy soil the horses made scarcely any noise, and the riders were upon them before they could prepare for defense. One of them, however, was quick, cool and ready. He leaped forward and fired a pistol just after Mr. Vernon had passed. His aim was deadly; a young creole threw up his hands and tumbled from his saddle.

Vasseur clutched Mr. Vernon, and cried out:

"Pierre Rameau! That was Pierre Rameau!"

There was a rush of charging men and a volley of musketry from behind a tangle of low trees. Bullets sang past, but not a horse or rider was hit. The movement opened a view of the enemy's line at this point and showed that it was strong.

"Did you see Pierre Rameau? Did you see Colonel Loring?" Vasseur kept repeating, from his seat behind Mr. Vernon.

The old man made no answer to the questions; but they did not fail to reach his ears. He had used his eyes with as much effect as had Vasseur and had seen by the red flare of the fire the tall form and perfectly calm face of Loring.

It was impossible to stop or turn back; the fate of Jackson's army, the fate of New Orleans might be depending on the success of this reconnaissance.

Meantime General Jackson was perfecting his line of battle and preparing for an advance upon the enemy. Livingston was at his side all the time and more than once remarked that when Mr. Vernon returned with his report the whole plan of attack might have to be changed. They heard the firing, and Jackson looked uneasy.

"Don't fear, general," said Livingston, "they will not capture Vernon; he knows what he's about I assure you."

"Well, we shall have to wait till he gets back."

The wait was not long. Mr. Vernon with Vasseur still clinging on at the crupper came straight to the spot. Jackson, who at the time was not mounted, leaned on the sweating neck of the old man's horse and heard the story of what had been seen along the British front.

"We must turn their right flank," Mr. Vernon added, after giving a rapid report. "We must drive them toward the river."

"Zat Pierre Rameau, zat Colonel Loring vat pull yo' nose, he is over zare, mo'sieu le general!" cried Vasseur, jumping nimbly and lightly to the ground. "I see 'eem zare, zat colonel, yah, sare!"

He skipped around like a jay, his gesticulations coming in the proportion of about three to a word.

"Yah, sare, 'ee pull yo' nose an' slap yo' an' zen 'ee go to ze *Anglais* an' shoot at us!"

He knew that Jackson could not understand French; therefore his effort to make himself plain in English.

"Shut your mouth or I'll smash it!" was all the notice that the general gave to him.

"Go to your place with Major Dacquin!" Mr. Vernon ordered, and Vasseur went.

"We had been planning," said Jackson, "and your suggestion is just what we were agreeing upon when you arrived. Your men are just to the left of us here. When you hear the guns of the *Carolina* out there in the river, march straight to the British lines. General Coffee is on our extreme left. He will turn the enemy's flank and drive them toward the river. You know your men. You know what to do when you find the redcoats. Blow 'em sky-high, sir—sky-high!"

Just before going to the place assigned to him, Mr. Vernon stooped from his saddle and, speaking low in General Jackson's ear, said:

"I am glad that you refused to have anything to do with Colonel Loring. I was wrong in urging his claim. You were right in your estimate."

"Yes, sir," replied Jackson, with vigorous promptness, "he's an infernal villain, a scoundrel and a traitor—cut-throat! I'm amazed that you— But let's talk no more. Go at the enemy and give them the devil! Remember the signal—the guns of the *Carolina*. Good luck, sir."

It was a ghostly night. The moon had risen, but it could not shine through the fog that momentarily thickened after the sun went down. Some trouble was had in forming the line, owing to the awkwardness and nervousness of the undisciplined troops; and this battle turned out to be, as every one knows, a wild confusion of hand-to-hand combats between straggling bands of both armies.

A signal-shot and then a whole broadside from the *Carolina* set the little, ill-formed line into motion just as a flight of flaming rockets lit up the whole British front.

Mr. Vernon had reported the ground as quite

unfavorable to cavalry operations, and so all the riders were dismounted. Even the officers set out upon that strange night-attack on foot, plashing through the mire and tumbling waist-deep into ditches, leading their men amid the darkness and fog, often utterly ignorant of the points of direction and unable to distinguish friend from foe. It was an enthusiastic, harum-scarum rush from the outset, each little division anxious to be the first to fire at the enemy.

General Coffee took Fairfax near him, and soon saw that he had made no mistake in doing it. If ever a man is a good soldier, it is when there is an object for him behind the enemy's lines. We are all selfish to this degree : the personal appeal is the strongest appeal. It was as lover bereft of his sweetheart more than as patriot risking all for his country that Fairfax rode on through the fog along the skirt of that awful swamp and into the first strong outpost of the British line.

General Coffee was almost a giant in stature and as brave and daring as a lion. He and Fairfax were side by side when they approached the enemy near the house of General Villeré. Here were some orchards of orange trees and some clusters of negro-huts inclosed by board fences. The firing began in a scattering line that zigzagged from the edge of the swamp across to the levee at the river, and was traceable only by the spurts of flame from musket and rifle and by the broad flashes from some field-guns that had been trundled along apace with the infantry.

So soon as Coffee felt that he had passed the British right flank, he wheeled to the right and charged toward the river, carrying everything before him, until he reached a piece of levee behind which the enemy had formed in strong force. Here he called a halt and fell back a space, as he found the position too well taken for him to risk attempting to storm it.

"Hurry to General Jackson and bring me his orders," he said to Fairfax; and he gave the same order to two other temporary aids, each of which was told to take a different direction from that pointed out to Fairfax; for, in the darkness and fog, no one was sure of the compass.

Thinking of Pauline, the lover stumbled away on his mission, trying his best to keep the course indicated by the general. Deprived for the time of the light of his companion's guns, as he ran everything seemed to come into his way. He bumped against trees, fell over fragments of fences, stepped into oozy ditches, struggled through prickly clumps of bushes and tore his clothes on the brush of fallen tree-tops.

A sword, and it a clumsy affair, was now his only weapon. This he carried naked in his hand, having thrown away the belt and scabbard because they hindered him.

It seemed to him that there was firing in every direction, north, south, east and west. Field-pieces here, musketry yonder, the heavy thunder of the vessel's guns to his left-oblique, and all around the keen "pang, pang," of the well-known woodsmen's rifles.

He pushed on as best he could, guessing his direction by what he knew of the position of the *Caroline* and of the probable whereabouts of Jackson in reference thereto, and, before long, he found himself in a focus of converging bullets. The missiles swarmed past him like fretful bees. Then there was a rush with loud yelling, and he was in the midst of a rough-and-tumble fight, where guns were clubbed, knives flashed and swords clinked savagely. He tried to fall in with his friends and take part in their behalf, but the struggle shifted the combatants so suddenly that before he could do anything he was surrounded by men wearing the uniform of the enemy. This he quickly noted by the flash of a rocket which fell, still burning, not far away.

Luckily, none of the excited and rushing British soldiers appeared to recognize his uniform. He was hastening to reach the cover of a hedge of bushes growing in an ill-kept fence-row, and had nearly reached it, when a tall man faced him and called out:

"Halt! Where do you belong?"

In the darkness, Fairfax, of course, could not make out the challenger's features; but the voice had a familiar sound, though his memory of it was not at the moment certain. He knew that he must answer instantly, and he did.

"I am Fairfax, of General Coffee's staff," said he.

"Then surrender!" came the short, stern command.

Fairfax responded with a sword-stroke as he leaped

toward his would-be captor. He was deceived by
the fog and the night's blackness, and so missed his
point and his blade cut only the air. This threw
him around just in time to disconcert the other's
aim, which else had been deadly.

The flash and report of a pistol came together on
the moment. By that instantaneous glare Fairfax
saw the dark, cool face of his antagonist.

It was the face of Pierre Rameau, the face of Colonel Loring, who was replacing his pistol in his belt
and drawing his sword.

The two men went toward each other ; the thought
of capture or surrender was vanished ; for recognition had been mutual, and both felt a deadly hatred
taking the place of mere soldierly animosity.

It would have gone ill with Fairfax, skillful fencer
though he was, if the combat had been permitted to
pass on to the end ; but their swords never crossed.
A heavy cannot-shot struck the ground between
them and buried itself. Loring sprang away, thinking it a shell that would explode.

Fairfax took advantage of the moment and jumped
through the line of weeds and bushes. It was not a
heroic way of escaping from an unequal fight ; but
he did not think of this. Like a flash it had come
into his mind that the fate of the American army
might depend upon his finding General Jackson.
The fall of the cannon-shot had reminded him that
he was in a battle, not in a personal conflict.

On he ran till at last he came to some of Major
Planché's men whom he knew. They had a torch
and were working heroically to assist a party of

artillerymen in getting a gun out of a little bog where its wheels had mired.

Just then General Jackson himself came up and exclaimed:

"By the Eternal, men, save that gun!"

Fairfax leaped into the mud and set his shoulder into the strain. It was as if Jackson's appeal had given new strength to all. Out came the gun, and was soon again in working order.

The gun was quickly wheeled into position and began bellowing away, its balls bumping and thumping and crashing among some negro cabins not far off.

A party of the enemy, guided by the flash, ran up to within short musket range and fired a heavy volley. The gunner fell dead.

"Stand by that cannon, men! Stand firm! Give it to 'em!" stormed Jackson.

Fairfax sprang to the piece and took the dead gunner's place.

Then came another and heavier volley. A bullet hit him hard in the breast, but he fired the gun, now loaded to the muzzle with grape. It was a destructive shot. By merest chance, the storm of missiles went straight to the light board-fence behind which the British were massed and swept them away almost to a man.

In the space of silence that followed, Fairfax reeled, groaned and fell across the gun.

CHAPTER XXII.

A TENDER NURSE.

Fairfax returned to consciousness after twelve hours of insensibility, and found himself in a beautifully furnished bedroom. There were bandages around his body, and his head was deep-sunk in a luxurious pillow. Around the pale-blue tester on the tall, heavily carved bed-posts clung a festoon of the most delicate and costly lace. The linen that covered him was fine, soft, fragrant, and on the walls of the chamber hung tapestries from ceiling to floor. A mahogany dressing-case, tall, slender, dark, with attenuated carved legs and claw-feet, stood across one corner, and opposite to it a narrow cheval glass, framed in gold, was flanked by curious dog-eared vases filled with roses.

The windows of the room were large and cut into minute square panes by heavy oak mullions that showed darkly through the close folds of the lace curtains. A beautiful old picture of Mary and the Christ child hung low at the foot of the bed, and close to the painting stood a quaint little blue cushioned *priedieu*, upon which lay a crucifix of ivory and gold.

On the dressing-case were various things suggestive of feminine needs and tastes—a gold thimble, a brass jewel-case finely decorated and surmounted by a sleeping Pan, a curious tortoise-shell comb, a fan of ebony and heron-plumes, a pair of wee gloves and a silver tray full of gay floss, scraps of embroidery silk and a pair of scissors.

The instant that Fairfax moved, a small, humpbacked man—Crapaud Crapoussin, in fact—arose from a low chair and slipped noiselessly out of the room. In a moment, he returned, following a *petite* brunette, whose face was saintly in its beauty. She was young, delicate, graceful, and the dead-black of her dress contrasted strangely with the soft, rose-like underglow of her cheeks and the bright flush of her ruby lips. Her hair, black and wavy, was simply done in a Greek knot, and it crinkled with charming effect around her low forehead.

She came straightway to the young man's bedside and stood there, looking down into his face, a rare smile on her half-parting lips, her head bent a little, and her dark eyes beaming softly with tender inquiry.

Crapaud slunk down again into his chair with a peculiar celerity and resumed reading a French novel bound in black leather. He had been a great admirer of Fairfax ever since the night when the young man rescued him from his burly antagonist in the street, and it was he who had asked the privilege of bringing Fairfax to New Orleans when it was found that he was badly wounded. Crapaud had volunteered as a soldier in Planché's battalion and had fought like a demon in the battle of the 23d. Dwarf though he was, he could shoot well, and he was as courageous as Jackson himself.

"Oh, you are awake! You have slept so well!" said the young woman, smoothing the snowy bed-clothes as she spoke.

On her tiny hands were rubies and emeralds and diamonds; at her throat an enormous pearl shimmered all alone.

"You feel refreshed, don't you? Ah, to be sure you do; and you are hungry. I will give you something good."

Her voice was so tender, so sweet, so soothing. It was the voice of a French creole speaking good English, but with an indescribable sub-accent engaging as it was strange and soft.

Fairfax looked steadily at her, but for a while did not speak.

"Some soup with a little brandy," she went on to say; "that will be nice for you. Go, Monsieur Crapoussin, and tell Felice to bring it."

Crapaud slipped away through the door in noiseless haste.

"You are so kind, mademoiselle," Fairfax presently found tongue to say, "so very good. Where am I? What is the matter with me?"

He was half beginning to remember the battle.

"Sh-h-h!" she exclaimed. "You must not speak; the doctor said so, and he knows. I will talk for both of us. You are not so badly hurt; you just need to keep quiet for a few days, and then you'll be all right, the doctor says. Sh-h-h! Don't try to speak."

The tapering, perfectly modeled finger that she touched her lip with had on it a superb sapphire.

Crapaud came in after a while, followed by a servant with a tray, on which steamed a bowl of broth beside a small bottle of brandy.

Fairfax could not move; indeed, he felt no inclination to; nor was he yet quite aware of what had happened to him. The young woman fed a few spoonfuls of the warm liquid and prattled to him the while. Crapaud was deep into the book again.

"The surgeon says your wound is really not a bad one," said she; "the ball only tore the muscles a little and did not touch your lung. But you must not speak to-day."

When she had given him enough to eat, she sent the servant out with the tray and sat down beside him.

"The general says that you fired the gun that turned the tide of the fight. Isn't it glorious to be wounded when that is said about you? No, no; don't try to answer. I'm to do the talking. I'm so proud to have you in my house and to have the honor of nursing you. I wish I were a man! Oh, how I would fight!"

Fairfax remembered everything now. The circumstances of the past few days came back to him all at once, and with a cold shiver he thought of

Pauline, a prisoner in the British camp. He closed his eyes and groaned.

"There, now, don't. You must bear up and be strong," spoke up the sweet-voiced little lady, rising and bending over him. She laid a cool, soft hand on his forehead and smoothed back the tumbled, brown hair. The touch was electrical and soothing. "You are my patient, and I am to make you well," she continued. "The doctor has gone down to the army; all the men who are not too old are gone; we women have to take care of the city and the wounded; we are making clothes for the men, making bandages, cooking food and sending it down to them. They are brave, brave men and will never let those English come here."

She stroked his temples and forehead until he dropped asleep again. For a good while she stood gazing at his pale, handsome, half-boyish face, then turning to Crapaud, said:

"Watch him all the time, and if he needs me come for me."

As she turned to go out of the room she paused before the cheval glass and looked into it over her shoulder. It was a quick, bird-like, comprehensive glance. She smiled, gave a little satisfied sigh, turned her eyes once more to the bed and, shaking her jeweled finger at Crapaud to signify that he must be watchful, went out,

Crapaud read on and on, now and again looking up when Fairfax drew a deeper breath than usual. The novel was one of mystery and adventure that stirred the hunchback's blood and set his imagination into ecstasy. When it was read he flung it on the cushion of the *priedieu* where it lay an hour later when the young woman returned.

She noticed it immediately and snatched it off with a chirruping cry of disapproval.

"A romance there!" she exclaimed, with the peculiar rising inflection of the upper-class creoles. "Why did you put it there? A novel on my crucifix and the Holy Mother looking down!"

Her little flurry disturbed Fairfax.

"Sh-sh-h-h!" she hissed at Crapaud, who had not so much as breathed aloud. "You'll wake him!"

The book was placed on the dressing-case; then she went to the bed and bent over the sleeper just as he opened his eyes.

"Pauline," he murmured, gazing wistfully, "Pauline, where are you?"

"There, now, be still," she said coaxingly, stroking his forehead until he again fell away into sleep.

"Crapaud," she presently spoke up, turning to the dwarf with sudden inquiry, "that's his sister's name, eh? Pauline is his sister, isn't she?"

"Yes, mademoiselle—"

"No—say, 'madame,' sir, say 'madame' to me!"

"Yes, madame, his sister, a beautiful young lady, that Pauline."

Crapaud had no particular object in telling this lie; it came to him promptly, spontaneously, just as his breath came and went forth and just as lightly.

"And she loves him very much, doesn't she?"

"Yes, madame, it is a beautiful love that sister has for him, very beautiful."

"And he loves her the same?"

"Oh, yes, madame."

She clasped her little hands, keeping outermost the one bearing the richest jewels, and turning her head to one side, looked admiringly at the wounded man's face.

"Is she like her brother, Crapaud?"

"Very like him, madame."

"How beautiful she must be, Crapaud, how very beautiful!"

An underglow showed in her dark cheeks.

"What did you say his name is?"

"Fairfax, madame."

"Ah, a fine name. I knew he was an American. Is he a good Catholic, Crapaud?"

"Oh, madame, the most devout that you ever saw," lied Crapaud.

She gave the bed-coverings some dainty touches and went out of the room, singing under her breath a snatch of old French song. It was not a church song.

The next day Fairfax was feverish and sleepless; his wound had inflamed a trifle.

"Crapaud," he inquired quickly, "who is this young woman who is so good to me?"

"It is Madame Souvestre, monsieur."

"This is her house?"

"Yes. She is a widow. She is very rich."

"How came I here?"

Crapaud told him all.

"But you must not talk, Monsieur Fairfax," he added. "She forbids it."

"Tell me, Crapaud," the young man persisted, paying no heed to the prohibitory command, "have you heard anything from—"

"The young lady—Mademoiselle Vernon? Oh, yes! I have heard. She's safe. She's at home. She came back. Oh, yes!"

Of course, he was glibly lying again. He had heard Fairfax talking in the half-delirium of his sleep and had made out his secret. He thought it would please him to be told that his sweetheart was safe at home.

It seemed easier for Fairfax to converse in English, so Crapaud drew upon his limited vocabulary in that language.

"Yah, sah, Mees Vernon she varee well at prayson, sah."

"When did you see her, Monsieur Crapoussin?"

"Yeestidy, I see uh. I waint down zere w'en yo's sleepin', sah. She look varee pooty—zes—lak—lak —lak a beauteous angel."

"Then she is not in the hands of the British? She is—"

"Oh, no, monsieur; she is at home. It was all a meestake. The ladies came home. Oh, yes, monsieur, they're all safe. I tole you zat paysantlee."

Fairfax smiled and slept again and murmured brokenly. Crapaud put his ear close to the pallid lips and caught every word.

The days went by, days of suspense and anguish to the women of New Orleans. Those were women of fine courage, however, and they did not fold their hands and cry. Madame Souvestre, in whose mansion Fairfax was receiving such tender nursing went out every day to sew for the army. At the Livingston home was where most of this work was done; at least, so far as Madame Souvestre's circle was concerned, and there, from early morning until the dinner hour, a throng of ladies cut and stitched and wrought with lively, if not happy, chatter, keeping up a brave show of nerve and confidence, while their husbands, fathers, brothers and lovers dug and shoveled with pick and spade in the muddy sand, building a line of breastworks from the river near Chalmette across to the swamp.

Madame Souvestre was considered the most favored one of all her circle. To have a brave, young soldier, wounded almost to death, as her special charge, to care for in her own house, with her own hands, seemed to all those noble-hearted and patriotic women the very highest possible honor.

"I am just as jealous of you as I can be," said Mrs. Livingston, one day, after the sewing task was over and the other ladies had gone away, "and I think it's selfish of you, dear, not to allow me even to see your brave young patient."

"But the doctor forbade it, you know, and said that he must see no one—no one must even speak to him—he must have absolute quiet. Yes, that was just what he said, absolute quiet."

"You will be falling in love with him, Hortense," Mrs. Livingston remarked, after a little further conversation had disclosed Madame Souvestre's enthusiastic admiration of the young man's personal appearance, "and that will be romantic—it will be like a novel. What did you say is his name?"

"Fairfax. It has a noble sound, hasn't it? But, no," with a little sigh, "there is no more romance for me."

Madame Souvestre's husband had been killed in a duel only a month after her marriage, two years gone by. He was a noted swordsman; but when he met Colonel Loring under the dueling oaks, it was Death that he fenced with, and he was run through at the third pass.

"Forgive me, dear," cooed Mrs. Livingston, taking the petite form in her arms, "I am always saying something foolish. You are too good and sweet to be the victim of my teasing tongue."

She kissed her and then held her at arms'-length to look lovingly at her.

"You are so beautiful, dear, that if I were a man, I know I should steal you. I couldn't help it!"

Madame Souvestre laughed, half-blushing at her friend's enthusiasm. She broke away and said:

"I must go back to him; he needs a great deal of care, that hero of mine."

Mrs. Livingston stood smiling by the door when her friend was gone.

"She loves him already, the little warm-hearted witch!" she mused, "and if he's even half a man, he will love her. Heigh-ho! I wish this war was over!"

She clasped her hands, and the light faded out of her face. It was so every evening after the ladies were all gone and the house had become silent. She nearly always went to her dinner with a tear-stained face and with feverish eyes.

Fairfax did not improve as rapidly as Madame Souvestre had hoped for; but he bore up bravely enough and showed little sign of dangerous restlessness until the night of the 7th of January, when Crapaud Crapoussin went back to the army.

"They need me." the dwarf said, "and I want to go. You can do without me for a few hours."

He smiled in his hideously affectionate way and fondled the sick man's bloodless hand.

Madame Souvestre tried to persuade him not to leave her; but he could not be influenced. He had received word that the battle would be on before daylight of the following day, and his creole blood was hot with fight.

"I will be back to bring you the news of the victory before sunset to-morrow," he said, with queer dramatic intonation.

Then he kissed the hand of Fairfax and was off.

Madame Souvestre cried a little and cast herself upon the *priedieu*, with hands held forth beseechingly to the Virgin.

Fairfax watched her as if through some sweet mist of tenderness. The plump little figure, the perfectly poised head, the softly rounded arms and beautiful, tiny hands were but bewitching auxiliaries to the pure, childlike, almost saintly face upturned in prayer.

When she arose and came to his bedside, he felt a deep comfort in her nearness to him.

"How good, how very good you are!" he murmured.

Then he closed his eyes and thought of Pauline.

Madame Souvestre stroked his pale forehead gently, slowly, her hands trembling with the exquisite thrill that was in her nerves. He sank into a soft slumber and dreamed that it was Pauline who thus soothed away his pain.

Slowly the hours of the night drew by. Madame Souvestre never left the bedside of the sleeping man save to walk the floor in the soft lamplight or to stand a moment before the glass and smile approvingly at her own face.

It was a while before dawn when she clasped her hands and bent over Fairfax to hear what he was saying in his dream.

"Sweet and beautiful," he murmured low, "you are so good, so pure, so true, so kind!"

She pressed one hand upon her heart.

"Oh, love? You have taken away all my pain!" he rambled on.

She started back, faltered, blushed, turned pale, then stood looking down upon his strong yet somewhat wasted face with a gaze of tenderest, sweetest import. The next moment she stooped and would have kissed him—nay, her lips did touch his, just as an awful roar of cannon shook the air.

He opened his eyes and smiled as one coming slowly out of a delicious experience.

Then the guns roared again.

"What's that?" he cried, trying to sit up.

She gently pushed him back on the pillow, and said:

"They are killing those English down there. Be calm. We shall hear good news this very day. So—so; now, don't try to get up, please; it will hurt you."

And then the din of battle was like a thunder-storm with wind and hail, and, looking out of the window, Madame Souvestre saw the gray of daylight.

CHAPTER XXIII.

THE NIGHT BEFORE THE BATTLE.

It was dark, foggy, dreary at Chalmette about the first hour of the eighth day of January, 1815, and the little army of the Americans lay in silence behind the oozy breastworks just completed. Most of the tired soldiers were asleep, their clothes all wet and muddy and their hands blistered by the friction of pick-helve, shovel-stave and spade-hilt. For whole days and nights on half-rations, and almost without sleep, they have delved in the ditches and on the embankments. Now they lay on their arms. A few sentinels walked to and fro with slow, weary tread. General Jackson and his staff were asleep in a plantation-house not far in rear of the line.

Mr. Vernon was, by his own request, officer of

the night, and all alone made the rounds, again and again, of the different commands in the little army, from the river to the swamp. He preferred this activity to any attempt to sleep. The terrible weight upon his heart and mind was only less crushing when he could find some exacting duty, the performance of which would force him to crowd the moment's demands to the front of his thoughts.

A few hours more, and the battle would come and be over with. How would it end? In the intense selfishness of love—the deepest love of husband and father—he was thinking only of the result to his dear ones in the case of victory or defeat. But behind the awful sense of danger to them from their captivity to an army whose brutality was at the time known the world over, there lay a vast, formless, yet certain and distinct cloud of calamity creeping closer and closer to their lives from out his past.

It was while he was standing near the river, at the west end of the breastworks, where a battery of two guns had been planted, that a hand touched his shoulder, and he turned to face old Burns.

It was as if the tall, wasted form had arisen out of the ground. Mr. Vernon did not at first recognize him, but when he spoke, the voice was unmistakable.

"There is no use trying to resist the force yonder," said the preacher. "They are five to your one. They will overwhelm you in the morning. I have been there; I know what I say."

"If they are a thousand to one," growled Mr. Vernon, "we will whip them."

"You cannot; they will pour right over these works."

"They will never cross that ditch."

"I tell you," said Burns with vehemence, "there must be ten thousand of them, all in columns, ready to move at daylight."

Mr. Vernon thrust his face close to that of the preacher and said:

"How do you know?"

"Did I not just say that I was there? It is not an hour since I stood within their lines and saw what I have spoken of," was the prompt answer.

"Then come with me to General Jackson; he must see you and speak with you. Come on!"

He clutched Burns's arm and led him toward the house where the general was sleeping.

When they had gone a little way, Burns stopped suddenly, as if some thought had demanded instant consideration, or as if he had on the moment formed the stubborn resolution not to go farther.

"Thomas MacCollough," he exclaimed, with deep emphasis, "I owe you my life, and now I would save yours in turn. You—"

"Hold!" said Mr. Vernon, interrupting him with peremptory firmness. "Not another word on that score. You owe me nothing."

"Well, then, you will not blame me if I kill him?"

"What do you mean?"

"I speak of Kirk MacCollough, your son!"

No mere presentation of the words can suggest the dramatic import of this terse colloquy.

Mr. Vernon turned a quarter about and seized Burns's other arm.

Behind them a little fire flickered in the fog; they could dimly see each other's faces, grim and grizzled, as they leaned closer and tried to stare into each other's eyes.

Lately Mr. Vernon had begun to dread even the thought of this man, who now seemed the one greatest danger to his happiness; for it was through him that the past seemed on the point of being unlocked and re-opened. Vasseur knew much; but Vasseur was easy to manage. One other knew all; but that one could always be bought to silence with money. Burns alone was unmanageable; because he alone was sincere and incorruptible.

When for years a man has been absolute master of himself and over all who have come within the circle of his life, it is hard for him to realize suddenly that his influence is about to fail. To Mr. Vernon this threatened failure meant much more than mere loss of power in the direction of any ordinary ambition. He had lived so long and so happily on the crust of a volcano, that, until Burns had come, he had forgotten what a fire lay under it. The worst of it was that a man like Mr. Vernon could but feel helpless and hopeless when dealing with one like Burns.

As they stood thus for a moment at arms'-length, with their faces thrust almost together, the two men felt for the first time clearly how much they were in each other's way. Burns was aware now that Mr. Vernon would stand between him and his one remaining desire. He had conferred with Vasseur, and from him had shrewdly drawn enough to confirm himself thoroughly in this thought.

Mr. Vernon's grip on Burns's arms drew them inward with such force that the old man's chest was almost folded together and his breathing became difficult.

"You, a minister of the gospel, a priest of the God of Heaven, come to tell me that you are going to assassinate—" Mr. Vernon stopped short and drew in a deep, shivering breath as if the words had almost choked him. "Shall I turn you over to Jackson to be dealt with?"

"Shall I turn you over to him?" calmly responded Burns.

There was something desperately reckless, beyond anything that Mr. Vernon had ever dreamed of, in the suggested significance of the words. He involuntarily loosed his hold and let fall his hands as if just released from a galvanic shock.

"True, true," he murmured, in a strangely changed voice; "I am not one to lead others to justice."

"You are better, far better than most men, even with your sins all counted," said Burns. "I owe everything to you and yours—"

"Everything?"

"Yes, everything. But the evil part is not—"

"Yes, yes, the evil and all is from me."

"I was hungry and you fed me. I was dying and you nursed me back to life."

"And now I ask you for more than life!" exclaimed Mr. Vernon, in a hoarse whisper.

"I know, I know," faltered Burns.

"No, you do not. You know enough, but not all."

"Yes, Thomas McCollough—"

Mr. Vernon flew at his throat and shut off his words.

"Speak that name again, and—" He did not complete the sentence; he was ashamed of himself instantly "Forgive me; I am not at myself," he went on, letting go his hold. His voice softened. "And you—you are going all wrong, Mr. Burns, you are permitting your passion to drag you along with it; let me beg of you to stop and give your conscience its freedom once more."

"I am sure," said Burns, with dry emphasis, "that you have shown less self-control than have I. I haven't tried to choke you."

"Forgive me, I repeat it, forgive me!" Mr. Vernon supplicated.

"There is nothing to forgive; I mentioned it only to remind you that it is not so easy to hold oneself in."

"But you are a good man, Mr. Burns, and I am not. Your life has been pure and clean and self-sacrificing. You have served God and kept his commandments. It is terrible for you to close up your long and noble career where mine began, in crime and violence. Think a moment, and—"

"No, no, when I think, it maddens me! I dare

not think! Don't ask me to. All my years of humble service in my calling have led up to this. It is fate. I have but one thing to live for and that I will accomplish before I die."

"Have you thrown off your Christianity, your obligation to God and your priestly sanctity, as one throws off a top-coat?"

"All these have been torn from me by the wayside thorns. I wore them till they fell in shreds at my feet. They were not the true—"

"There, ta! You do violence to yourself and to your sacred profession."

"Violence, violence, ah! I have felt what it is. I am not violent! I am simply God's blade of vengeance. I am not a living man as you are; I am dead, save for the one little spark that lights me to my purpose. You do not understand me; you cannot; you have not suffered enough to realize my meaning."

"Ta! You are unreasonable."

"Am I? So I am. It is well that I am. If I were reasonable I could not do what is to be done. Behind me is desolation, a desert, a scorched and blackened way, a life made as a cinder by Kirk MacCollough. Reasonable, reasonable! To kill him is the only reasonable thing!"

Burns's words fell upon Mr. Vernon's ears with a strange power. It was not the crazed old preacher's purpose that struck with most terrible effect. It was what lay beyond even the most perfect consummation of revenge. There seemed little probability, indeed, that Burns could ever do harm to the man he was trying to follow ; but what he might do with the mere breath of his frenzied lips was incomparably dreadful to think of.

Strange it is that, although Mr. Vernon had not the slightest assurance of the safety of his wife and daughter from even the most horrible consequences that could come out of their captivity, he felt their danger from that source far less than what would befall them were his past to be made known to them. Somehow, so long as he had Jackson's army with him, he could not lose the hope that all would be well, so far as retaking his loved ones was concerned.

This was but a matter of fight. But the other! That was not to be fought back, once it should find the way to reach them. He felt that Burns, in his monomania, was likely at any moment to make an end of all this beautiful, precious dream of happiness. Happiness? Ah! He had been happy—no man happier—but now, what was coming? Where were his wife and daughter? He felt his brain swim and waver.

Suddenly he grasped Burns's arms again with all his giant strength.

"Tell me right here and now," he muttered huskily, "tell me: Are you going to betray me? are you going to disclose the secret of my life? Speak or—"

"I will not speak, save to shout for help, while you assault me like this," said Burns.

"Forgive me; I forgot."

Mr. Vernon took off his hands from the old man's arms as he spoke.

"But you can see how terrible it would be. Think of my wife and daughter!"

"Think of Margaret! But—but—to be sure, you never harmed her, and I owe my life to you and yours," said Burns. He stood a moment in silence, and then added:

"Your secret is safe with me so long as you do not interfere with—with my purpose. To accomplish that I would, if I could, destroy heaven and earth and all that is in them. I tell you that Kirk MacCollough shall not live!"

His tone was solemnly awful. Mr. Vernon felt helpless before him. They stood there in silence after that until, suddenly, a light flashed forth from the house where General Jackson had his headquarters.

"Gentlemen, it is time to be up!" they heard the gruff commander exclaim, as if to awaken his sleeping staff; "the redcoats will be upon us before we are ready if we don't step spry. Come, come, gentlemen, fall out?"

Immediately there were a stir and bustle in the house. Lights shown at the windows and the clinking of latches and the opening of doors told how promptly the officers responded to the call of their leader. A moment later Jackson himself came forth, followed by the enthusiastic but sleepy aids, who were buckling on their side-arms.

"Ah, Mr. Vernon; is that you?" he demanded, as he came near the two old men. "How goes everything? Any stir among the redcoats?"

"Not yet," replied Mr. Vernon, "save that they seem to be making ready for an advance."

"Let them come; we are ready. Who is this you have with you?"

The general peered askance at Burns through the fog and dust.

"It is a friend of mine," said Mr. Vernon, without offering further introduction.

The members of Jackson's staff were coming around him for orders, which he began giving with his usual swift and clear understanding of what the moment called for. Meantime Burns managed to disappear.

CHAPTER XXIV.

ENOS PEEVY'S RIFLE-PRACTICE.

At a little after daybreak, though the fog was still heavy and the breeze too light to remove it, it was observed that the British were steadily advancing.

Jackson had everything ready and was nervously eager for the fray to begin; but he preserved a cool expression of face, and gave orders that there be not a shot fired until the enemy were within certain range of the guns.

Mr. Vernon hastened to make his presence felt among the men, who looked to him for the encouragement that such beings always need in the supreme hour of danger. He found them chilled and hungry; but they responded vehemently to his few low words, and showed that they meant to be brave.

A fiery rocket whizzed up from the British front and curved through the slowly thinning fog; then another arose from a different point.

"They are coming," said Jackson to Lieutenant Ballanche. "Let us go to Spotts's battery."

They walked along the line at a rapid gait and, just as they came near, they heard a low order, and then out boomed the gun. The long, red blaze leaped far out through the fog-curtain, and they saw for the first time the glint of red uniforms away off by the line of woods across the open level land.

The column was moving at a swift pace right down upon them.

Old Enos Peevy came near the general and saluted.

"Well, Enos," said Jackson, "is Mary Ann in good order?"

"Ye'll see poorty soon, gin'r'l. I air jes' er waitin' for 'em air fellers ter come close enough for Mary Ann ter talk to 'em; she air got some remarks to say to 'em, an she'll make 'em sick, shore 'nuff."

He rubbed the long, heavy barrel of his rifle while he spoke, and wagged his head grimly.

And now the breeze strengthened and began to lift away the fog.

Spotts's gun bellowed once more, shaking the wet ground with its tremendous concussion.

The British column came right on; all the batteries in front of it opened bravely and sent their heavy missiles plowing through it.

Soon enough the rifles of Tennessee and Kentucky began to crack, keen and clear; and when the range became certain, the effect was terrible to see.

Peevy stood on top of the earthwork, with the brim of his old cap turned up in front. He lifted his gun and fired at an officer, who, sword in hand, was leading the column. It was a deadly shot. Down fell the brave man; but the column bore right on. Not far, however, for there was that fatal ditch in its way, and the bullets and cannon-shot were cutting men down like weeds.

"Give it to them, boys!" shouted Jackson, as he tramped back and forth behind his brave little army, the fire of battle lighting up his careworn face. "Give it to them while they are wavering!"

The British recoiled, shattered, bleeding, confused, their front ranks breaking into and destroying the order of those behind. At first it appeared that the fight was over; for how could those scattered and widely fleeing men ever be rallied and re-formed?

It was then that the brave Pakenham showed himself at the front waving his hat aloft and galloping to and fro and calling on his men to remember the honor of England. They heard his manly voice above the roar of the patriot guns that were playing upon them, and they turned and set their faces once more toward those low, dark breastworks along which flickered and sparkled and flamed the rifle-blazes of marksmen who shot with the aim of veteran woodsmen. The bullets, like level swarms of furious bees, hummed along the crisp air of the morning.

"Aim well, men! Get a fine bead on them!" shouted Jackson. "Blow them to hell!"

"That's the talk, gin'r'l!" responded Peevy, as he stood deliberately reloading Mary Ann. "I'm er doin' that air very thing!"

There was Vasseur wildly excited and trembling like a freezing lamb, but fighting like a mad lion.

Not far off, Crapaud Crapoussin, who came from the city but an hour before, was crouching behind the wet earthwork and firing away as best he could. Fiddler Dick was there, too, with an enormously heavy gun, which was so long, that he had to rest the butt of it far back on the ground behind him when he was loading it. Indeed, it seemed that all classes of men to be found on the gulf coast, gentlemen and cut-throat, dandy and ragamuffin, upright citizen and scowling *forban*, all the noted characters of city or swamp were to be seen in that oozy trench fighting for the country of their birth or adoption, regardless of self, their whole energy centered in the one desire to drive back the British. Only one of the well-known men of New Orleans who might well have been looked for in the line was missing. Yes, two. Colonel Loring and Lafitte.

The latter had been sent by Livingston to bear Mrs. Livingston and her child to a place of safety, should the battle be lost.

Down the line where Mr. Vernon's men were stationed, the roar of the guns was continuous, like the long, rattling roll of summer thunder. The

British bullets sang keenly overhead or tossed up little puffs of sand along the embarkment.

"I'll git thet air feller on the hoss yit," muttered Peevy, taking aim at Pakenham, "thet is, ef Mary Ann kin carry thet fur."

He fired, and down went that brave officer's horse, pitching his rider headlong.

"Thet thar stopped his cavortin', anyhow!" the scout bawled out, though everybody was too excited to hear. "'Rah fur Gin'r'l Jackson!"

About this time Burns came shambling along the line, apparently quite unconscious of danger. He was haggard and wild-looking, his hair unkempt and his long, thin, white beard tangled across his face.

He saw Vasseur and approached him.

"Have you seen him yet?" he inquired, bending over the excited little half-breed, "have you seen him yet?"

A round-shot cast up a splash of mud and water in front of them.

"He not there at prayson," stammered forth poor Vasseur. "Mebbe he not care about zis t'ing varee likely."

The front of the British column dashed up to the ditch; a few brave fellows floundered through it and rushed right into the muzzles of the American guns.

But it was not for mortal courage to stem that humming current of missiles. A thirty-two-pounder was loaded to the muzzle with musket-balls and fragments of metal. Just as the column thickened close along the ditch, the gunner, with steady hand, lowered the piece so that the dreadful charge would rake the level surface of the ground and fired. Never, perhaps, in the history of warfare was there another so destructive a shot. The historians tell (what is too incredible even for romance) that two hundred British soldiers were killed outright by that storm of lead and iron, that one blast of the breath of war!

The whole front of the charging column had melted down.

Peevy still stood on the breastwork, peeping through the battle-smoke, trying always to aim at some particular one of the enemy before firing Mary Ann.

Pakenham had been given another horse, and although one of the scout's bullets had hit him, he mounted and went to the head of the column once more to re-form it. But he was doomed. A grape-shot dashed him, dying, to the ground.

General Gibbs took command. Peevy saw him and signaled him out for his aim.

Mary Ann was merciless. Officer after officer fell. Down dropped Gibbs; over went Keane; Dale fell dead; indeed, it seemed that no man who undertook to lead the columns could escape those special messages of Mary Ann when directed by the imperturbable aim of the scout.

So the battle went; the British recoiled, plunged forward, tumbled in bleeding heaps, broke, rallied, charged again and again. That little, muddy ditch, with its slippery banks and slow, dark tide, was the line of death. No man crossed it and lived.

At the last desperate moment, a man, superbly mounted, was seen calling together the bravest spirits of the English army. He rode like a king; his face was as cold as marble and yet scintillant with magnetic energy.

General Jackson leveled his old field-glass upon him and actually recoiled.

"That devil!" he exclaimed, and his bronzed and jaundiced visage showed a sudden excitement. "A renegade, by the eternal!"

Vasseur saw the new leader and leaned over the breastwork to gaze at him. So attracted was he by the apparition that he forgot his fear.

Mr. Vernon looked and turned pale. The enemy's line re-formed, the Highlanders in front, and came on again, this time with a steady sweep that appeared resistless.

Peevy was still at his stand, reloading Mary Ann as calmly as if he were going to shoot a squirrel.

"He air a long ways off, Mary Ann," muttered he, "but we mus' re'ch 'im, ole gal!"

He lifted the rifle and took deliberate sight over the long barrel. The sharp report was lost in the general roar of the fight. Had he missed? There was no sign to the contrary.

"Pierre Rameau! *Violà!* See! It's Pierre Rameau!" screamed Vasseur, dancing around wildly.

General Jackson came almost running along the line, the white foam of excitement fringing his bloodless lips.

"Shoot that eternal, infernal scoundrel for me, Peevy!" he shouted, pointing his long, emaciated finger toward the new British leader. "Shoot him! Kill him!"

"Thet air 's jes' w'at I tole Mary Ann," replied the scout, priming his rifle.

Jackson snatched up an old musket that had been flung down by some one and aimed it. It snapped harmlessly. He dashed it aside with furious emphasis and stood gazing in stark anger.

On came that steady, shining line, the regiment of Highlanders stepping all as one man.

"Blow 'em up!" yelled Jackson. "Blow 'em to the devil! Shoot that officer! Everybody aim at him! Do you hear? Shoot that man on the horse!"

"Thet 's the doctrine w'at I'm er preachin' ter Mary Ann," responded Peevy.

Vasseur was so excited that he forgot to prime his gun and, when at last he did prime it, he had rammed home three loads, and so, when he fired, it almost kicked him over. He thought he was wounded in the shoulder. He cursed in three languages.

The horseman rode right up to the ditch and waved his hand to signal the charging troops to cross it.

Peevy fired. The man's right arm fell to his side; but he took the bridle reins in his teeth and waved his hat with his left hand.

"Shoot that devil, I tell you, Peevy, shoot him!"

"Ef ye'll shet erp yer mouth, gin'r'l, an' quit er botherin' me wi' yer talk, I'll do it yit!" cried the scout, with peevish fretfulness in his voice. "Mary

Ann cayn't stan' no sich jawin' es this yar 'at ye'r' a-givin' us! Go on erbout yer own business an' le' me erlone!"

The general probably did not hear these words; but if he did he made no response, for Peevy was a privileged character.

Mr. Vernon stood mute and motionless, his eyes fixed upon that desperate horseman.

"Order your men to shoot at that officer—that renegade yonder!" Jackson stormed in the old man's ear.

Mr. Vernon made no response, but turned and walked away.

Just then the batteries and the rifles of Carroll's men all roared out as one. A level flood of destruction poured across the ditch. For a few moments the smoke enveloped the American line so that nothing could be seen. Still the marksmen had the range and kept on firing by guess, doing frightful havoc.

When the cloud lifted, the whole British army had apparently melted away. All over the level field lay heaps and windrows of the slain. A few scattered redcoats shone in the distance, their wearers in precipitate flight. Broken cannon, tumbled fascines and crushed ladders marked the straggling route of the British Forty-fourth Regiment, which had been assigned to the duty of making the ditch crossable. One company, not far from the river, was seen trying to re-form, although half of its men were already dead and the living ones nearly all wounded.

The rider who had been so boldly conspicuous was urging his sorely crippled horse away across the field toward the wood. He still had the reins in his teeth, while both arms dangled at his sides.

The terrible thirty-two-pounder was fired once more, and the horse went down, torn into shreds; but up rose that dark, determined cavalier and steadily continued his retreat on foot.

A yell of admiration burst forth from the victorious Americans as they gazed.

Then a still stranger sight met their eyes. A tall old man, who had climbed over the breastworks from the American side, set off at a tottering but singularly swift gait in the direction of the British lines. When he reached the fatal ditch, beyond which the ground was heaped with slain, he floundered through it and arose, muddy and dripping, on the farther bank. There he paused for a moment, wiped the ooze from his face and then went right on.

It was Max Burns, the preacher. And who was that little man running after him? The onlookers had scarcely had time to make out before the cloud of smoke settled down again and hid both from view.

Mr. Vernon stood like a grim statue while this was going on. Very well he knew what it was that impelled both Burns and Vasseur.

CHAPTER XXV.

PRISONERS.

When Lapin recoiled before the incoming men out at the plantation-house and uttered the name of Pierre Rameau, Mrs. Vernon, Pauline and Mademoiselle de Sezannes began to shriek, rushing together into one another's arms.

Colonel Loring entered, followed by two or three ill-favored men. If he was surprised at seeing the three ladies so frightened at the mere mention of his name—the name he had come to like best—he did not show it in his calm, cold face, or by even the slightest movement.

He stood a moment as if to make sure of his vision and then stalked forward in his peculiar half-graceful, half-dogged way to where the group of frightened and crying women stood.

"Why, Madame Vernon!" he cried. "Is this you? And you, Miss Pauline! And Mademoiselle de Sezannes!"

He looked at them askance, but with no particular interest.

"Oh, it is Colonel Loring!" cried Mrs. Vernon,

springing toward him, almost as if to embrace him, in her sudden sense of relief. "I was frightened nearly out of my senses; oh, I'm so very glad!"

The man smiled so that his face for the moment flashed forth a fascinating light from its almost stolid features. He took Mrs. Vernon's hand, and at the same time looked at Pauline and Mademoiselle de Sezannes.

"I am making my way to my friends," he said, "and came in here thinking to get some information. I did not dream of the pleasure of finding you here."

He told the lie with consummate ease and naturalness.

The young ladies now came forward smiling through their tears and greeted him warmly. For the moment even Mademoiselle de Sezannes forgot that he had made himself odious to her.

Meantime Lapin stood open-mouthed and wondering to see that terrible robber received so considerately by his mistress and Pauline.

"I am on my way to join the British army," Loring went on to say, with perfect indifference in his tone. "I think they are quite near here."

Mrs. Vernon recoiled from him, horrified. Pauline's face whitened.

"But you are jesting," said Mademoiselle de Sezannes. "You would not do that."

"Why not?" he demanded, with something like brutal emphasis. "What should hinder me? These Americans have set a price on my head; and, besides, I am a Scotchman. I owe my allegiance to my country."

The scene in the theatre rose in Mademoiselle de Sezannes's memory at once, and so vividly that she clasped her hands and uttered a little cry of pain and anger.

Loring smiled sardonically, feeling her thought, as it were, flung upon him.

"This country is too small for both me and my enemies," he smiled, "and so for a few days I leave them in possession; but when I return," and his face showed a sudden concentration of passion, "when I return, they will be glad to get out of my way."

He turned and waved his hand, and his men retired from the house.

"Go give them something to eat," he said to Lapin.

Then he began tramping heavily back and forth across the floor.

Pauline went to him and timidly yet with a certain firmness laid her hand on his arm. She walked beside him. It was a strange picture they made. The girl's impulse could not have been explained by her; she felt as if she could save him, as if some great spring in her nature compelled her to try.

The thought that the British army was very near her had affected Mrs. Vernon to such a degree that she could not feel the full force of what was impelling Pauline. As for Mademoiselle de Sezannes, she stood shivering with a chill of blended emotions while she gazed at Loring.

It is the last refinement of torture when we feel that we hate and detest and yet have to admire-

Loring compelled Mademoiselle de Sezannes's admiration in some mysterious way. His manly beauty, marred with the gloom of evil as it was, had yet the fascination which captivates while it repels. As he walked with Pauline hanging on his arm, it was like Satan leading an angel of heaven and still there came from his dark face the unmistakable and irresistible demand for sympathy.

"Do not go," murmured Pauline; "stay with us. I do not know why, but I feel that I cannot let you go."

Her appeal was so simply spoken, so earnest, so evidently straight from the heart that Loring looked down into her face with sudden softening of his cruel eyes. He did not speak, but she saw his look.

"You know that it is not right for you to—"

"Right!" he interrupted. "I never did a right thing in my life. Doing right would be a new experience."

"Begin now," she urged. "You will find it very comforting."

"Do you know who I am?" he demanded, almost gruffly.

"Yes, I know."

"No, you do not. If you did, you would not touch me, speak to me, look at me. You would abhor me."

"I heard your name just a while ago."

"Ah, that name! Yes, you heard that. Is it not dreadful to you?"

"You might be a good man yet."

"The words come easily; but deeds are not so

lightly fashioned. If I had always had one like you to influence me—"

"It is yourself that must do that. You are no child to be influenced. I am scarcely more than a child myself, but I know that—"

"You know absolutely nothing."

"I know that, if you would try, you could be a good man. Forgive me, if I say that you are bad; but—"

He laughed outright and looked at her as one looks at a child when it has said some laughable thing.

She let go his arm and stood facing him. Her attitude and her fresh and delicate beauty made her look like a tall, graceful flower.

He reached a hand and half caressingly touched her hair. It was the thing that a brother would have done; there was no way of resenting it.

"I'd rather have a biscuit and a glass of wine than a lecture," he said, lightly enough. "Can't you offer me something to eat and drink? I'm hungry."

"Yes, certainly."

They together approached Mrs. Vernon and Mademoiselle de Sezannes, who had been standing helplessly looking upon what was to them an inexplicable scene.

"Colonel Loring has not had dinner," Pauline said to her mother; "we must be hospitable."

Mademoiselle de Sezannes shrank away as they came up.

Loring noticed this and gave her a smile which

made his face show all of its evil beauty. He waved his hand at her and said :

"You hate me because I punished Ballanche for his impudence." His lip curled.

"He and Jackson will be apt to remember me," he added, after a moment's pause.

Mrs. Vernon hastened to set some food for him, and he ate and drank heartily.

Pauline was in a strange state of mind. She felt irresistibly urged from within to do something, she knew not what, for the benefit of this dark, wicked, fascinating man. It made her shudder to see him, and she shrank from the thought of his past life— knowing now that he was Pierre Rameau, the outlaw—but yet some fountain in her heart bled for him, some center of sympathy in the deepest chamber of her soul sent forth a thrill in his behalf. She was, to a degree, like one in a dream, albeit she realized to the full the hopelessness of the desire that was forming in her breast. How could she do anything to turn this strong man back from evil? She remembered that she had, when a child, seen the officials taking a young man to the scaffold to be executed. He was a mere youth, hard-faced and repulsive ; but ever since she had regretted that she could not go to him and show him that one of all the world was sorry for him. Why should she recall that scene at this moment? The human heart beats through mysterious rhythms. We can never say by what labyrinths the roots of sympathy travel to reach their end. If Pauline could have known all the history of this man, she might have felt none of the inexplicable fascination which came to her like a vague but powerful reminder of something sadly but unmistakably imperative in her nature; but she was aware now of just enough to arouse all the romance as well as all the pity that an inexperienced young girl's heart can compass.

When Loring arose from the table at which he had eaten, he turned to Mademoiselle de Sezannes and appeared about to speak, but he checked himself.

"Thank you," he said to Mrs. Vernon. "I was very hungry. I will now go to the British lines, unless"—he hesitated just for a breath—"unless you will permit me to help you and the young ladies back to New Orleans. Indeed, this is no place for you."

He had scarcely ceased speaking, when one of his men unceremoniously broke into the room and exclaimed, with blunt, rough vehemence:

"We're surrounded! The British are all around the place!"

When Loring's companion ran in with the cry, "We are surrounded! The British are all around the place!" the ladies were dumbfounded. They stood like white-faced statues.

Loring did not appear to find anything startling in the situation.

"Do not be alarmed," he said, shrugging his shoulders and again touching Pauline's hair with a half-playful yet perfectly respectful expression of regard. "I shall not be long settling with my friends. Excuse me for a few moments."

He walked boldly out through the front door, followed by his man. As he passed close to Mrs. Vernon, he stooped toward her and said, with a ring of impatience in his voice :

"Your husband must have been quite out of his senses when he sent you ladies out here. But be calm. You shall not be ill-treated."

There was a stir out-of-doors—a sound of voices. Some low commands were given. Mrs. Vernon and Mademoiselle de Sezannes became hysterical, but Pauline, though pale as a ghost, seemed to have found ample strength to bear whatever was to come. She thought she heard her father's voice at the door. It was Loring speaking with the British officer. The two entered a moment later.

"They must be taken to some place where they can be protected," Loring was saying.

"Certainly, if it can be done," the officer replied. "But we are in no condition to take care of ladies."

"Send them to New Orleans."

"No, sir. That is against positive orders. We are to permit no white person to go from us to the enemy. No ; we must take them. If you are what you claim to be, the general will receive you kindly and give the ladies the best comforts that he can command. That is all that I can say."

"I advise you to treat me with respect, sir," said Loring, very calmly, and fixing his eyes with a malignant stare on those of the officer. "You will know more of me."

"Do as I command you!" exclaimed the sturdy Englishman. "I'm not to be bullied by a prisoner !

Bundle up these women and put them on your horses. You will walk. There's no time for talk. Move along!"

Loring compressed his lips, but said not another word. He saw that for once he had found a check to his arrogance. He explained to the ladies that all were prisoners and that they would have to go to the British commander's headquarters."

"I commend you to the good-will of Lieutenant Barnaby," he said, bowing with perfect ease toward the officer. "He feels as big as a drum-major at present."

"Silence, sir, or I'll have you gagged in an instant!" exclaimed the lieutenant.

"You could not gag a hen!" sneered Loring.

The lieutenant whipped out his sword; his face was ablaze with choler.

The ladies began to shriek. Pauline sprang between the men. Loring put her gently but forcibly aside; then lifted the lapel of his coat and leaned forward.

"Put your sword-point through that!" he exclaimed, laying his finger on a shining badge that covered his heart. "Thrust away, young man! Thrust away!"

The face of the officer paled as suddenly as it had reddened. He stood as if faltering for a moment, and then saluted.

Loring responded with lofty indifference, and turning to Mrs. Vernon bade her make haste to go with her captors.

"I will protect you all," he said, turning to Mademoiselle de Sezannes. "You will be safer with the army than in New Orleans." After a moment he turned to the lieutenant and said :

"Hurry things up, let us be off."

It was a curious change ; the prisoner seemed to be in command.

"You will ride my horse," he said to Pauline, taking her gently by the arm, "and I am going to walk along beside you. Wrap yourself up well, for it is chilly out in this night fog.

CHAPTER XXVI.

ACROSS THE BATTLE-FIELD.

After the great battle was over, Lieutenant Ballanche was sent by General Jackson to confer with the British officers regarding the burial of the dead lying so thickly tumbled together on that bloody plain. In the course of the interview he did not fail to make inquiries concerning the captive ladies, and when he was told that they were in a small country house not far from the battle-field, he felt his heart leap. He had to smother impatience, however, and go on with his military duties just as though love were a matter of subordinate importance, and as if the burial of a few hundred invaders were of higher obligation than rescuing a beautiful and adorable sweetheart from a situation of suffering and danger. A young man must be under good discipline to be thus wedded to military duty; but it may be remembered that Andrew Jackson had a way of making every one about him regard orders as absolutely binding beyond even life itself.

What set the terrible sting of doubt in the lieutenant's heart and made him chafe through every moment of that seemingly interminable conference, was the fact that none of the British officers could tell him whether or not the captives were still safe from harm. All that they could say was to the effect that the ladies had been kindly treated and safely guarded up to the time of the battle. Since then no one had seen them or heard of them. And what might have happened during that wild rush of overthrow, when the whole British army was torn and scattered, and when the exasperated soldiers were left to shift for themselves without officers to restrain them? The thought was one to chill the young man's blood; but he went on with the conference, his agitation showing only in a certain austerity of manner which the British officers attributed to native churlishness. When at last he had finished the matter, he hastened to General Jackson with his report.

Mr. Vernon was present when he arrived at headquarters and had already asked leave to go in search of his family. The old man's face lighted up wonderfully when Ballanche told what he knew.

"And they are safe!" he exclaimed, showing more passionate excitement than any one had ever witnessed in him before. "They told you that they were safe?" A singularly beseeching note rang through his words.

The lieutenant could not have the heart to tell him that there was a doubt.

General Jackson would not permit any precipitate action. He reminded Mr. Vernon that a truce was pending and that due formalities must be observed in the matter of penetrating the British lines for any purpose. The old man bore the delay in the spirit of a caged lion. It seemed to him that a year might have elapsed since he parted from his wife and daughter; every moment now dragged by like a snail.

What added a peculiar dread to the situation was the thought of Loring, Vasseur and old man Burns all going in the direction which might lead them to where Mrs. Vernon and Pauline had been left by their captors. Mr. Vernon's whole mind dwelt on the fear that his wife and daughter might be told the secret of his past life. His imagination, which was as vigorous and lawless as his frame was stalwart, built up all manner of dark prophecies and filled him with forebodings too dreadful for any thought to give them definite form. He accused himself with all the bitterness of which self-accusation is possible. Why had he not left his loved ones at home where they would have been so safe now? What demon had possessed him to send them (of all places in the world) to that plantation-house right in the path of the British army?

When at last, after hours of delay, all necessary formalities had been observed and everything was ready, General Jackson ordered six men detailed to accompany Mr. Vernon and Lieutenant Ballanche on their journey of love.

Old Enos Peevy was one of the squad. A young British officer joined them to see them safe to their destination. They were all mounted; but three of the horses were to bear the ladies back to the American lines.

A rough bridge had been hastily cast across the ditch of death, and over this Mr. Vernon led the way, passing into the awful swaths of war's reaping. Peevy rode beside him, sitting awkwardly but firmly on a little creole pony, his long, bony legs reaching down so far that his feet almost touched the blood-tinged ground. He was very much interested in noting the condition of the dead British as he passed along.

"Thar's a feller 'at I plumpted a hole through," he exclaimed presently with great satisfaction, pointing toward a stalwart Highlander outstretched on his back. "I put it to 'im jes' ez 'e war—"

"Hush, man!" said Mr. Vernon in an undertone, "remember that we have an English officer with us."

"Oh, tarnation take the officer! W'at air I er keerin' fer 'im?" grumbled the scout. "I wush 'at I'd er got a bead onter him. Ef I hed it 'd er ben good-bye 'at Mary Ann 'd said to 'im."

If the English officer heard what was said he discreetly kept silent.

As they rode along, picking their way between the heaps of slain, their horses stumbling over the ruts made by cannon-balls, Lieutenant Ballanche looked back toward the low breastworks behind which he had fought, and it required but a glance to comprehend the fatal mistake made by the British. The deadly ditch looked harmless enough from this side—a man would think he could jump across it.

Mr. Vernon could not bear a moderate pace. As soon as they were well beyond the first windrow of the battle he urged his horse to a canter, then into a gallop. Ballanche spurred forward and joined him. A mighty impatience was burning the blood of the two men.

"How far is it yet!" Mr. Vernon huskily demanded, after they had gone beyond the battle-field proper and passed through a stretch of wet, plashy woods.

"Just yonder, around the point of magnolias," was the almost breathless answer. "The house is behind those trees."

The old man leaned forward in his saddle and put his horse to its best.

"I fear that we shall run into trouble at this rate," said the English officer who had chanced to come side by side with Enos Peevy.

"Ef we do," said the scout, with a grim leer, "I'll pop you the fust one. Mary Ann yer, w'at I hev in my han', kinder wants ter mek yer 'quaintance anyhow."

The conversation ended at once. The Englishman bit his lip and drew in his horse so as to fall behind. Soon enough he was out of sight, and the

Americans saw him no more. He was tired of the ride.

Mr. Vernon and Lieutenant Ballanche were too much absorbed in the thought of reaching the magnolia point and coming within view of the house to note the absence of the officer until Peevy called to them :

"Thet air feller hey snoke off," he cried, in his shrill treble. "That etarnal orficer air gone!"

They slackened their pace to let him come up with them.

"Let him go," said Mr. Vernon, when he understood the matter, "we don't need him." And again they spurred on.

Lieutenant Ballanche had a fresher, stronger horse than the one that bore Mr. Vernon and by the time that they had swung round the point with the little plantation-house full in view he was considerably in the lead.

It was with an indescribable stifling sensation that he leaned over his saddle-horn and gazed between straggling orange trees toward the low doorway beyond a broken gate. The place looked lonely and desolate ; it was a picture of silence set against a gray background of wilderness.

Mr. Vernon and Ballanche had ridden into the enclosure and were approaching the house. The walk or pathway was narrow and Mr. Vernon was now in advance. Suddenly he drew his horse back with such force that it almost stood upright on its haunches ; at the same time he uttered a deep ejaculation of surprise and horror.

A man lay dead, doubled up across the path near the front-door of the house. Mr. Vernon recognized the face instantly, although it was pinched and distorted.

Peevy saw that something startling had been discovered and hurried through the gate.

"W'at air the matter now, fellers?" he inquired. Then, seeing the dead body, he added: "W'y, it air thet thar feller 'at went er cavortin'—"

He was interrupted by a sharp cry from the house, and the door was flung wide open.

"Etarnal Jerusalem!" he exclaimed. "Jes' look, will ye!"

Mr. Vernon and Ballanche were already looking. They had seen many dead men that day, had ridden past them and over them, but this one demanded more than a glance, at least from Mr. Vernon, who did not look at once, even when the voice rang out from the opening door of the house.

CHAPTER XXVII.

A WOUNDED LION.

Meantime, Mrs. Vernon, Pauline and Mademoiselle de Sezannes had not been ill-treated beyond what the exigencies of life in the immediate vicinity of the British camp made inevitable. The commanding officer ordered them to be kept in the small house already described and furnished them food and a guard. Under the circumstances, this was the best that he could do. He felt that to send them through the lines would be a dangerous proceeding, as he was relying upon surprising the Americans.

Colonel Loring found no difficulty in securing the favor of General Keane, and, later, General Pakenham himself recognized him as one who had done him a great and dangerous service years before. Moreover, Loring brought with him perfect maps and drawings of all the American defenses and full descriptions and reports of all the troops under Jackson and the probable order of their distribution, nor did he neglect to exhibit, as if half by accident, the newspapers containing the sensational accounts of his daring assault upon General Jackson's nose. He volunteered to lead a reconnoitering party in the direction of the American lines, and the result was a full confirmation of his previous statements regarding the probable plans of Jackson for the defense of New Orleans. All this aided him, but his personal magnetism went much farther. There was something in him that drew men of daring and reckless courage to him and held them there. His voice, his manner, his steady, fearless eyes and the look of absolute self-assurance which seemed to be the natural expression of his face made way for him even in the councils of the generals. Men of iron found him a man of adamant, nor did they look through to the darker side of his being; men rarely trouble themselves with what is not most available in their fellows.

Loring found time to be kind to the captive women, and especially to Pauline he showed almost tender solicitude in seeking her comfort. He did not often enter into conversation with her, nor were his visits more than merely formal. Pauline, however, in her great desire to know what was going on and what was likely to be the outcome of the impending battle watched for his coming each day, with the hope that he would have something to say which would lessen the strain of suspense.

Day after day went by, meantime, with nothing to break the dread monotony or to soften the horror of seeing the English troops swell in numbers and of hearing the preparation of an overwhelming column of attack which was meant to sweep the little American band before it like dry leaves before a breeze.

Mademoiselle de Sezannes hated Loring more and more as the time dragged on. She treated him with the cold courtesy of a scornful politeness when she was forced to accept a favor at his hands; but he appeared not to notice her mood. His whole mind seemed occupied with the thought of contributing all that he could to insuring the best disposition and direction of the British forces. The little and yet in some way strangely significant marks of attention shown by him to Pauline were the only signs of any turning, even for a moment, from his concentrated singleness of interest.

The house on which our attention for the present centers stood at the edge of a dark wood bordering a swamp. Its front looked toward the plain upon which were being made the preparations for battle. Westward and not far away the muddy current of the Mississippi tumbled along darkly behind a low levee. It was a rough wooden building plainly furnished and but recently abandoned in great haste by its owner. Two elderly slave-women were appointed to serve the captives.

After the night-fight already hastily sketched, Loring came to the house and reported that the Americans had shown their strength and mode of warfare and that now it would be an easy thing to attack them in force and destroy them. He appeared somewhat more animated than Pauline had ever before seen him; but she could not be sure what his excitement indicated; it may have been, she thought after he was gone, no more than the after-glow of the battle-spirit. It was evident, even to her inexperienced mind, that the British had not been successful in the engagement; but when, later on, the reinforcements landed and poured across the plain, when the great cannon went lumbering by, when the flags streamed out and the thousands of red uniforms shone in thick array, seen in the distance through the straggling orange-grove, she felt that all hope was indeed gone.

Mrs. Vernon and Mademoiselle de Sezannes had been despondent and given over to moaning and tears from the first. Pauline, even when despair came, preserved her composure. Loring noted this steadfastness of will in the girl, and it seemed to appeal to him as through a strain of likeness to his own character, strange as such a comparison might be; and once, when Mademoiselle de Sezannes looked at the two standing near each other, she saw, as by a flash of sudden revelation, a striking resemblance between their faces, especially in the way of lengthening and narrowing the eyes in moments of deep feeling.

"I hate you, almost," she said to Pauline, when Loring was gone, "because you look like that man."

"Look like him!" exclaimed Mrs. Vernon. "What a horrid jest!"

"It is horrible, but it is no jest," said Mademoiselle de Sezannes, with emphasis. "Just now their eyes were precisely alike."

Pauline was offended, and drew herself up to turn away. The quick rush of resentment, well repressed though it was, exemplified the theory of Mademoiselle de Sezannes. Madame Vernon saw the flattening and leveling of the beautiful eyelids and caught the momentary gleam from the lengthening eyes.

She started hysterically, and would have spoken had not Loring returned rather hastily to say that the battle would open on the following morning—this had just been determined upon—and that it was absolutely necessary for them to remain close shut in the house until all should be over.

And so when, in the small hours of the following night, the low, wide stir began, the women knew that the British columns were forming for the great assault.

The day was a terrible one for them. They

could not see any part of the battle ; but the grinding roar of it rolled over the house, which shook as if with an earthquake. It seemed to them that they could hear the despairing cry of the Americans as they fell crushed and bleeding under the victorious columns of their enemies. Mrs. Vernon clasped the tiny gold crucifix which hung at her throat and kneeling in agony prayed and wept. Mademoiselle de Sezannes cast herself upon a couch and hid her face in the pillows ; but Pauline stood at a front window straining her eyes and ears to see and hear.

Before the middle of the forenoon the thunder and the patter of the fight gradually ceased, and soon enough the broken and fear-crazed columns of the British came wildly straggling back across the plain. What had been solid walls of red uniformed soldiers moving with rhythmic vigor and steadiness was now a confused rabble, leaderless and dispersed, all flying away from an imaginary charging column of Americans.

"Heaven be praised!" cried Pauline. "They are flying! They are defeated! They are driven back all wild and routed!"

She precipitated herself upon her mother in an ecstasy of joy.

Mademoiselle de Sezannes sprang up and ran to the window. Off in the distance, as she looked between the orange trees, she saw men bearing litters, rolling cannon, running, limping, gesticulating, assisting wounded comrades, leading horses on which lay dead officers—it was a terrible sight : but in the first rush of her realization of triumph she felt no horror from the scene. She clasped her hands together and gazed with wide open tearless eyes.

It was nearly noon when the servants brought in breakfast; meantime the British had disappeared, and a great silence lay upon the plain and the woods. The ladies had eaten nothing for twenty-four hours, and now, with the great reaction from the strain of terrible anxiety, there came hunger. But food did not seem to attract them; they ran to the windows and doors every minute or two only to turn away, disappointed, from the desolate scene.

At last, however, a footfall on the doorsteps was accompanied by the voice of Colonel Loring.

"Miss Pauline, will you let me in, please?" he called.

Pauline ran to the door and opened it. At first she did not notice that Loring was bloody. He stood quite erect, and his face showed no sign of suffering.

"Come in," she cried, "come in, Colonel Loring. It is so good of you—we are so frightened, so bewildered, so lonely."

She extended both hands with the impulse of her delight at the relief his presence afforded.

He inclined his hatless head and smiled in acknowledgment of her greeting, and now she saw that both his arms hung powerless, dangling and bloody.

"Oh, you are hurt, wounded!" she exclaimed. "You have been shot!"

"It is of no consequence; some light hurts that

will give no trouble. Is there any wine in the house?"

He came in with a firm step and sat down in a large armed chair.

There was a half-bottle of claret, which Pauline fetched. He drank the whole of it thirstily.

"It is a wonder that this is left," he said, nodding toward the empty bottle after Pauline had poured the last drop down his throat.

"General Gibbs sent it to us," she said.

"And he is killed; so is Pakenham; indeed, they are all killed; the army is destroyed, it destroyed itself. What a set of dolts they all were!" Loring spoke rapidly, but seemingly without much feeling.

Before he had finished there was a knock at the door. Mademoiselle de Sezannes, who chanced to be nearest it, flung it open.

Vasseur came in without ceremony and stood before Loring, his face twitching with the ecstasy of terrible passion. Immediately he began to pour forth the most horrible curses, and between them he sandwiched what he knew of Loring's past history. It was a denunciation at once eloquent and brutal beyond description. Loring for once was unable to meet an exigency with a prompt bar. He sat calmly enough; but he could not stop the current. Vasseur, in his wild wrath, seeing that his victim was apparently helpless, went with a rush into the revolting details of the life which he and Loring had passed together as outlaws in Spain. They had robbed a convent, killing a nun to get the jewels and precious stones afterward taken from Vasseur by Pierre Rameau. He went on to tell how Loring and Pierre Rameau were the same man, and how Margaret, the robber's wife, had been murdered by him in cold blood because she sought the protection of a priest to escape brutality.

It was a story to chill the blood of any hearer, and its double climax was reached when Vasseur dwelt upon the whipping that Rameau had caused him to submit to and the attempt to murder old man Burns in the wilderness of the Pearl-River country.

The ladies retreated before the blasphemous torrent of mingled confession, denunciation and profanity.

Vasseur spoke so rapidly that his say was soon ended, and then he sprang at Loring with a dagger.

"Die, Pierre Rameau!" he shrieked, in creole patois. "Die! Die!"

But Pierrre Rameau had heard such tragic commands before this. He had played a part in tragedy too often to be taken by surprise and laid out so easily.

"Fool!" was all that he said; and, rising with the promptness of a steel spring, he kicked the little man through the open doorway into the yard.

Vasseur arose from where he had fallen, put his hands on his chest, tottered for a few paces along the walk toward the gate, then sank down, all doubled together, and lay still.

Pierre Rameau stood gazing at the crumpled body for a moment, and when, presently, he lifted his calm, almost stolid eyes, he saw a tall form coming through the gate.

It was Burns. The old man saw him, and quickened his pace almost to a run.

Rameau turned about and passed through the house without a word. Going out, he crossed what had been a vegetable garden, kicked some palings from a fence, went through and was soon in the depth of the wood.

He was feeling the effect of his wounds. Not only were both his arms badly hurt; but a gun-shot rent in his breast, though it bled little, was weakening him rapidly.

Pauline saw him going away and ran after him entreating him to return and have his hurts cared for. Something in his face had told her that he was desperate, hopeless, and she felt a great swell of pity for him rising in her heart.

She had not noticed the fall of Vasseur or the approach of Burns. Just within the gloom of the moss-hung forest she overtook Rameau and sprang lightly before him.

He stood still and looked at her. A smile stole into his face; he tried to lift a hand; but could only twitch a shoulder. She was flushed and panting, her lips apart, her bright hair disheveled. Her appearance seemed to touch him with some deep emotion.

"My sweet sister," he murmured, then as if shaking off an illusion, he sprang past her while she was pouring forth entreaties, and fairly ran away from her into the gloomy swamp wood.

Pauline stood, like one in a dream, with the words, "my sweet sister," ringing strangely as if from distance to distance through her soul.

She saw, without fairly realizing it, the tall, gaunt form of Burns go by with long, half-feeble, half-vigorous strides.

CHAPTER XXVIII.

A GLIMPSE OF LOVE.

That morning of the eighth day of January was one of awful suspense to the patriotic women of New Orleans. Everything that could make life worth living depended upon the issue of the fight whose heavy billows of sound came rolling up the river to shake the foundations of the city.

Madame Souvestre, as she stood at the window of the chamber in which Fairfax lay, held one hand upon her heart. She felt it leaping heavily with mingled dread and joy. Each throb was for the brave men battling down there in the fog of morning, and each throb was also for the handsome soldier lying within four paces of her, weak and wounded, in her sole care.

The window-panes jarred with every palpitation of the battle-thunder. She turned now and again to look at Fairfax.

"Do not try to move," she would say; "it will

hurt you. Be brave and patient; it will come out well."

Then she would go and smooth his pillows or adjust the snowy spread of his couch. Her tiny hands trembled, and a bright rosy spot showed under the petal-like skin of either cheek.

He tried to talk to her about the battle, but she put one sweet hand over his mouth and shook her head.

"Listen and be calm, but do not speak," she commanded; and he had to obey.

"Monsieur Crapaud Crapoussin will return after a while," she went on, "and he will tell us glorious news. I know that our brave men are killing those British; I feel it in every drop of my blood. Hear how our guns crash and roll!"

She clasped her hands before her and stood in an attitude of intense, passionate attention to the tumbling and bounding din as it seemed to fill all space by jars and throbs.

Fairfax gazed at her through the crepuscular shadows of the chamber, and, to his feverish and misty imagination, she appeared to irradiate a heavenly light, so that a pale, tender aureole trembled about her. A peaceful languor seized him, and he slept.

The streets were deserted and silent, and as the fog grew tenuous and vanished before the coming of the sun, the cannon roar seemed more distant.

Madame Souvestre wandered around in the chamber, moving noiselessly, covering her face now and again with her hands.

Slowly the moments passed. She looked at her jeweled watch; it was nine o'clock, and the guns had almost ceased their thunder. Fairfax was breathing heavily, but his sleep seemed natural. She bent over him and touched his hair with a furtive tender movement. How could he feel so light a stroke on his loosely tumbled locks?

"Ah, Pauline; you have come to me again! How kind, how sweet!" he murmured. "And the battle is over, and we shall not be parted any more!"

The little woman drew back from the sleeper and tured pale; then a hot glow suffused her cheeks. She trembled and held her brow with both hands.

"Pauline! Pauline!" she whispered. "He loves some one—Pauline! Pauline! But it may be his sister. Yes, yes, his voice was so gentle and calm; Pauline is his sister."

Once more she cast herself upon the *priedieu* and lifted prayerful eyes to the Virgin.

A black woman, with a spotless white turban on her head came in, carrying a silver tray with coffee which she placed on the table. She glanced askance at Madame Souvestre, and then silently withdrew.

The rich brew in the shining pot filled the room with its fragrance. A plump-faced masculine saint looked down from a dark frame on the wall; his lips appeared ready to ask for a cup.

Fairfax awoke.

"Pauline! Pauline!" he gently called.

Madame Souvestre sprang up.

"Oh! Ah!" he murmured, looking at her inquiringly.

"You have had a good sleep," she remarked, "and you look refreshed. Here is some coffee."

"I have been dreaming," he said, smiling apologetically, "and at first—"

"At first you thought Mademoiselle Pauline was here."

"How do you know?"

"You are not reserved. You speak freely when you dream."

"Do I? Well, it is all right if I did not disturb you."

"Disturb me? Oh, no, not at all. I only heard you calling for Mademoiselle Pauline. She is your sister?"

"It was a most vivid dream. But the battle! Have you heard? Do you know how it is going?"

"You do not hear any more guns," she said, turning to help him with his coffee, "but no word has arrived yet. Surely, Monsieur Crapoussin will arrive soon."

She put one hand under his head and with the other held the cup to his lips, while he took a hearty draught of the pungent black liquid.

"Thank you, madame. That was delicious—the best coffee that I ever tasted; and I feel so much better. Surely, there will be good news. But what is that noise?"

Madame Souvestre set the coffee on the table and hastened to the window. People were rushing along the street, shouting, gesticulating, grimacing wildly. Men, women, children, all appeared to be possessed by an uncontrollable excitement. Hats flew up into the air, old men were behaving like boys. She turned toward Fairfax with a great light in her face and said :

"It is victory! I hear them rejoicing! Listen!"

The tumult increased momentarily, and above it all they heard voices singing the "Marseillaise."

A servant admitted Crapaud Crapoussin whose left ear was under a white bandage that showed a stain of blood.

"It is glorious!" cried he, pirouetting across the floor, "and see, I am wounded! A bullet tore a gash in my ear; I shall have honorable mention! But, oh, it is a great victory! We tore them all to rags!"

He went to the bedside and took a hand of Fairfax between both of his.

"Ah, monsieur, the whole plain down yonder is red with dead British soldiers, and our army is not hurt," he went on rapidly, almost out of breath.

"Crapaud," said Fairfax, "go fetch Mademoiselle Pauline Vernon here to me."

Madame Souvestre started and looked quickly back and forth, from Fairfax to the dwarf.

"Mademoiselle Pauline Vernon," she repeated, with a confused expression in her face, "oh, to be sure; but—" she hesitated.

"I made a foolish request," said Fairfax, quickly. "Of course it cannot be done. Forgive me, I fear my strength has fallen off until my mind is weak."

"No, no, monsieur; but you talk too much; you

must not do it. Certainly, though, Mademoiselle Vernon can come to my house to see you. Go, Crapaud, order my carriage and bring the mademoiselle here."

She followed Crapaud out of the room, and when they were on the stair she stopped him and said:

"Is Mademoiselle Vernon his cousin or other kin?"

"No, madame."

"Is he her lover?"

"Yes, madame."

"Crapaud Crapoussin, if you bring her here, I will kill you, do you hear?"

"Yes, madame."

She wrung her hands and looked down into the distorted face of the dwarf.

"No, no, Crapaud!" she presently added, her voice softening and the tears rising in her eyes, "no, no, I am foolish—I do not mean that— Here Crapaud!" She drew forth her purse and gave him some pieces of gold, pieces hard to get in those days. "Take this, and make haste! Go bring Mademoiselle Vernon. Do you hear? Hurry!"

"But, madame," said Crapaud, with a sheepish smile as he pocketed the money, "Mademoiselle Vernon is a prisoner in the hands of the British. I had to speak as I did to Monsieur Fairfax, because he ought not to know that the mademoiselle is a prisoner. It would excite him, kill him, to know."

Madame Souvestre's face paled, and she trembled from head to foot.

"These are terrible times, Crapaud," she faltered,

with a meaningless intonation in her voice, "terrible times."

He saw her gasp and loose her balance. He caught her in his sturdy arms, lifted her with ease and bore her up the steps into a chamber where he laid her on a couch; then he ran for her maid and sent her to her mistress.

"Bah! It is very bad," he muttered to himself, "this way of the women. It is always love and spasm with them. Bah!"

He fumbled the bandage over his ear and grimaced hideously as he looked at the blood that had oozed out upon his fingers.

Fairfax waited for what seemed an age to him before Madame Souvestre returned. She was pale, but the smile on her lips and the ready cleverness of her manner hid from him the fact that she had been suffering. He knew that she had a brother in Jackson's army, a young fellow just coming to manhood; she had spoken of him often, and he attributed her excitement to uneasiness about him.

Crapaud Crapoussin returned at the end of an hour and said that Pauline was not at home.

"She is very well, though," he volunteered to remark, "the servants told me so."

"Thank you! I am glad you did not find her. I was half dreaming when I asked you to fetch her; it was absurd."

Fairfax was looking at Madame Souvestre while he spoke. Something in the depth of her eye as she momentarily returned his gaze was a revelation; he felt a strange, sorrowful thrill go through him.

After all, her kindness to him had brought her but suffering. He was aware of this now ; the knowledge came to him through one of those obscure but ever reliable veins of consciousness by which we receive all of the most precious and many of the most saddening impressions of life.

Just then she thought of her brother. Why had she not inquired about him of Crapaud Crapoussin? She felt guilty and abashed, and her heart throbbed painfully. Turning upon the dwarf with a sudden flare of fretfulness in her face, she demanded :

"Why have you not told me of my brother, Emile ?"

Crapaud's countenance grew ashen-gray, and his usual clever glibness forsook him wholly.

" Oh, yes, your brother—your brother Emile is— oh, he is very well ; yes, he—"

" Monsieur Crapoussin !"

" Yes, madame, your brother—"

" Monsieur !"

" Monsieur Emile, your brother is—"

" Crapaud !"

" Is dead—shot—killed !"

Crapaud bubbled these words forth as if frightened almost out of his senses.

That afternoon they brought the dead soldier home to his sister's house and prepared him for burial.

CHAPTER XXIX.

AT LAST.

Burns, when he caught sight of Pierre Rameau making his way through the woods into the swamp, rushed after him with the energy of one who feels that the spurt of strength vouchsafed to him is to be short and final.

The old man knew that to fail now meant to fail forever. The terrible excitement, exposure and effort of the past fortnight had drained the cup of his vitality almost to the bottom. The fire of monomaniacal frenzy had burned so fiereely in his breast of late that his eyes showed the effect by a wild, steadfast, strained stare, not unlike that of a dead man. When he shambled past Pauline at the edge of the swamp, he did not see her, so intently was his gaze set upon the retreating figure of the victim he longed for.

"Kirk MacCollough!" he called, and the name rasped the woods like a file. "Kirk MacCollough, I am coming!"

At the sound of the voice, the dark man halted and turned about.

"You had better come no farther!" he coolly said. "Stop right there!"

Burns slackened his pace, but came steadily upon him, fumbling meantime for the knife in his bosom, his drawn feature set and rigid.

Rameau retreated, walking slowly backward, fixing his tiger-like eyes steadily on the old man's face.

Pauline ran back to the house as soon as Rameau left her; so she did not hear the voices of the two men, although they rang with strange distinctness through the moss-hung aisles of the forest.

"Max Burns," growled the outlaw, with a certain harsh accentuation, "I do not wish to injure you. Keep off!"

"Ha! Ha! Injure me! You cannot; I am beyond that. Injury is already hardened upon me like a mail. Death itself cannot find a loose joint." He was speaking with the preacher's intonation and his words had a suggestion of the pulpit. "Though you be Satan himself, I will prevail over you! Yea, now is your time come to die!"

"You are crazy! I pity you! But you'd better stop!" Rameau muttered, still stepping backward and watching steadily every movement that Burns made.

Both men were just then recalling the scene in the Pearl-River woods.

"I will make sure work this time if you force me to it!" Rameau added.

"This time you die!" said Burns.

"I have been told that many a time before, Max Burns; but it was always a lie; it is a lie now."

Rameau stopped suddenly as he spoke, and poised himself to kick Burns as he had Vasseur.

The old man, with uplifted knife, pressed right on. Now, for the first time, he saw that Rameau's arms were both useless and that his clothes were saturated with blood. The discovery caused him to falter involuntarily.

Rameau lifted his foot, and as he did so he slipped and fell heavily backward on the ground, with one of his broken arms doubled up under him.

Burns stood glaring at him, while he made feeble efforts to rise. He had fallen so that he could not even turn himself over, and, although he showed no sign of pain, his torture must have been extreme.

"I am at your mercy. Kill me and be done," he remarked, with the old tone of indifference. "You had better be quick if you value revenge, for I am bleeding inwardly. This fall has started the flow."

Burns stooped over him and gazed into his eyes. The long knife in the old man's hand trembled so that it flickered like a cold ray of light amid the shadows of the funereal wood.

"You are losing precious time," urged Rameau. "Strike the coward's blow and enjoy the assassin's triumph. When next you preach, take 'Thou shalt not kill,' for a text."

Burns stooped lower, his face growing livid, his whole frame shaking as with an ague.

"Hypocrite of hypocrites," continued Rameau, "and fools of fools! End up your long Christian career with murdering a helpless and dying man! What a lovely thing this Christianity is! Stab away, why don't you?"

Rameau was very weak, and over his firm, strangely complacent face was creeping an ashy pallor.

Burns knelt down astride of him and grasped the collar of his coat with his left hand, while with his right he slowly lifted the knife. He did not strike, however, but lowered the weapon and gazed vaguely around him and up, as if he had heard something that troubled him.

The wood was strangely silent, save that, far aloft, the breeze sighed in the tree-tops.

"Ah, your courage fails you, does it?" Rameau sneered. "Your dyspeptic soul shrinks and falters in its hour of triumph! Pluck up a little spirit, Max Burns; don't let your last grand opportunity slip away from you!"

Again the old man began to lift the knife; but his hand seemed uncontrollable. What was it overhead that made him look up with such an expression in his eyes? His lips moved dumbly.

Rameau's narrow gaze grew awfully intense.

"You are to blame for my life and yours!" he growled hoarsely. "You are to blame for everything! You set your selfish, hypocritical, canting objections between Margaret and me; poisoned our lives with your driveling, sanctimonious deceit and bigotry; drove her from home; made a brute of me, and now here we are dying together! Stab, you cowardly old assassin, stab!"

If Burns had heard him, he gave no sign; his face was still upturned and over his emaciated features and into his sunken eyes had come a look of supplication. Was he praying?

"None of that here!" exclaimed Rameau, noticing the rapt stare and the moving lips. "You shall not make an altar of me for your infernal mummery!"

As he spoke, he feebly lifted one of his half-paralyzed legs and tried to strike Burns in the back with his knee.

It was a futile attempt, and the exhausted outlaw settled down with grim resignation to await the end, whatever it might be.

Burns drew his left hand, which had been clutching Rameau's collar, across his forehead and eyes, as if to clear his vision, and looked all around, then up into the tree-tops. One seeing him would have been sure that the old man had heard a familiar voice calling him. He was now sitting heavily on Rameau's breast and his shoulders were collapsed.

"Margaret! Margaret!" he presently cried in a strange, far-reaching half-whisper. "Did you call me, Margaret?"

"Idiot!" snarled Rameau, in whose throat the breath was rattling ominously. "Can't you see that I am dying? You are going to lose your revenge if you don't strike soon! What do you see? What are you staring at?"

"Margaret! Come nearer, Margaret!"

"Fool, make haste!"

"Speak, Margaret! Speak to me again!"

Burns leaned and gazed; the cold sweat stood on

his wrinkled forehead; his eyes glowed with some inexpressible ecstasy.

"Dolt! Dotard! Do the dead ever speak? Your own selfish stubbornness killed her, not my hand; and now you ask her to speak! Take your knife and strike your own heart with it as you struck hers with your—"

Rameau was speaking rapidly, huskily; his voice seemed to flutter in his throat, when Burns stopped him with a throttling grasp.

"Hush!" cried the old man. "You frighten her, and she will not speak."

Was it a smile or a swift spasm of pain that lighted up the outlaw's face? The breathing of the two men whispered strangely in the silent wood.

"What is that on your breast, Margaret? A wound? Oh, my poor child! Who did it?"

"I did it! I told you that long ago! I did it!" gasped Rameau.

"You! You did it!" screamed Burns, supporting his weight again on his knees and uplifting the knife with an arm as rigid now as steel. "Kirk MacCollough—"

"Yes, I, Kirk MacCollough!"

Once more the old man faltered and listened, his eyes turning in every direction. Suddenly he looked up, and a great cry escaped his lips:

"Heavenly Master—is it Thou?"

His face changed; it was like transfiguration; it was illumination.

* * * * * * *

When Mr. Vernon and Lieutenant Ballanche came

upon the scene of this last meeting between Max Burns and Kirk MacCollough, they found both men lying dead.

The outlaw's face was still strangely handsome, and wore, even in that awful repose, a trace of the old reckless indifference to consequences.

Burns's face was downward, and his knife was driven to the hilt in the damp ground.

Mr. Vernon stood for a long while looking at the dead. What he thought has never been revealed.

CHAPTER XXX.

CONCLUSION.

General Jackson, with the caution which the occasion demanded, held his little army well together and did not relax his vigilance until he was sure that the British had abandoned all thought of further efforts to take New Orleans. He permitted Mr. Vernon to conduct Mrs. Vernon, Pauline and Mademoiselle de Sezannes to the city, but Lieutenant Ballanche was ordered, much to his chagrin, to remain with the army.

Kirk MacCollough, old man Burns and Vasseur had been buried temporarily in shallow graves near where they had fallen. Later, Mr. Vernon had all three brought to New Orleans and interred in a cemetery where to this day a heavy brick tomb stands under a spreading oak, and until recently its tablet bore this simple inscription :

> *Ci-Gît*
>
> PHILIP LORING
>
> *Tué en Bataille Rangée.*

A few years ago, the walls of this tomb were crumbling to ruin; but in 1889 some kind hand restored them and covered the whole with durable stucco. Singularly enough, by mistake, no doubt, the inscription slab also was covered with this rock-like substance.

There was a tumult of rejoicing which lasted for many days and nights in New Orleans. Never, perhaps, in the history of wars was there a battle of such consequence that caused so little mourning to the victors. The killed and wounded were so few that the face of sorrow scarcely showed itself amid the general flare of glorification.

The de Sezannes's mansion was thrown open late in January for a grand reception to General Jackson and his officers. All the world was there, as the creoles expressed it, and, next to the grim commander himself, Fairfax, who was able to attend as the only wounded soldier present, was the hero of the occasion, especially in the eyes of the ladies.

"Ah, if I could have been touched with a shot!"

exclaimed Lieutenant Ballanche, as he joined the group that had gathered around the pale yet radiantly happy young man.

"But then we should not have had the pleasure of being rescued by you," said Pauline.

"Oh, that was a tame affair on my part."

"Tame, indeed!" remarked Mademoiselle de Sezannes. "You do not appreciate romance."

"But I do, mademoiselle; only the romance did not make me a man of note. I am horribly jealous of Fairfax."

"And here I must sit, like a cat on a rug, while you dance with all these charming ones," said Fairfax. "It is I who lose most if accounts are properly squared."

Mr. Vernon was present, passing among the thronging guests, his stalwart form and his massive head distinguishing him as one cast in no common mold. He appeared to have grown older, and the expression of his face suggested some inward reserve of gloom, albeit he smiled and conversed with much of his accustomed stately vivacity. To him General Jackson showed more marked respect than to any other person in the house.

"You will not think me neglectful of your gallant husband's inestimable services to me and the country, madame," said the general to Mrs. Livingston, "if I say frankly that I owe more to Mr. Vernon than to any man in my army."

"You may trust me not to misunderstand you, general," replied that lady, with frank earnestness. "Mr. Vernon has always been a man of remarkable influence and executive power. My husband has often relied upon him, and never without avail, in matters apparently beyond hope. But do you know," and she lowered her voice, "that he is wholly mysterious?"

"Yes; I confess that he is the only man that I ever met whose motives and whose character I could not even guess at."

"It is comforting to hear you say so; it confirms me in my romance." She smiled reminiscently and then added: "I have always imagined that some great secret was locked in his breast."

"It is the secret of greatness hampered by some controlling fate," said Jackson, half in seriousness, perhaps, but guided by his chivalrous impulse to assist Mrs. Livingston in her romantic notion.

"Do you know that his word is law with the *forbans* and outlaws?" she suddenly inquired. "My husband says that he controls them perfectly."

General Jackson looked at her, and then, without replying, masked his face in an expression of impenetrable reserve. He knew that Livingston himself had been accused of standing close in with the Lafittes and other noted law-breakers, and doubtless he feared that the wife of his friend might go too far with her disclosures. Long afterward, in his old age, he remarked to a friend in Nashville that, at the time he was commanding at New Orleans, society there knew no line of division between gentlemen and robbers. "But," he added, "the gentlemen were gentlemen; the robbers, patriots; and the women were charming; they were angels, sir—angels!"

The people thronging the de Sezannes mansion were, indeed, drawn together without regard for fitness as we now view it, and little did certain of them dream that the great battle over which they were rejoicing had rung the note of change and reform; that the flash of those guns had kindled the fire of destruction under the very foundations of outlawry.

It is true that Murrell organized his band of robbers and thieves in Mississippi and held them together for some years; but in New Orleans, as if by a wave of a hand, when Mr. Vernon withdrew his influence, the *Chats-Huants* disappeared, and the power of the Lafittes was broken forever.

The de Sezannes reception was the last notable social event under the old *régime*. After that, there followed disclosures which led to governmental investigation and legal procedure. Steps were taken to administer the criminal laws with great vigor in the State, and the United States government enforced its authority along the coast. These changes speedily brought about a new social order, especially in New Orleans, and the city at once took a high place as a center of refinement, luxury and culture, in which the lines of division between the fit and the unfit were drawn with extreme exclusiveness.

Wilfred Parker made his last appearance in New Orleans society on the occasion of Mademoiselle de Sezannes's marriage. M. de Sezannes had insisted on inviting him, although Marie offered as an objection that she had never been able to rid herself of the belief that Parker had stolen her ruby on the evening of the party at Chateau d'Or. Lieutenant Ballanche heartily disliked the suave little adventurer, without knowing just why; but he pooh-poohed Marie's suspicion of felonious behavior.

The very next day Parker was identified as John A. Murrell, and with great difficulty made his escape into Mississippi. The crime of which he was accused was horse-stealing, and when he left New Orleans, it was astride of Ballanche's favorite mare that he rode into the swampy woods and evaded the officers.

When Pauline and Fairfax were married, the guests at their wedding were chosen with a care that surprised not a few who had expected to be invited. It was Mr. Vernon himself who had most insisted on this exclusiveness.

Fairfax had his drop of bitter to swallow with all his nuptial sweets. On the day of his marriage, he learned that Madame Souvestre had made over her fortune to the church and had retired to a convent. He could in no wise blame himself for this, and yet he knew that into that sweet young woman's life his sojourn in her house had cast ineradicable sorrow.

Mr. Vernon insisted upon having his children, as he now called Pauline and Fairfax, live at Chateau d'Or, where they watched him go gently down the decline of life. He outlived Mrs. Vernon many years, and died at the age of ninety-one. For years before his death, he spent much time at an old mahogany desk, writing what afterward was found to be both a will and a history. In the testamentary part of the huge document he left all his property to his daughter, and she was surprised to find that a large part of the bequest consisted of landed estates in Scotland. The will was signed "Thomas MacCollough," and among the annexed papers were all the directions, facts and documentary proofs necessary to establish the truth of a strange and startling autobiography.

One thing was left without a word of explanation: In the package of papers was inclosed the amethyst cross, still shut in the old, worn leather case.

Pauline refused to make public claim to the estates in Scotland; but after her death, which was in 1849, her children offered the proofs and possessed the property, which was valued at nearly a million dollars.

Fairfax never reached eminence as an artist. Indeed, after his marriage, he made no more than occasional efforts with his brush. One of his pictures, however, has been recently attracting much attention. By some means, it passed from the hands of the friend in New Orleans to whom Fairfax gave it, and is now in the collection of "Masterpieces by Obscure Artists," made by the late Marquis de Montluzin.

The picture is scarcely more than a study of the face of Kirk MacCollough, sketched by Fairfax long before his marriage and before he had proof that Pierre Rameau and Colonel Loring were but one man. It is, nevertheless, a powerful piece of work, in which is caught with perfect cunning the indescribable fascination of the strange outlaw's countenance.

Under it, on the darkened margin of the canvas, is written in heavy red letters:

> THE KING OF HONEY ISLAND.

THE END.

www.ingramcontent.com/pod-product-compliance
Lightning Source LLC
Chambersburg PA
CBHW031855220426
43663CB00006B/634